SPEECHES
THAT CHANGED
WORLD
THE

SPEECHES THAT CHANGED THE WORLD

INCLUDES FREE AUDIO CD
GREAT SPEECHES OF THE WORLD

ALAN J. WHITICKER

JAICO PUBLISHING HOUSE

Ahmedabad Bangalore Bhopal Bhubaneswar Chennai
Delhi Hyderabad Kolkata Lucknow Mumbai

Published by Jaico Publishing House
A-2 Jash Chambers, 7-A Sir Phirozshah Mehta Road
Fort, Mumbai - 400 001
jaicopub@jaicobooks.com
www.jaicobooks.com

Originally published by
New Holland Publishers (Australia) Pty. Ltd.
of 1/66 Gibbes Street
Chatswood NSW 2067
AUSTRALIA

To be sold only in India, Bangladesh, Bhutan,
Pakistan, Nepal, Sri Lanka and the Maldives.

SPEECHES THAT CHANGED THE WORLD
With Audio CD
ISBN 978-81-8495-084-7

First Jaico Impression: 2010
Seventeenth Jaico Impression: 2018

Printed by
SRG Traders Pvt. Ltd.
B-41, Sector 67,
Noida 201301, U.P.

Dedication

For my teachers—who instilled and fostered a love of history
in their students ... of whom I was just one.

Contents

The Cold War, 1950-1959   113

Revolution, 1960-1969   151

Absolute Power, 1970-1979   183

The Big Chill, 1980-1989 217

The Dawn of Enlightenment, 1990-1999   237

The New Millennium, 2000-   273

Sources   287

Acknowledgements

There are many people whom I would like to thank for their assistance in the writing and publishing of this book: Fiona Schultz, Lliane Clarke, Michael McGrath, Natasha Hayles and all the team at New Holland; my wife Karen and family for their patience and support in meeting yet another deadline.

Introduction:

The Power of Persuasion

Rhetoric ... is the artificer of a persuasion which creates belief
about the just and unjust, but gives no instruction about them...
(Socrates, quoted in Plato's *Gorgias*).

This book: *Speeches that Changed the World* is not meant to be a definitive list of the 'greatest' speeches of all time–that has been done by other authors. This collection takes recurring themes such as politics and diplomacy, war and peace, freedom and justice, civil rights and human rights, and puts them into a historical context. These themes ring out across the decades, but they have in common the rhetoric–the power of persuasion.

The philosopher and mathematician Aristotle studied the use of language as a tool of persuasion. In *The Rhetoric*, he argues that rhetoric is neither good nor bad, but an art form. Plato claimed that 'the rhetorician need not know the truth about things; he only has to discover some way of persuading the ignorant that he has more knowledge than those who know ...' Whether a course of action is 'just or unjust' depends on the character of the speaker and the context of the speech.

An example of the power of speech to move the masses is–Jesus Christ's 'Sermon on the Mount'. Even if one disregards the religious context of the speech and considers Jesus purely as a teacher or civil rights leader, his words have moved millions during the past two thousand years. These simple words, written and recorded in the gospels, changed the world:

'And seeing the multitudes, (Jesus) went up into a mountain: and when
he was set, his disciples came unto him:
    And he opened his mouth, and taught them, saying:
    'Blessed are the poor in spirit: for theirs is the kingdom of heaven.
    Blessed are they that mourn: for they shall be comforted.
    Blessed are the meek: for they shall inherit the earth.
    Blessed are they which do hunger and thirst after righteousness: for
    they shall be filled.

Blessed are the merciful: for they shall obtain mercy.

Blessed are the pure in heart: for they shall see God.

Blessed are the peacemakers: for they shall be called the children of God.

Blessed are they which are persecuted for righteousness' sake: for theirs is the kingdom of heaven.

Blessed are ye, when men shall revile you, and persecute you, and shall say all manner of evil against you falsely, for my sake.'

A more contemporary example is Abraham Lincoln's Gettysburg Addresss. Dedicating a national cemetery on November 19, 1863 on the former battlefield of Gettysburg, Pennsylvania, Lincoln took out his handwritten notes and delivered a speech that lasted barely two minutes:

'Four score and seven years ago our fathers brought forth on this continent, a new nation, conceived in liberty, and dedicated to the proposition that all men are created equal.

Now we are engaged in a great civil war, testing whether that nation, or any nation so conceived and so dedicated, can long endure. We are met on a great battlefield of that war. We have come to dedicate a portion of that field, as a final resting place for those who here gave their lives that that nation might live. It is altogether fitting and proper that we should do this.

But in a larger sense, we cannot dedicate—we cannot consecrate—we cannot hallow—this ground. The brave men, living and dead, who struggled here, have consecrated it, far above our poor power to add or detract. The world will little note, nor long remember, what we say here, but it can never forget what they did here. It is for us the living, rather, to be dedicated here to the unfinished work which they who fought here have thus far so nobly advanced. It is rather for us to be here dedicated to the great task remaining before us—that from these honored dead we take increased devotion to that cause for which they gave the last full measure of devotion—that we here highly resolve that these dead shall not have died in vain—that this nation, under God, shall have a new birth of freedom—and that government of the people, by the people, for the people, shall not perish from the earth.

These 275 words did not initially resonate with Lincoln's audience, but once published in newspapers and journals, over time they (especially the final sentence, 'government of the people, by the people, for the people') have come to define a nation of people. Although Lincoln's Gettysburg Address belongs to a world now long gone, it resonated with the public via the media and as such, it can be viewed as the starting point of this book.

This collection of speeches reflects not only events of one of the most cataclysmic centuries known to humanity, they also represent a fair share of the century's heroes and villains, martyrs and monsters. In this book the speeches of Josef Stalin, Mahatma Gandhi, Adolf Hitler, Nelson Mandela, Joseph McCarthy, the Kennedy family, Fidel Castro and Pope John Paul II, are presented side-by-side.

Selecting the speeches that shaped a century of human endeavour is no easy task, not least because any list was always going to be dominated by Americans and men. If modern rhetoric is an art from (although Socrates would disagree) then it is an American art form. The 'public address' is such an important part of American political life that any list of important speeches is dominated by United States politicians. However, these are balanced by the views of civil rights leaders, peace activists, women and voices from other nations—15 countries are represented here—to provide equilibrium of social conscience and political views.

Although there are only 9 speeches by women they are among the most powerful and influential of the last 100 years. Emmeline Pankhurst, Margaret Sanger, Golda Meir, Indira Ghandi and the indefatigable Arundhati Roy— speak on everything from women's suffrage to human rights.

Some speeches, such as Winston Churchill's 'Our Finest Hour', John F Kennedy's 'Cuban Missile Crisis' and Martin Luther King's 'I Have a Dream'— which was voted the most important speech of last century—were obvious choices. Others, such as Soviet leader Nikita Khrushchev's denouncement of Stalin, German Cardinal Clement von Galen's criticism of Hitler and George S Patton's D-Day address to his troops, are relatively unknown.

In this book I have provided an historical context for each speech and a biographical background of each speaker. I have however, wherever possible, avoided offering my own critique of the merits of each speech. Let the words speak for themselves ... they are, after all, the *Speeches That Shaped the Modern World*.

Speeches that Changed the World

The Old World
1901-1919

The Duke of Cornwall and York

'The Opening of the Australian Federal Parliament'

Exhibition Building, Melbourne, 9 May 1901.

On January 1, 1901, a new nation came into being. The Commonwealth of Australia, a member nation of the British Empire, was proclaimed at a ceremony in Sydney's Centennial Park attended by Governor General Lord Hopetoun, the country's newly appointed Prime Minister Edmund Barton, and the members of his Executive Council.

Australia's road to federation—the union of the six British colonies on the continent under one constitution, one flag and one federal government—had started much earlier. In 1891 the First National Australasian Convention in Sydney, New South Wales had drafted a federal constitution. In 1898 referendums in favour of federation were held in New South Wales, Victoria, Tasmania and South Australia while Western Australia (1899) and Queensland (1900) soon followed suit. On July 9, 1900 the Commonwealth of Australia Constitution Act was passed by the British Parliament and received Royal assent from Queen Victoria.

Queen Victoria did not live to see the formation of the first Australian Parliament—she died on 22 January 1901, and was succeeded by her son, King Edward VII. The Australian Parliament met in Melbourne's Exhibition Building on 9 May, 1901, for the first sitting of the nation's newly-elected federal representatives. Australia's First Parliament House was not opened for another 26 years in Canberra (in the Australian Capital Territory) on 9 May, 1927. Sixty one years after that, on the same date during Australia's Bicentenary, the country's new Parliament House building was opened by Queen Elizabeth II.

At exactly 12 o'clock, on 9 May, 1901, His Royal Highness, the Duke of Cornwall and York (who, a decade later, would be crowned King George V) accompanied by his wife, the Duchess of Cornwall and York, entered the Exhibition Building. They stood alongside their Excellencies the Governor-General, the Earl of Hopetoun, and the Countess of Hopetoun. The orchestra played the National Anthem, not surprisingly, England's 'God Save the King.'

'Hysterical sensationalism is the very poorest weapon wherewith to fight for lasting righteousness.'

After the Clerk of the Parliaments read the Proclamation to the Senate, the clerk of the House of Representatives read the same Proclamation to the members of that chamber. The Proclamation stated:

'Whereas, by the Commonwealth of Australia Constitution Act, it is amongst other things enacted that the Governor-General may appoint such times for holding the sessions of the Parliament as he thinks fit; and whereas, by the said Act, it is further enacted that the Parliament shall sit at Melbourne until it meets at the seat of Government; and whereas, it is expedient now to appoint the time for holding the first session of the Parliament of the Commonwealth: Now, therefore, I, John Adrian Lewis, Earl of Hopetoun, the Governor-General aforesaid, in exercise of the power conferred by the said Act, do by this my Proclamation appoint Thursday, the ninth day of May instant, as the day for the said Parliament to assemble ... '

His Royal Highness the Duke of Cornwall and York then motioned to the Usher of the Black Rod to inform the House of Representatives that he, authorised by virtue of His Majesty's commission, desired the immediate attendance of the Members of the House of Representatives. Several minutes later the Members, headed by the Prime Minister Edmund Barton, entered the main hall of the building.

The Hundredth Psalm was then sung with accompaniment by the orchestra. Following a short prayer, the Clerk of Parliaments read His Majesty the King's Commission to His Royal Highness the Duke of Cornwall and York to open the Australian Parliament. The following message from His Majesty, King George V, was delivered by His Royal Highness the Duke of Cornwall and York who advanced to the edge of the dais, placed his hat on his head and read the following speech.

' Gentlemen of the Senate and Gentlemen of the House of Representatives...

My beloved and deeply-lamented grandmother, Queen Victoria, had desired to mark the importance of the opening of this the first Parliament of the Commonwealth of Australia, and to manifest her special interest in all that concerns the welfare of her loyal subjects in Australia, by granting to me a special commission to open the first session. That commission had been duly signed before the sad event which has plunged the whole Empire into mourning, and the King, my dear father, fully sharing her late Majesty's wishes, decided to give effect to them, although His Majesty stated, on the occasion of his opening his first Parliament, that a separation from his son at such a time could not be otherwise than deeply painful to him.

His Majesty has been pleased to consent to this separation, moved by his sense of the loyalty and devotion which prompted the generous aid afforded by all the colonies in the South African War, both in its earlier and more recent stages, and of the splendid bravery of the colonial troops. It is also His Majesty's wish to acknowledge the readiness with which the ships of the Special Australasian Squadron were placed at his disposal for service in China, and the valuable assistance rendered there by the Naval Contingents of the several colonies.

His Majesty further desired in this way to testify to his heartfelt gratitude for the warm sympathy extended by every part of his dominions to himself and his family in the irreparable loss they have sustained by the death of his beloved mother.

His Majesty has watched with the deepest interest the social and material progress made by His people in Australia and has seen with thankfulness and heartfelt satisfaction the completion of that political union of which this Parliament is the embodiment.

The King is satisfied that the wisdom and patriotism which have characterised the exercise of the wide powers of self-government hitherto enjoyed by the colonies will continue to be displayed in the exercise of the still wider powers with which the united Commonwealth has been endowed. His Majesty feels assured that the enjoyment of these powers will, if possible, enhance that loyalty and devotion to his throne and Empire of which the people of Australia have already given such signal proofs.

It is His Majesty's earnest prayer that this union so happily achieved may, under God's blessing, prove an instrument for still further promoting the welfare and advancement of his subjects in Australia, and for the strengthening and consolidation of his Empire.

'His Majesty has watched with the deepest interest the social and material progress made by His people in Australia.'

Gentlemen of the Senate and Gentlemen of the House of Representatives. It affords me much pleasure to convey to you this message from His Majesty. I now, in his name, and on his behalf, declare this Parliament open.'

And so, in a bloodless recognition of constitutional power, the Commonwealth of Australia was born. Never far from 'Mother England' Australia followed her into both World Wars during the next fifty years, after which it aligned itself more closely with the United States (Vietnam, Iraq and the 'War on Terrorism') whilst searching for its own identity amongst its Asian and Islander neighbours in the South Pacific. Interestingly, when given the chance to become an independent republic in a 1999 referendum (thereby having an Australian as head of state), the majority of Australians opted to stay a member of the British Commonwealth.

Mary Church Terrell

'Being Coloured in the Nation's Capital'

Speech to United Women's Club, Washington, DC, 10 October 1906.

The life of Mary Church Terrell (1863-1954) bridged an expanse of history from the emancipation of the slaves in the American Civil War (1861-65) to the US Supreme Court decision to end segregation in schools (Brown v Board of Education, 1954).

Terrell spent her life at the forefront of the fight for civil rights. In 1884 she was the first African-American woman to earn a college degree and later studied education in Europe for two years. A high school teacher and principal, she became the first black woman in America to be appointed to an Education Board (District of Columbia).

As the first president of the National Association of Colored Women, Mary Church Terrell spoke out in support of women's suffrage and an end to racial segregation. In October 1906, Terrell addressed the United Women's Club in Washington DC about the discrimination faced by black women because of both their race and their gender. Terrell's speech is considered to be one of the most influential speeches on race in the 20th century.

‘ Washington DC has been called 'The Colored Man's Paradise'. Whether this sobriquet was given to the national capital in bitter irony by a member of the handicapped race, as he reviewed some of his own persecutions and rebuffs, or whether it was given immediately after the war by an ex-slaveholder who for the first time in his life saw colored people walking about like free men, minus the overseer and his whip, history saith not. It is certain that it would be difficult to find a worse misnomer for Washington than 'The Colored Man's Paradise' if so prosaic a consideration as veracity is to determine the appropriateness of a name.

For fifteen years I have resided in Washington, and while it was far from being a paradise for colored people when I first touched these shores, it has been doing its level best ever since to make conditions for us intolerable. As a colored woman I might enter Washington any night, a stranger in a strange land, and walk miles without finding a place to lay my head. Unless I happened to know colored people who live here or ran across a chance acquaintance who could recommend a colored boarding-house to me, I should be obliged to spend the entire night wandering about. Indians, Chinamen, Filipinos, Japanese and representatives of any other dark race can find hotel accommodations, if they can pay for them. The colored man alone is thrust out of the hotels of the national capital like a leper...

As a colored woman I cannot visit the tomb of the Father of this Country, which owes its very existence to the love of freedom in the human heart and which stands for equal opportunity to all, without being forced to sit in the Jim Crow section of an electric car which starts from the very heart of the city—midway between the Capitol and the White House. If I refuse thus to be humiliated, I am cast into jail and forced to pay a fine for violating the Virginia laws...

As a colored woman I may enter more than one white church in Washington without receiving that welcome which as a human being I have a right to expect in the sanctuary of God. Sometimes the color blindness of the usher takes on that peculiar form which prevents a dark face from making any impression whatsoever upon his retina, so that it is impossible for him to see colored people at all. If he is not so afflicted, after keeping a colored man or woman waiting a long time, he will ungraciously show these dusky Christians who have had the temerity to thrust themselves into a temple where only the fair of face are expected to worship God to a seat in the rear, which is named in honor of a certain personage, well known in this country, and commonly called Jim Crow.

'If I try to enter many of the numerous vocations in which my white sisters are allowed to engage, the door is shut in my face.'

MARY CHURCH TERRELL   19

Unless I am willing to engage in a few menial occupations, in which the pay for my services would be very poor, there is no way for me to earn an honest living, if I am not a trained nurse or a dressmaker or can secure a position as a teacher in the public schools, which is exceedingly difficult to do. It matters not what my intellectual attainments may be or how great is the need of the services of a competent person, if I try to enter many of the numerous vocations in which my white sisters are allowed to engage, the door is shut in my face.

From one Washington theater I am excluded altogether ... [After explaining that] in some of the theaters colored nurses were allowed to sit with the white children for whom they cared, the ticket seller told me that in Washington it was very poor policy to employ colored nurses, for they were excluded from many places where white girls would be allowed to take children for pleasure.

If I possess artistic talent, there is not a single art school of repute which will admit me. A few years ago a colored woman who possessed great talent submitted some drawings to the Corcoran Art School, of Washington, which were accepted by the committee of awards, who sent her a ticket entitling her to a course in this school. But when the committee discovered that the young woman was colored, they declined to admit her, and told her that if they had suspected that her drawings had been made by a colored woman, they would not have examined them at all...

'With the exception of the Catholic University, there is not a single white college in the national capital to which colored people are admitted, no matter how great their ability ...'

With the exception of the Catholic University, there is not a single white college in the national capital to which colored people are admitted, no matter how great their ability, how lofty their ambition, how unexceptionable their character or how great their thirst for knowledge may be. A few years ago the Columbian Law School [in Washington] admitted colored students, but in deference to the Southern white students the authorities have decided to exclude them altogether...

I might go on citing instance after instance to show the variety of ways in which our people are sacrificed on the altar of prejudice in the capital of the United States and how almost insurmountable are the obstacles which block our paths to success. Early in life many a colored youth is so appalled by the helplessness and the hopelessn of his situation in this country that, in a sort of stoical despair he resigns himself to his fate. 'What is the good of our trying to acquire an education? We can't all be preachers, teachers, doctors and lawyers. Besides those professions, there is almost nothing for colored people to do but engage in the most menial occupations, and we do not need an education for that.' More than once such remarks, uttered by young men and women in our public schools who possess brilliant intellects, have wrung my heart.

> 'The chasm between the principles upon which this Government was founded ... and those which are daily practiced under the protection of the flag, yawns ... wide and deep.'

It is impossible for any white person in the United States, no matter how sympathetic and broadminded, to realise what life would mean to him if his incentive to effort were suddenly snatched away. To the lack of incentive to effort, which is the awful shadow under which we live, may be traced the wreck and ruin of scores of colored youth. And surely nowhere in the world do oppression and persecution based solely on the color of the skin appear more hateful and hideous than in the capital of the United States, because the chasm between the principles upon which this Government was founded, in which it still professes to believe, and those which are daily practiced under the protection of the flag, yawns so wide and deep. '

The fact that Church Terrell's speech was delivered in the national capital—the centre of American democracy—contrasted the ideals of the country's founding fathers with the realities experienced by many of the city's minorities. Martin Luther King exposed the same paradox 57 years later when he delivered his famous 'I Have a Dream' speech on the steps of the Lincoln Memorial (see Revolution, 1960-69). In 1953, a year before her death at 91, Mary Church Terrell led a campaign to end the segregation of public facilities in Washington, DC.

Emmeline Pankhurst

'Freedom or Death'

Fundraising Speech, Hartford, Connecticut, United States, 13 November 1913.

Emmeline Pankhurst (1857-1928) is arguably the most famous representative of the struggle for Votes for Women. The English barrister drafted the first women's suffrage bill in Britain and founded the Women's Franchise League in 1899.

Pankhurst took the fight for women's suffrage to a new level. Public demonstrations and rallies often resulted in police violence and the arrest of her and her followers. Under arrest, Pankhurst and her fellow suffragettes staged hunger and thirst strikes and had to be force-fed by the police—usually through a funnel thrust down their throats. The police released the women until they were nursed back to health and re-arrested them. The cycle—known as the 'cat and mouse game'—would start all over again. The damage to the women's health was 'astounding', and Pankhurst would often speak at rallies from a stretcher.

In November 1913 Pankhurst made her third 'fundraising' tour of the United States, where her tactics had received widespread publicity since the turn of the century.

' I do not come here as an advocate, because whatever position the suffrage movement may occupy in the United States of America, in England it has passed beyond the realm of advocacy and it has entered into the sphere of practical politics. It has become the subject of revolution and civil war, and so tonight I am not here to advocate women's suffrage. American suffragists can do that very well for themselves. I am here as a soldier who has temporarily left the field of battle in order to explain——it seems strange it should have to be explained—what civil war is like when civil war is waged by women. I am not only here as a soldier temporarily absent from the field of battle; I am here—and that, I think, is the strangest part of my coming—I am here as a person who, according to the law courts of my country, it has been decided, is of no value to the community at all; and I am adjudged because of my life to be a dangerous person, under sentence of penal servitude in a convict prison. So you see there is some special interest in hearing so unusual a person address you. I dare say, in the minds of many of you—you will perhaps forgive me this personal touch—that I do not look either very like a soldier or very like a convict, and yet I am both. '

It would take too long to trace the course of militant methods as adopted by women, because it is about eight years since the word militant was first used to describe what we were doing; it is about eight years since the first militant action was taken by women. It was not militant at all, except that it provoked militancy on the part of those who were opposed to it. When women asked questions in political meetings and failed to get answers, they were not doing anything militant. To ask questions at political meetings is an acknowledged right of all people who attend public meetings; certainly in my country, men have always done it, and I hope they do it in America, because it seems to me that if you allow people to enter your legislatures without asking them any questions as to what they arc going to do when they get there you are not exercising your citizen rights and your citizen duties as you ought.

At any rate in Great Britain it is a custom, a time-honoured one, to ask questions of candidates for Parliament, and ask questions of members of the government. No man was ever put out of a public meeting for asking a question until Votes for Women came on to the political horizon. The first people who were put out of a political meeting for asking questions were women; they were brutally ill-used; they found themselves in jail before twenty-four hours had expired. But instead of the newspapers, which are largely inspired by the

'I am here as a soldier who has temporarily left the field of battle in order to explain ... what civil war is like when civil war is waged by women. '

politicians, putting militancy, and the reproach of militancy, if reproach there is, on the people who had assaulted the women, they actually said it was the women who were militant and very much to blame.

It was not the speakers on the platform who would not answer them who were to blame, or the ushers at the meeting; it was the poor women who had had their bruises and their knocks and scratches, and who were put into prison for doing precisely nothing but holding a protest meeting in the street after it was all over. However, we were called militant for doing that, and we were quite willing to accept the name, because militancy for us is time-honoured; you have the church militant and in the sense of spiritual militancy we were very militant indeed.

> 'We will put the enemy in the position where they will have to choose between giving us freedom or giving us death.'

We were determined to press this question of the enfranchisement of the women to the point where we were no longer to be ignored by the politicians as had been the case for about fifty years, during which time women had patiently used every means open to them to win their political enfranchisement.

Experience will show you that if you really want to get anything done, it is not so much a matter of whether you alienate sympathy; sympathy is a very unsatisfactory thing if it is not practical sympathy. It does not matter to the practical suffragist whether she alienates sympathy that was never of any use to her. What she wants is to get something practical done, and whether it is done out of sympathy or whether it is done out of fear, or whether it is done because you want to be comfortable again and not be worried in this way, doesn't particularly matter so long as you get it. We had enough of sympathy for fifty years; it never brought us anything; and we would rather have an angry man going to the government and saying, my business is interfered with and I won't submit to its being interfered with any longer because you won't give women the vote, than to have a gentleman come on to our platforms year in and year out and talk about his ardent sympathy with woman suffrage.

'Put them in prison,' they said, 'that will stop it.' But it didn't stop it. They put women in prison for long terms of imprisonment, for making a nuisance of themselves—that was the expression when they took petitions in their hands to the door of the House of Commons; and they thought that sending them to prison, giving them a day's imprisonment, would cause them to all settle down again and there would be no further trouble. But it didn't happen so at all: instead of the women giving it up, more women did it, and more and more and more women did it until there were three hundred women at a time, who had not broken a single law, only 'made a nuisance of themselves' as the politicians say.

'... they actually said it was the women who were militant and very much to blame ... the poor women who had their bruises and their knocks and scratches, and who were put into prison for doing precisely nothing but holding a protest meeting in the street.'

The whole argument with the anti-suffragists, or even the critical suffragist man, is this: that you can govern human beings without their consent. They have said to us, 'Government rests upon force; the women haven't force, so they must submit.' Well, we are showing them that government does not rest upon force at all; it rests upon consent. As long as women consent to be unjustly governed, they can be; but directly women say: 'We withhold our consent, we will not be governed any longer so long as that government is unjust,' not by the forces of civil war can you govern the very weakest woman. You can kill that woman, but she escapes you then; you cannot govern her. And that is, I think, a most valuable demonstration we have been making to the world.

' Now, I want to say to you who think women cannot succeed, we have brought the government of England to this position, that it has to face this alternative; either women are to be killed or women are to have the vote. I ask American men in this meeting, what would you say if in your State you were faced with that alternative, that you must either kill them or give them their citizenship—women, many of whom you respect, women whom you know have lived useful lives, women whom you know, even if you do not know them personally, are animated with the highest motives, women who are in pursuit of liberty and the power to do useful public service? Well, there is only one answer to that alternative; there is only one way out of it, unless you are prepared to put back civilisation two or three generations; you must give those women the vote. Now that is the outcome of our civil war.

You won your freedom in America when you had the Revolution, by bloodshed, by sacrificing human life. You won the Civil War by the sacrifice of human life when you decided to emancipate the negro. You have left it to the women in your land, the men of all civilised countries have left it to women, to work out their own salvation. That is the way in which we women of England are doing. Human life for us is sacrificed, but we say if any life is to be sacrificed it shall be ours; we won't do it ourselves, but we will put the enemy in the position where they will have to choose between giving us freedom or giving us death.'

'We had enough of sympathy for fifty years; it never brought us anything; and we would rather have an angry man going to the government ... because you won't give women the vote, than to have a gentleman come on to our platforms and talk about his ardent sympathy for women's suffrage.'

Emmeline Pankhurst was detained on Ellis Island Immigration Station, New York during this tour, which was not unusual for her. She was arrested several times during her life—for conspiracy in 1912 and for inciting violence under the 'Cat and Mouse' Act in 1913. (She was arrested twelve times during 1914.) Her call was 'freedom or death' and some took Pankhurst at her word. In June 1913, suffragette Emily Davidson threw herself in front of King George V's horse, Anmer, as it competed in the English Derby. The 40 year old Miss Davidson lingered on for six days before she died—the women's movement's first heroine and martyr.

Despite New Zealand granting women the vote in 1889 (the first country to do so) and Australian women achieving suffrage in 1902, World War I put the issue of 'Votes for Women' in England and the United States on hold for four years. In England, women over the age of thirty were finally granted the vote in 1918 with full suffrage achieved in 1928. In 1920 the Nineteenth Amendment to the US Constitution was passed giving American women the right to vote, one year after Pankhurst had returned to America and settled in Canada after remarrying.

Historians now credit the work of suffragists Millicent Fawcett (England) and Carrie Chapman Catt (USA) as the driving force which led to women achieving the right to vote in the two largest democracies in the world at the time. However, it was Emmeline Pankhurst who put the movement—through her own example and sacrifice—on the world stage.

Patrick Pearse

'Ireland Unfree Shall Never Be At Peace'

Glasnevin Cemetery, Dublin, 1 August 1915.

Padraic Henry Pearse (1879-16) graduated from the King's Inn Law School in Dublin before gaining his BA in linguistics. A foundation member of the Irish Volunteers militia, Pearse was committed to the establishment of an Irish republic after centuries of unrest over British occupation of Ireland. However, the outbreak of World War I further delayed the implementation of legislation that would have restored the Dublin parliament. The Irish Republican Brotherhood (the forerunner of the Irish Republican Army) saw England's preoccupation with the war as its opportunity to press—by force if necessary—for independence.

Pearse had already travelled to America in 1914 to raise money for weapons and ammunition to force the British out of Ireland and campaigned for the use of force against the British. He gave this speech at the funeral of Jeremiah O'Donovan Rossa at Glasnevin Cemetery in Dublin in August 1915 and used the opportunity to agitate for Irish rebellion. O'Rossa was one of the old Fenian Republicans, who had been imprisoned in England and had died in exile in America after a long illness. In front of thousands of mourners, Pearse's speech became a rallying cry for armed resistance in Northern Ireland, which culminated in the failed Easter Uprising of 1916.

> 'Life springs from death; and from the graves of patriot men and women spring living nations.'

' It has seemed right, before we turn away from this place in which we have laid the mortal remains of O'Donovan Rossa, that one among us should, in the name of all, speak the praise of that valiant man, and endeavour to formulate the thought and the hope that are in us as we stand around his grave. And if there is anything that makes it fitting that I, rather than some other, I rather than one of the grey-haired men who were young with him and shared in his labour and in his suffering, should speak here, it is perhaps that I may be taken as speaking on behalf of a new generation that has been rebaptised in the Fenian faith, and that has accepted the responsibility of carrying out the Fenian programme. I propose to you then that, here by the grave of this unrepentant Fenian, we renew our baptismal vows; that, here by the grave of this unconquered and unconquerable man, we ask of God, each one for himself, such unshakable purpose, such high and gallant courage, such unbreakable strength of soul as belonged to O'Donovan Rossa.

Deliberately here we avow ourselves, as he avowed himself in the dock, Irishmen of one allegiance only. We of the Irish Volunteers, and you others who are associated with us in today's task and duty, are bound together and must stand together henceforth in brotherly union for the achievement of the freedom of Ireland. And we know only one definition of freedom: it is Tone's definition, it is Mitchel's definition, it is Rossa's definition. Let no man blaspheme the cause that the dead generations of Ireland served by giving it any other name and definition than their name and their definition.

We stand at Rossa's grave not in sadness but rather in exaltation of spirit that it has been given to us to come thus into so close a communion with that brave and splendid Gael. Splendid and holy causes are served by men who are themselves splendid and holy. O'Donovan Rossa was splendid in the proud manhood of him, splendid in the heroic grace of him, splendid in the Gaelic strength and clarity and truth of him. And all that splendour and pride and strength was compatible with a humility and a simplicity of devotion to Ireland, to all that was olden and beautiful and Gaelic in Ireland, the holiness and simplicity of patriotism of a Michael O'Cleary or of an Eoghan O'Growney. The clear true eyes of this man almost alone in his day visioned Ireland as we of today would surely have her: not free merely but Gaelic as well; not Gaelic merely, but free as well.

In a closer spiritual communion with him now than ever before or perhaps ever again, in a spiritual communion with those of his day, living and dead, who suffered with him in English prisons, in communion of spirit too with our own dear comrades who suffer in English prisons today, and speaking on their behalf as well as our own, we pledge to Ireland our love, and we pledge to English rule in Ireland our hate. This is a place of peace, sacred to the dead, where men should speak with all charity and with all restraint; but I hold it a Christian thing, as O'Donovan Rossa held it, to hate evil, to hate untruth, to hate oppression, and, hating them, to strive to overthrow them.

Our foes are strong and wise and wary but, strong and wise and wary as they are, they cannot undo the miracles of God who ripens in the hearts of young men the seeds sown by the young men of a former generation. And the seeds sown by the young men of (18)65 and '67 are coming to their miraculous ripening today. Rulers and Defenders of Realms had need to be wary if they would guard against such processes. Life springs from death; and from the graves of patriot men and women spring living nations. The Defenders of this Realm have worked well in secret and in the open. They think that they have pacified Ireland. They think that they have purchased half of us and intimidated the other half. They think that they have foreseen everything, think that they have provided against everything; but the fools, the fools, the fools! They have left us our Fenian dead, and while Ireland holds these graves, Ireland unfree shall never be at peace. '

Although many rebels questioned whether the Irish Brotherhood was ready for armed battle with the British, a major uprising began on 23 April (Easter Sunday) in 1916. Pearse was a teacher and poet, and although he described himself as 'commandant-general' he did not have a military background. Only 1700 rebels took part, mainly in Dublin itself. The following day, on the steps of the captured general Post Office, Pearse proclaimed the Irish Republic. But the uprising was routed by 20 000 British troops and with Dublin ablaze and many innocent civilians killed, the rebels surrendered. Those who signed the republican proclamation as part of the provisional government–Thomas J Clarke, Sean MacDiarmada, Thomas MacDonagh, Eamonn Ceannt, James Connolly, Joseph Plunkett and Padraic Pearse–were among 16 rebels executed on 3 May, 1916.

From the dock during his trial, Pearse foretold of the century of bitter struggle for Irish independence: 'You cannot conquer Ireland. You cannot extinguish the Irish passion for freedom. If our deed has not been sufficient to win freedom, then our children will win it by a better deed.'

Woodrow Wilson

'War Message'

Address to Extraordinary Session of US Congress, Washington DC, 2 April 1917.

Thomas Woodrow Wilson (1856-24) was a lawyer, Princeton University Professor and Democratic Governor of New Jersey before elected President of the United States of America in 1912. This was a time when war clouds were gathering in Europe. For three years America stayed out of the conflict and Wilson was re-elected in 1916 on the slogan: 'He kept us out of the War'. However, within three months of his inauguration he reversed America's isolationist stance, despite his personal commitment to peace and neutrality. In this speech, Wilson cites submarine attacks in the Atlantic, which led to the sinking of the commercial liner Lusitania in 1915, and declares Germany's sponsorship of Mexico's bid for lost territory in Texas as reasons for entering the war.

' I have called the Congress into extraordinary session because there are serious, very serious, choices of policy to be made, and made immediately, which it was neither right nor constitutionally permissible that I should assume the responsibility of making ...

With a profound sense of the solemn and even tragic character of the step I am taking and of the grave responsibilities which it involves, but in unhesitating obedience to what I deem my constitutional duty, I advise that the Congress declare the recent course of the Imperial German Government to be in fact nothing less than war against the government and people of the United States; that it formally accept the status of belligerent which has thus been thrust upon it, and that it take immediate steps not only to put the country in a more thorough state of defense but also to exert all its power and employ all its resources to bring the Government of the German Empire to terms and end the war.

> 'It is a fearful thing to lead this great peaceful people into war, into the most terrible and disastrous of all wars, civilization itself seeming to be in the balance.'

What this will involve is clear. It will involve the utmost practicable cooperation in counsel and action with the governments now at war with Germany, and, as incident to that, the extension to those governments of the most liberal financial credit, in order that our resources may so far as possible be added to theirs.

It will involve the organisation and mobilisation of all the material resources of the country to supply the materials of war and serve the incidental needs of the Nation in the most abundant and yet the most economical and efficient way possible. It will involve the immediate full equipment of the navy in all respects but particularly in supplying it with the best means of dealing with the enemy's submarines. It will involve the immediate addition to the armed forces of the United States already provided for by law in case of war at least five hundred thousand men, who should, in my opinion, be chosen upon the principle of universal liability to service, and also the authorisation of subsequent additional increments of equal force so soon as they may be needed and can be handled in training.

It will involve also, of course, the granting of adequate credits to the Government, sustained, I hope, so far as they can equitably be sustained by the present generation, by well conceived taxation. I say sustained so far as may be equitable by taxation because it seems to me that it would be most unwise to base the credits which will now be necessary entirely on money borrowed. It is our duty, I most respectfully urge, to protect our people so far as we may against the very serious hardships and evils which would be likely to arise out of the inflation which would be produced by vast loans.

In carrying out the measures by which these things are to be accomplished we should keep constantly in mind the wisdom of interfering as little as possible in our own preparation and in the equipment of our own military forces with the duty—for it will be a very practical duty—of supplying the nations already at war with Germany with the materials which they can obtain only from us or by our assistance. They are in the field and we should help them in every way to be effective there.

I shall take the liberty of suggesting, through the several executive departments of the Government, for the consideration of your committees, measures for the accomplishment of the several objects I have mentioned. I hope that it will be your pleasure to deal with them as having been framed after very careful thought by the branch of the Government upon which the responsibility of conducting the war and safeguarding the Nation will most directly fall.

While we do these things, these deeply momentous things, let us be very clear, and make very clear to all the world what our motives and our objects are. My own thought has not been driven from its habitual and normal course by the unhappy events of the last two months, and I do not believe that the thought of the Nation has been altered or clouded by them. I have exactly the same things in mind now that I had in mind when I addressed the Senate on the twenty-second of January last, the same that I had in mind when I addressed the Congress on the third of February and on the twenty-sixth of February.

Our object now, as then, is to vindicate the principles of peace and justice in the life of the world as against selfish and autocratic power and to set up amongst the really free and self-governed peoples of the world such a concert of purpose and of action as will henceforth insure the observance of those principles. Neutrality is no longer feasible or desirable where the peace of the world is involved and the freedom of its peoples, and the menace to that peace and freedom lies in the existence of autocratic governments backed by organised force which is controlled wholly by their will, not by the will of their people. We have seen the last of neutrality in such circumstances. We are at the beginning of an age in which it will be insisted that the same standards of conduct and of responsibility for wrong done shall be observed among nations and their governments that are observed among the individual citizens of civilized states.

We have no quarrel with the German people. We have no feeling towards them but one of sympathy and friendship. It was not upon their impulse that their government acted in entering this war. It was not with their previous knowledge or approval. It was a war determined upon as wars used to be determined upon in the old, unhappy days when peoples were nowhere consulted by their rulers and wars were provoked and waged in the interest of dynasties or of little groups of ambitious men who were accustomed to use their fellow men as pawns and tools.

'We desire no conquest, no dominion. We seek no indemnities for ourselves, no material compensation for the sacrifices we shall freely make. We are but one of the champions of the rights of mankind.'

Self-governed nations do not fill their neighbor states with spies or set the course of intrigue to bring about some critical posture of affairs which will give them an opportunity to strike and make conquest. Such designs can be successfully worked out only under cover and where no one has the right to ask questions. Cunningly contrived plans of deception or aggression, carried, it may be, from generation to generation, can be worked out and kept from the light only within the privacy of courts or behind the carefully guarded confidences of a narrow and privileged class. They are happily impossible where public opinion commands and insists upon full information concerning all the nation's affairs.

A steadfast concert for peace can never be maintained except by a partnership of democratic nations. No autocratic government could be trusted to keep faith within it or observe its covenants. It must be a league of honor, a partnership of opinion. Intrigue would eat its vitals away; the plottings of inner circles who could plan what they would and render account to no one would be a corruption seated at its very heart. Only free peoples can hold their purpose and their honor steady to a common end and prefer the interests of mankind to any narrow interest of their own.

Does not every American feel that assurance has been added to our hope for the future peace of the world by the wonderful and heartening things that have been happening within the last few weeks in Russia? Russia was known by those who knew it best to have been always in fact democratic at heart, in all the vital habits of her thought, in all the intimate relationships of her people that spoke their natural instinct, their habitual attitude towards life. The autocracy that crowned the summit of her political structure, long as it had stood and terrible as was the reality of its power, was not in fact Russian in origin, character, or purpose; and now it has been shaken off and the great, generous Russian people have been added in all their naive majesty and might to the forces that are fighting for freedom in the world, for justice, and for peace. Here is a fit partner for a League of Honor.

One of the things that has served to convince us that the Prussian, autocracy was not and could never be our friend is that from the very outset of the present war it has filled our unsuspecting communities and even our offices of government with spies and set criminal intrigues everywhere afoot against our national unity of counsel, our peace within and without, our industries and our commerce. Indeed it is now evident that its spies were here even before the war began; and it is unhappily not a matter of conjecture but a fact proved in our courts of justice that the intrigues which have more than once come perilously near to disturbing the peace and dislocating the industries of the country have been carried on at the instigation, with the support, and even under the personal direction of official agents of the Imperial Government accredited to the Government of the United States. Even in checking these things and trying to extirpate them we have sought to put the most generous interpretation possible upon them because we knew that their source lay, not in any hostile feeling or purpose of the German people towards us (who were, no doubt, as ignorant of them as we ourselves were), but only in the selfish designs of a Government that did what it pleased and told its people nothing. But they have played their part in serving to convince us at last that that Government entertains no

'We are glad, now that we see the facts with no veil of false pretense about them to fight thus for the ultimate peace of the world and for the liberation of its peoples, the German peoples included.'

real friendship for us and means to act against our peace and security at its convenience. That it means to stir up enemies against us at our very doors the intercepted note to the German Minister at Mexico City is eloquent evidence.

We are accepting this challenge of hostile purpose because we know that in such a Government, following such methods, we can never have a friend; and that in the presence of its organised power, always lying in wait to accomplish we know not what purpose, there can be no assured security for the democratic Governments of the world. We are now about to accept gauge of battle with this natural foe to liberty and shall, if necessary, spend the whole force of the nation to check and nullify its pretensions and its power. We are glad, now that we see the facts with no veil of false pretense about them to fight thus for the ultimate peace of the world and for the liberation of its peoples, the German peoples included: for the rights of nations great and small and the privilege of men everywhere to choose their way. of life and of obedience. The world must be made safe for democracy. Its peace must be planted upon the tested foundations of political liberty. We have no selfish ends to serve.

We desire no conquest, no dominion. We seek no indemnities for ourselves, no material compensation for the sacrifices we shall freely make. We are but one of the champions of the rights of mankind. We shall be satisfied when those rights have been made as secure as the faith

'We have no quarrel with the German people. We have no feeling towards them but one of sympathy and friendship.'

and the freedom of nations can make them. Just because we fight without rancor and without selfish object, seeking nothing for ourselves but what we shall wish to share with all free peoples, we shall, I feel confident, conduct our operations as belligerents without passion and ourselves observe with proud punctilio the principles of right and of fair play we profess to be fighting for.

I have said nothing of the Governments allied with the Imperial Government of Germany because they nave not made war upon us or challenged us to defend our right and our honor. The Austro-Hungarian Government has, indeed, avowed its unqualified endorsement and acceptance of the reckless and lawless submarine warfare adopted now without disguise by the Imperial German Government, and it has therefore not been possible for this Government to receive Count Tarnowski, the Ambassador recently accredited to this Government by the Imperial and Royal Government of Austria-Hungary; but that Government has not actually engaged in warfare against citizens of the United States on the seas, and I take the liberty, for the present at least, of postponing a discussion of our relations with the authorities at Vienna. We enter this war only where we are clearly forced into it because there are no other means of defending our rights....

It is a distressing and oppressive duty, Gentlemen of the Congress, which I have performed in thus addressing you. There are, it may be many months of fiery trial and sacrifice ahead of us. It is a fearful thing to lead this great peaceful people into war, into the most terrible and disastrous of all wars, civilization itself seeming to be in the balance.

But the right is more precious than peace, and we shall fight for the things which we have always carried nearest our hearts—for democracy, for the right of those who submit to authority to have a voice in their own Governments, for the rights and liberties of small nations, for a universal dominion of right by such a concert of free peoples as shall bring peace and safety to all nations and make the world itself at last free. To such a task we can dedicate our lives and our fortunes, every thing that we are and everything that we have, with the pride of those who know that the day has come when America is privileged to spend her blood and her might for the principles that gave her birth and happiness and the peace which she has treasured. God helping her, she can do no other. '

Despite his personal misgivings, Woodrow Wilson asked for a declaration of war and received thunderous applause from Congress. That night, as he reflected on the historic day, he remarked, 'My message today was a message of death for our young men. How strange it seems to applaud that.' Wilson then laid his head down and wept.

In January 1918, ten months before the end of World War I, Wilson appeared before a joint session of Congress and outlined possible peace terms to end World War I. The Fourteen Points outlined in his speech served as both the basis for peace and the establishment of a 'League of Nations' to promote post-war understanding and peaceful relations. But the war dragged on until the end of 1918, until Germany's allies collapsed or surrendered and English, French and American forces were poised to invade Germany itself.

'Neutrality is no longer feasible or desirable where the peace of the world is involved.'

In August, the Chancellor of Germany, Prince Max of Baden, appealed for an armistice based upon Wilson's Fourteen Points but by the time the war ended—at 11am on 11 November—nearly 40 million people had perished. As for Wilson's idealism, his 'Fourteen Points' were but a memory when the victors met in Versailles, France in 1919, and punished Germany under the guise of a peace treaty. While England and France listened politely to Wilson, they were intent on exacting reparations from Germany.

Wilson was forced to compromise heavily to bring his dream of a 'League of Nations' into a reality. Despite winning the Nobel Peace Prize in 1919, the Republican-dominated US Congress rejected the 'Treaty of Versailles' that Wilson presented to it. Despite his best efforts the American President had lost the confidence of the Congress and suffered a complete physical and mental breakdown. The President who had lost the support of his own country had outlined his personal dream of future international security based upon an idealism for which the world was not yet ready. Woodrow Wilson died a broken man in 1924.

Vladimir Ilyich Lenin

'Constructing the Socialist Order'

Address to the First Congress of the Communist International, 2 March 1919.

Vladimir Ilyich Lenin (originally Ulyanov) was born in Simbirski, Russia in 1870 and studied law at Kazan State University. A Marxist revolutionary, Lenin was exiled to Serbia from 1897 to 1900. He became the leader of the Social Democratic Workers' Party and, after the overthrow of Tsar Nicholas in March 1917, returned to St Petersberg from Zurich and urged his followers to seize control from the provisional government led by Alexander Kerensky. Lenin marshalled the Bolshevik forces and captured government buildings, the Winter Palace in St Petersberg and finally all of Moscow.

Lenin headed the Russian Communist Party (formerly the Social Democratic Workers Party) but the Bolsheviks performed poorly in the election of a constituent assembly and had to seize power by force. The Bolsheviks executed the Tsar's family and sought peace with Germany, giving up sovereignty to 1.3 million square miles of land in the Treaty of Brest Litovsk.

News of the Russian Revolution reverberated all over the world and resonated with workers in England, France, Germany and America. In March 1919, Lenin addressed the First Congress of the Communist International, advocating the Soviet system's 'dictatorship of the proletariat'.

' On behalf of the Central Committee of the Russian Communist Party
I declare the First Congress of the Communist International open. First
I would ask all present to rise in tribute to the finest representatives of
the Third International: Karl Liebknecht and Rosa Luxemburg.

Comrades, our gathering has great historic significance. It testifies to the collapse of all the illusions cherished by bourgeois democrats. Not only in Russia, but in the most developed capitalist countries of Europe, in Germany for example, civil war is a fact.

The bourgeois are terror-stricken at the growing workers' revolutionary movement. This is understandable if we take into account that the development of events since the imperialist war inevitably favors the workers' revolutionary movement, and that the world revolution is beginning and growing in intensity everywhere.

The people are aware of the greatness and significance of the struggle now going on. All that is needed is to find the practical form to enable the proletariat to establish its rule. Such a form is the Soviet system with the dictatorship of the proletariat. Dictatorship of the proletariat—until now these words were Latin to the masses. Thanks to the spread of the Soviets throughout the world this Latin has been translated into all modern languages; a practical form of dictatorship has been found by the working people. The mass of workers now understand it thanks to Soviet power in Russia, thanks to the Spartacus League in Germany and to similar organisations in other countries, such as, for example, the Shop Stewards Committees of Britain. All this shows that a revolutionary form of the dictatorship of the proletariat has been found, that the proletariat is now able to exercise its rule.

'The imperialist war inevitably favours the workers' revolutionary movement, and that the world revolution is beginning and growing in intensity everywhere.'

Comrades, I think that after the events in Russia and the January struggle in Germany, it is especially important to note that in other countries, too, the latest form of the workers' movement is asserting itself and getting the upper hand. Today, for example, I read in an anti-socialist newspaper a report to the effect that the British government had received a dedication from the Birmingham Workers' Council and had expressed its readiness to recognise the Councils as economic bodies. The Soviet system has triumphed not only in backward Russia, but also in the most developed country of Europe—in Germany, and in

Britain, the oldest capitalist country.

Even though the bourgeoisie are still raging, even though they may kill thousands more workers, victory will be ours, the victory of the worldwide Communist revolution is assured.

Comrades, I extend hearty greetings to you on behalf of the Central Committee of the Russian Communist Party. I move that we elect a presidium. Let us have nominations.'

> 'Even though the bourgeoisie are still raging, even though they may kill thousands more workers, victory will be ours, the victory of the worldwide Communist revolution is assured.'

In 1922, after the end of the Russian Civil War between the Bosheviks (Reds) and the anti-Bolsheviks (Whites), the Union of Soviet Socialist Republics was formed. In April 1922, Josef Stalin was elected General Secretary of the Communist Party. The following month Lenin suffered the first of several strokes that would eventually claim his life in January 1924. Although he warned the Party in his final will and testament to remove Josef Stalin from power, Stalin survived Lenin's criticism from the grave and out-manoeuvred—and gradually purged—the Communist Party of his political rivals, including Trotsky. In 1924 the Soviet Union adopted a constitution based on the dictatorship of the proletariat and the public ownership of land and all means of production. The revolution was complete.

Between
the Wars
1920-1939

Margaret Sanger

'The Children's Era'

Address to The Birth Control League, New York, March 1925.

Margaret H. Sanger (1883-1966) was the founder of the American birth control movement and fought for the revision of archaic rules which prohibited the publication of facts about contraception. Sanger's mother died at the age of 49 after 18 pregnancies (seven children died). As a practising nurse in New York's impoverished lower East Side, Sanger learnt first hand about the relationship between high infant and maternal mortality rates and poverty. Of most concern was the methods used by some women to induce abortion.

Sanger resolved to seek out the 'root of the evil'—the lack of education about birth control. In 1914 she began publishing material about contraception and opened the first American birth control clinic in Brooklyn. Sanger also argued—controversially for the time—that birth control would 'fulfill a critical psychological need by enabling women to fully enjoy sexual relations free from the fear of pregnancy'. Opposition to Sanger was strong and many of her speeches were greeted with shouts of abuse. She fled to England under an alias in 1914 to escape prosecution, and spent 30 days in the workhouse in 1917 for 'maintaining a public nuisance'. Her greatest opposition came from the Catholic Church.

Sanger founded the American Birth Control League in 1921, serving as its president for seven years, and offered women an alternative that the Church could not—the ability to control their own lives. In March 1925, Sanger addressed a Birth Control League conference in New York.

‘ My subject is 'The Children's Era'. The Children's Era! This makes me think of Ellen Key's book—The Century of the Child. Ellen Key hoped that this twentieth century was to be the century of the child.

The twentieth century, she said, would see this old world of ours converted into a beautiful garden of children. Well, we have already lived through a quarter of this twentieth century. What steps have we taken toward making it the century of the child? So far, very, very few.

Why does the Children's Era still remain a dream of the dim and the distant future? Why has so little been accomplished? In spite of all our acknowledged love of children, all our generosity, all our good-will, all the enormous spending of millions on philanthropy and charities, all our warm-hearted sentiment, all our incessant activity and social consciousness? Why?

Before you can cultivate a garden, you must know something about gardening. You have got to give your seeds a proper soil in which to grow. You have got to give them sunlight and fresh air. You have got to give them space and the opportunity (if they are to lift their flowers to the sun), to strike their roots deep into that soil. And always—do not forget this—you have got to fight weeds. You cannot have a garden, if you let weeds overrun it. So, if we want to make this world a garden for children, we must first of all learn the lesson of the gardener.

So far we have not been gardeners. We have only been a sort of silly reception committee, a reception committee at the Grand Central Station of life. Trainload after trainload of children are coming in, day and night—nameless refugees arriving out of the Nowhere into the Here. Trainload after trainload—many unwelcome, unwanted, unprepared for, unknown, without baggage, without passports, most of them without pedigrees. These unlimited hordes of refugees arrive in such numbers that the reception committee is thrown into a panic—a panic of activity. The reception committee arouses itself heroically, establishes emergency measures: milk stations, maternity centers, settlement houses, playgrounds, orphanages, welfare leagues, and every conceivable kind of charitable effort. But still trainloads of

'There can be no hope for the future of civilization, no certainty of racial salvation, until every woman can decide for herself whether she will or will not become a mother, and when and how many children she cares to bring into the world.'

children keep on coming—human weed crop up that spread so fast in this sinister struggle for existence, that the overworked committee becomes exhausted, inefficient, and can think of no way out.

When we protest against this immeasurable, meaningless waste of motherhood and child-life; when we protest against the ever-mounting cost to the world of asylums, prisons, homes for the feeble-minded, and such institutions for the unfit, when we protest against the disorder and chaos and tragedy of modern life, when we point out the biological corruption that is destroying the very heart of American life, we are told that we are making merely an "emotional" appeal. When we point to the one immediate practical way toward order and beauty in society, the only way to lay the foundations of a society composed of happy children, happy women, and happy men, they call this idea indecent and immoral.

It is not enough to clean up the filth and disorder of our overcrowded cities. It is not enough to stop the evil of child labour—even if we could! It is not enough to decrease the rate of infantile mortality. It is not enough to open playgrounds, and build more public schools in which we can standardise the mind of the young. It is not enough to throw millions upon millions of dollars into charities and philanthropies. Don't deceive ourselves that by so doing we are making the world 'Safe for Children'.

Those of you who have followed the sessions of this Conference must, I am sure, agree with me that the first real step towards the creation of a Children's Era must lie in providing the conditions of healthy life for children not only before birth but even more imperatively before conception. Human society must protect its children—yes, but prenatal care is most essential! The child-to-be, as yet not called into being, has rights no less imperative.

We have learned in the preceding sessions of this Conference that, if we wish to produce strong and sturdy children, the embryo must grow in a chemically healthy medium. The blood stream of the mother must be chemically normal. Worry, strain, shock, unhappiness, enforced maternity, may all poison the blood of the enslaved mother. This chemically poisoned blood may produce a defective baby—a child foredoomed to idiocy, or feeble-mindedness, crime, or failure.

Do I exaggerate? Am I taking a rare exception and making it a general rule? Our opponents declare that children are conceived in love, and that every new-born baby converts its parents to love and unselfishness. My answer is to point to the asylums, the hospitals, the ever-growing institutions for the unfit. Look into the family history of those who are feeble-minded; or behind the bars of jails and prisons. Trace the family histories; find out the conditions under which they were conceived and born, before you attempt to persuade us that reckless breeding has nothing to do with these grave questions.

> **'We want to free women from enslavery and unwilling motherhood. We are fighting for the emancipation for the mothers of the world, of the children of the world, and the children to be.'**

There is only one way out. We have got to fight for the health and happiness of the Unborn Child. And to do that in a practical, tangible way, we have got to free women from enforced, enslaved maternity. There can be no hope for the future of civilization, no certainty of racial salvation, until every woman can decide for herself whether she will or will not become a mother, and when and how many children she cares to bring into the world. That is the first step.

I would like to suggest Civil Service examinations for parenthood! Prospective parents after such an examination would be given a parenthood license, proving that they are physically and mentally fit to be the fathers and mothers of the next generation.

This is an interesting idea—but then arises the questions: 'Who is to decide?', 'Would there be a jury, like a play jury?' Would a Republican administration give parenthood permits only to Republicans—or perhaps only to Democrats? The more you think of governmental interference, the less it works out. Take this plan of civil service examination for parenthood. It suggests Prohibition: there might even be bootlegging in babies!

No, I doubt the advisability of governmental sanction. The problem of bringing children into the world ought to be decided by those most seriously involved—those who run the greatest risks; in the last analysis—by the mother and the child. If there is going to be any Civil Service examination, let it be conducted by the Unborn Child, the Child-to-be.

Just try for a moment to picture the possibilities of such an examination. When you want a cook or housemaid, you go to an employment bureau. You have to answer questions. You have to exchange references. You have to persuade the talented cook that you conduct a proper well-run household. Children ought to have at least the same privilege as cooks.

Sometimes in idle moments I like to think it would be a very good scheme to have a bureau of the Child-to-be. At such a bureau of the unborn, the wise child might be able to find out a few things about its father—and its mother. Just think for a moment of this bureau where prospective parents might apply for a baby. Think of the questions they would be asked by the agent of the unborn or by the baby itself.

First: "Mr. Father, a baby is an expensive luxury. Can you really afford one?"

"Have you paid for your last baby yet?"

"How many children have you already? Six? You must have your hands full. Can you take care of so many?"

"Do you look upon children as a reward—or a penalty?"

"How are your ductless glands—well balanced?"

"Can you provide a happy home for one! A sunny nursery? Proper food?"

"What's that you say? Ten children already? Two dark rooms in the slums?"

"No, thank you! I don't care to be born at all if I cannot be well-born. Good-bye!"

And if we could organise a society for the prevention of cruelty to unborn children, we would make it a law that children should be brought into the world only when they were welcome, invited, and wanted; that they would arrive with a clean bill of health and heritage; that they would possess healthy, happy, well-mated, and mature parents.

And there would be certain conditions of circumstances which would preclude parenthood. These conditions, the presence of which would make parenthood a crime, are the following:

1. Transmissible disease
2. Temporary disease
3. Subnormal children already in the family
4. Space out between births
5. Twenty-three years as a minimum age for parents
6. Economic circumstances adequate
7. Spiritual harmony between parents.

In conclusion, let me repeat: we are not trying to establish a dictatorship over parents. We want to free women from enslavery and unwilling motherhood. We are fighting for the emancipation for the mothers of the world, of the children of the world, and the children to be. We want to create a real Century of the Child—usher in a Children's Era. We can do this by handling the terrific gift of life in bodies fit and perfect as can be fashioned. Help us to make this Conference, which has aroused so much interest, the turning point toward this era. Only so can you help in the creation of the future. '

Margaret Sanger had many of her writings labelled lewd, even pornographic. She was charged with nine counts of violating the postal act regarding the distribution of 'vulgar' material and travelled to England to escape prosecution. Lies were spread about her teachings regarding 'planned parenthood' and much was misrepresented in the press in order to discredit her.

In 1927 Margaret Sanger organised the first World Population Conference in Geneva, Switzerland, and was the first president of the International Planned Parenthood Federation. Jailed eight times during her adult life, one of the compromises she had to make was to secure her message among the upper and middle classes, thereby missing her target audience—the poor and uneducated.

In the late 1950s, with donations from her supporters, she funded the development of the birth control pill based on the research of the Worcester Foundation, at a time when the transference of birth control information was still a criminal act in some American states.

Franklin D Roosevelt

'The Only Thing We Have To Fear is Fear Itself'

Inaugural Presidential Address, Washington DC, 4 March 1933.

Franklin Delano Roosevelt (1882-1945) rose from being governor of New York in 1928 to President of the United States in 1932, despite being stricken with polio in 1921, which left him partially paralysed in the legs and necessitated the use of a wheelchair in later years. 'FDR' as he was known, was elected President in November 1932 at a time when America, and the world, was beset by economic depression after the Wall Street crash of October 1929. In this speech, Roosevelt outlines his plan for a 'New Deal' and economic recovery.

'This is a day of national consecration, and I am certain that on this day my fellow Americans expect that, on my induction into the presidency, I will address them with a candor and a decision which the present situation of our people impels.

This is pre-eminently the time to speak to truth—the whole truth, frankly and boldly. Nor need we shrink from honestly facing conditions in our country today. This great nation will endure as it has endured, will revive and will prosper. So, first of all, let me assert my firm belief that the only thing we have to fear is fear itself—nameless, unreasoning, unjustified terror, which paralyzes needed efforts to convert retreat into advance.

In every dark hour of our national life a leadership of frankness and vigor has met with that understanding and support of the people themselves which is essential to victory. I am convinced that you will again give that support to leadership in these critical days.

In such a spirit on my part and yours, we face our common difficulties. They concern, thank God, only material things. Values have shrunk to fantastic levels; taxes have risen; our ability to pay has fallen; government of all kinds is faced by serious curtailment of income; the means of exchange are frozen in the currents of trade; the withered leaves of industrial enterprise lie on every side; farmers find no markets for their produce; the savings of many years, in thousands of families, are gone.

'Let me assert my firm belief that the only thing we have to fear is fear itself—nameless, unreasoning, unjustified terror, which paralyzes needed efforts to convert retreat into advance.'

More important, a host of unemployed citizens face the grim problem of existence, and an equally great number toil with little return. Only a foolish optimist can deny the dark realities of the moment.

And, yet our distress comes from no failure of substance. We are stricken by no plague of locusts. Compared with the perils which our forefathers conquered, because they believed and were not afraid, we have still much to be thankful for. Nature still offers her bounty, and human efforts have multiplied it. Plenty is at our doorstep, but a generous use of it languishes in the very sight of the supply.

Primarily, this is because the rulers of the exchange of mankind's goods have failed through their own stubbornness and their own incompetence, have admitted their failure and have abdicated. Practices of the unscrupulous money-changers stand indicted in the court of public opinion, rejected by the hearts and minds of men.

True, they have tried, but their efforts have been cast in the pattern of an outworn tradition. Faced by the failure of credit, they have proposed only the lending of more money. Stripped of the lure of profit by which to induce our people to follow their false leadership, they have resorted to exhortations, pleading tearfully for restored confidence. They know only the rules of a generation of self-seekers. They have no vision, and when there is no vision, the people perish.

Yes, the money-changers have fled from their high seats in the temple of our civilization. We may now restore that temple to the ancient truths!

FRANKLIN D ROOSEVELT   49

> **'I am prepared under my constitutional duty to recommend the measures that a stricken nation in the midst of a stricken world may require.'**

The measure of the restoration lies in the extent to which we apply social values more noble than mere monetary profit. Happiness lies not in the mere possession of money; it lies in the joy of achievement, in the thrill of creative effort. The joy and moral stimulation of work no longer must be forgotten in the mad chase of evanescent profits.

These dark days will be worth all they cost us if they teach us that our true destiny is not to be ministered unto but to minister to ourselves and to our fellow men. Recognition of the falsity of material wealth as the standard of success goes hand in hand with the abandonment of the false belief that public office and high political position are to be valued only by the standards of pride of place and personal profit. There must be an end to a conduct in banking and in business which too often has given to a sacred trust the likeness of callous and selfish wrongdoing.

Small wonder that confidence languishes, for it thrives only on honesty, on honor, on the sacredness of obligations, on faithful protection, and on unselfish performance. Without them it cannot live.

Restoration calls, however, not for changes in ethics alone. This nation asks for action, and action now! Our greatest primary task is to put people to work.

This is no unsolvable problem if we face it wisely and courageously. It can be accomplished, in part, by direct recruiting by the Government itself, treating the task as we would treat the emergency of a war, but at the same time, through this employment, accomplishing greatly needed projects to stimulate and reorganise the use of our natural resources.

Hand in hand with that, we must frankly recognise the overbalance of population in our industrial centers and, by engaging on a national scale in a redistribution, endeavor to provide a better use of the land for those best fitted for the land. Yes, the task can be helped by definite efforts to raise the values of agricultural products and with this the power to purchase the output of our cities. It can be helped by preventing realistically the tragedy of the growing loss, through foreclosure, of our small homes and our farms. It can be helped by insistence that the Federal, State, and local governments act forthwith on the demand that their cost be drastically

> 'Happiness lies not in the mere possession of money; it lies in the joy of achievement, in the thrill of creative effort.'

reduced. It can be helped by the unifying of relief activities, which today are often scattered, uneconomical, and unequal. It can be helped by national planning for and supervision of all forms of transportation and of communications and other utilities that have a definite public character.

There are many ways in which it can be helped, but it can never be helped merely by talking about it! We must act, we must act quickly. Finally, in our progress toward a resumption of work, we require two safeguards against a return of the evils of the old order: There must be a strict supervision of all banking and credits and investments; there must be an end to speculation with other people's money. And there must be provision for an adequate but sound currency.

There are the lines of attack. I shall presently urge upon a new Congress, in special session, detailed measures for their fulfillment, and I shall seek the immediate assistance of the 48 States!

Through this program of action, we address ourselves to putting our own national house in order and making income balance outgo. Our international trade relations, though vastly important, are in point of time and necessity secondary to the establishment of a sound national economy! I favor, as a practical policy, putting of first things first. I shall spare no effort to restore world trade by international economic readjustment, but the emergency at home cannot wait on that accomplishment.

The basic thought that guides these specific means of national recovery is not narrowly nationalistic. It is the insistence, as a first consideration, upon the interdependence of the various elements in all parts of the United States; a recognition of the old and permanently important manifestation of the American spirit of the pioneer. It is the way to recovery. It is the immediate way. It is the strongest assurance that the recovery will endure!

FRANKLIN D ROOSEVELT   51

In the field of world policy, I would dedicate this Nation to the policy of the good neighbor; the neighbor who resolutely respects himself and, because he does so, respects the rights of others; the neighbor who respects his obligations and respects the sanctity of his agreements in and with a world of neighbors.

If I read the temper of our people correctly, we now realise as we have never realised before our interdependence on each other; that we can not merely take but we must give as well; that if we are to go forward, we must move as a trained and loyal army willing to sacrifice for the good of a common discipline, because without such discipline no progress is made, no leadership becomes effective. We are, I know, ready and willing to submit our lives and property to such discipline, because it makes possible a leadership which aims at a larger good. This, I propose to offer, pledging that the larger purposes will bind upon us—bind upon us all—as a sacred obligation with a unity of duty hitherto evoked only in times of armed strife.

With this pledge taken, I assume unhesitatingly the leadership of this great army of our people dedicated to a disciplined attack upon our common problems. Action in this image, and to this end, is feasible under the form of government which we have inherited from our ancestors. Our Constitution is so simple and practical that it is possible always to meet extraordinary needs by changes in emphasis and arrangement without loss of essential form. That is why our constitutional system has proved itself the most superbly enduring political mechanism the modern world has ever seen. It has met every stress of vast expansion of territory, of foreign wars, of bitter internal strife, and of world relations.

And, it is to be hoped that the normal balance of executive and legislative authority may be wholly adequate to meet the unprecedented task before us. But it may be that an unprecedented demand and need for undelayed action may call for temporary departure from that normal balance of public procedure.

I am prepared under my constitutional duty to recommend the measures that a stricken nation in the midst of a stricken world may require. These measures, or such other measures as the Congress may build out of its experience and wisdom, I shall seek, within my constitutional authority, to bring to speedy adoption.

'We require safeguards against a return of the evils of the old order—there must be a strict supervision of all banking and credits and investments; there must be an end to speculation with other people's money.'

But, in the event that the Congress shall fail to take one of these two courses, and in the event that the national emergency is still critical, I shall not evade the clear course of duty that will then confront me. I shall ask the Congress for the one remaining instrument to meet the crisis—broad executive power to wage a war against the emergency as great as the power that would be given to me if we were in fact invaded by a foreign foe!

For the trust reposed in me, I will return the courage and the devotion that befit the time. I can do no less.

We face the arduous days that lie before us in the warm courage of the national unity; with the clear consciousness of seeking old and precious moral values; with the clean satisfaction that comes from the stern performance of duty by old and young alike. We aim at the assurance of a rounded, a permanent national life. We do not distrust the future of essential democracy.

The people of the United States have not failed. In their need they have registered a mandate that they want direct, vigorous action. They have asked for discipline and direction under leadership. They have made me the present instrument of their wishes. In the spirit of the gift, I take it.

In this dedication of a nation, we humbly ask the blessing of God. May He protect each and every one of us! May He guide me in the days to come.'

Franklin D. Roosevelt's 'bold, persistent' leadership sought to make government and its institutions responsible for the economic well-being of the American people. (It was once facetiously reported that he ordered 'a grilled millionaire' for breakfast each morning). FDR created government agencies, closed banks and even took on the Supreme Court in order to facilitate economic recovery. But although he held more power than any other American President before or since, he never lost the common touch with the people.

Roosevelt used a powerful new communication medium—radio—to speak to the American people in a series of historic speeches he called 'fireside' chats. He served four consecutive terms as President (1933-45)—a feat unprecedented in the history of the country and one not allowable today because of constitutional amendment. It was a situation borne out of the incredible events of that time—the Depression, the conflict in Europe, the unprovoked attack on Pearl Harbour by Japanese forces and finally, World War II itself.

For Roosevelt's part, he proved an inspirational war-time commander-in-chief despite being confined to a wheelchair in later life. Winning the war became his number one priority, even in the face of criticism of the internment of 112 000 Japanese-Americans, the failure of his government to articulate an adequate response to Hitler's treatment of the Jews in Europe and the apparent appeasement of Russian leader Josef Stalin at the Yalta Conference in 1945. However, Roosevelt was fated never to see victory; he succumbed to a cerebral haemorrhage, aged 63, on 12 April, 1945.

The irony remains: would the American people have elected a partially crippled man to the White House if they had had televisions and television networds during the 1930s?

Josef V Stalin

'Election Speech'

A Meeting of the Voters of the Stalin Electoral District, Bolshoi Theatre, Moscow, 11 December 1937.

Under Stalin's leadership, millions of Russian peasants were either executed or sent to forced labour camps and their properties confiscated by the state. Conservative figures put the loss of life from the resulting 1931-32 famine at 10 million people. In this 'impromptu' address to members of his own electorate in December 1937, the hypocrisy behind the façade of 'elections'—as Stalin gives 'advice' to his 'electors'—is patently clear.

'First of all, I would like to express my thanks to the electors for the confidence they have shown me.

I have been nominated as candidate, and the Election Commission of the Stalin District of the Soviet capital has registered my candidature. This, comrades, is an expression of great confidence. Permit me to convey to you my profound Bolshevik gratitude for this confidence that you have shown the Bolshevik Party of which I am a member, and me personally as a representative of that Party.

I know what confidence means. It naturally lays upon me new and additional duties and, consequently, new and additional responsibilities. Well, it is not customary among us Bolsheviks to refuse responsibilities. I accept them willingly.

For my part, I would like to assure you, comrades, that you may safely rely on Comrade Stalin. You may take it for granted that Comrade Stalin will be able to discharge his duty to the people, to the working class, to the peasantry and to the intelligentsia.

Further, comrades, I would like to congratulate you on the occasion of the forthcoming national holiday, the day of the elections to the

Supreme Soviet of the Soviet Union. The forthcoming elections are not merely elections, comrades, they are really a national holiday of our workers, our peasants and our intelligentsia. Never in the history of the world have there been such really free and really democratic elections—never! History knows no other example like it. The point is not that our elections will be universal, equal, secret and direct, although that fact in itself is of great importance. The point is that our universal elections will be carried out as the freest elections and the most democratic compared with elections in any other country in the world.

Universal elections exist and are also held in some capitalist countries, so-called democratic countries. But in what atmosphere are elections held there? In an atmosphere of class conflicts, in an atmosphere of class enmity, in an atmosphere of pressure brought to bear on the electors by the capitalists, landlords, bankers and other capitalist sharks. Such elections, even if they are universal, equal, secret and direct, cannot be called altogether free and altogether democratic elections.

Here, in our country, on the contrary, elections are held in an entirely different atmosphere. Here there are no capitalists and no landlords and, consequently, no pressure is exerted by propertied classes on non-propertied classes. Here elections are held in an atmosphere of collaboration between the workers, the peasants and the intelligentsia, in an atmosphere of mutual confidence between them, in an atmosphere, I would, say, of mutual friendship; because there are no capitalists in our country, no landlords, no exploitation, and nobody, in fact, to bring pressure to bear on people in order to distort their will.

That is why our elections are the only really free and really democratic elections in the whole world ...

Further, comrades, I would like to give you some advice, the advice of a candidate to his electors. If you take capitalist countries you will find that peculiar, I would say, rather strange relations exist there between deputies and voters. As long as the elections are in progress, the deputies flirt with the electors, fawn on them, swear fidelity and make heaps of promises of every kind. It looks as though the deputies are completely dependent on the electors. As soon as the elections are over, and the candidates have become deputies, relations undergo a radical change. Instead of the deputies being dependent on the electors, they become entirely independent. For four or five years, that is, until the next elections, the deputy feels quite free, independent of the people, of his electors. He may pass from one camp to another, he may turn from the right road to the wrong, he may even become entangled in machinations of a not altogether savoury character, he may turn as many somersaults as he likes—he is independent.

Can such relations be regarded as normal? By no means, comrades. This circumstance was taken into consideration by our Constitution and it made it a law that electors have the right to recall their deputies before the expiration of their term of office if they begin to play tricks, if they turn off the road, or if they forget that they are dependent on the people, on the electors.

This is a wonderful law, comrades. A deputy should know that he is the servant of the people, their emissary in the Supreme Soviet, and that he must follow the line laid down in the mandate given him by the people. If he turns off the road, the electors are entitled to demand new elections, and as to the deputy who turned off the road, they have the right to send him packing. This is a wonderful law. My advice, the advice of a candidate to his electors, is that they remember this electors' right, the right to recall deputies before the expiration of their term of office, that they keep an eye on their deputies, control them and, if they should take it into their heads to turn off the right road, to get rid of them and demand new elections. The Government is obliged to appoint new elections. My advice is to remember this law and to take advantage of it should need arise.

And, lastly, one more piece of advice from a candidate to his electors. What, in general, must one demand of one's deputies, selecting from all possible demands the most elementary?

The electors, the people, must demand that their deputies should remain equal to their tasks; that in their work they should not sink to the level of political philistines; that in their posts they should remain

> **'The electors, the people, must demand that their deputies should remain equal to their tasks; that in their work they should not sink to the level of political philistines; that in their posts they should remain political figures of the Lenin type.'**

political figures of the Lenin type; that as public figures they should be as clear and definite as Lenin was that they should be as fearless in battle and as merciless towards the enemies of the people as Lenin was that they should be free from all panic, from any semblance of panic, when things begin, to get complicated and some danger or other looms on the horizon; that they should be as free from all semblance of panic as Lenin was that they should be as wise and deliberate in deciding complex problems requiring a comprehensive orientation and a comprehensive weighing of all pros and cons as Lenin was that they should be as upright and honest as Lenin was that they should love their people as Lenin did.

Can we say that all the candidates are public figures precisely of this kind? I would not say so. There are all sorts of people in the world, there are all sorts of public figures in the world. There are people of whom you cannot say what they are, whether they are good or bad, courageous or timid, for the people heart and soul, or for the enemies of the people. There are such people and there are such public figures. They are also to be found among us, the Bolsheviks. You know yourselves, comrades, there are black sheep in every family. Of people of this indefinite type, people who resemble political philistines rather than political figures, people of this vague, uncertain type, the great Russian writer, Gogol, rather aptly said: 'Vague sort of people,' says he, 'neither one thing nor the other, you can't make head or tail of them, they are neither Bogdan in town nor Seliphan in the country.' There are also some rather apt popular sayings about such indefinite people and public figures: 'A middling sort of man—neither fish nor flesh', 'neither a candle for god nor a poker for the devil'.

I cannot say with absolute certainty that among the candidates (I beg their pardon, of course) and among our public figures there are no people who resemble political philistines more than anything else, who in character and make up resemble people of the type referred to in the popular saying: 'Neither a candle for god nor a poker for the devil.' I would like you, comrades, to exercise systematic influence on your deputies, to impress upon them that they must constantly keep before them the great image of the great Lenin and imitate Lenin in all things.

> 'Never in the history of the world have there been such really free and really democratic elections—never!'

The functions of the electors do not end with the elections. They continue during the whole term of the given Supreme Soviet. I have already mentioned the law which empowers the electors to recall their deputies before the expiration of their term of office if they should turn off the right road. Hence, it is the duty and right of the electors to keep their deputies constantly under their control and to impress upon them that they must under no circumstances sink to the level of political philistines, impress upon them that they must be like the great Lenin.

Such, comrades, is my second piece of advice to you, the advice of a candidate to his electors.

Josef Stalin (1879-1953) was born Iosif Vissarionovich Dzhugashvili in Gori, Georgia (he adopted the name 'Stalin'—which literally means 'man of steel'—during his political career). Expelled from the Tiflis Orthodox Theological Seminary for spreading Marxist ideology he joined the Social Democratic Workers' Party, was arrested several times and twice exiled to Siberia during the period 1902-13. After playing a major role in the October 1917 Revolution, Stalin emerged as a leading Bolshevik figure during the Russian Civil War (1918-20). He became a member of the Communist Party Politburo and was appointed General Secretary of the Party in 1922—a position he held until his death thirty years later.

After securing the undisputed leadership of the Party following Lenin's death in 1924, Stalin denounced his main rival, Trotsky, and allied himself with Nikolay Bukharin. After attacking the 'united opposition' of Zinoviev, Kamenov and Trotsky, Stalin removed Bukharin from the Politburo. During the next decade Stalin's agents murdered political opponents (Kirov) and

> 'Here elections are held in an atmosphere of collaboration between the workers, the peasants and the intelligentsia, in an atmosphere of mutual confidence between them ...'

paraded rivals in 'show trials' before executing them (Zinoviev, Kamenov, Bukharin and Rykov among others). In June 1937 he began a purge of the army, and tried and executed many of his top generals.

In 1928 Stalin began the first of his 'five year plans' requiring the forced collectivism of all agriculture and the industrialisation of the Soviet economy. When the kulak class of land-owners resisted, millions of peasants were executed or sent to forced labour camps and their properties confiscated. But Stalin's position in power—and the propagation of his 'cult of personality'—were so entrenched there was no way of deposing him.

Nothing could match Stalin's hypocrisy in signing a 'non-aggression' pact with Germany in August 1939. This treaty, which stated that the Soviet Union would not intervene if Hitler attacked neighbouring Poland from the East, was the precursor to World War II. After the start of the war in September 1939, Soviet troops occupied Lithuania, Latvia and Estonia while Romania succeeded Bessarabia and North Bukovian to the USSR.

In April 1941 the Soviets signed a similar agreement with Japan but these 'non-aggression' pacts bought only momentary peace for the Russians. In June 1941 Germany launched a surprise attack on the Russian border and by mid-July the Nazis had pushed 450 miles inland to Smolensk.

Adolf Hitler

'The Jewish Question'

The Reichstag, Berlin, 30 January 1939.

I n this speech marking the sixth anniversary of his ascension to power, Adolf Hitler (1889-1945) reveals the paranoia and obsession that drove him to become one of the most evil dictators of the twentieth century. The tactic of playing on people's insecurities—especially about the economy, nationalism and the shame of losing World War I, as Hitler did—was not unusual in politics, but Hitler directed this fear at one ethnic minority. Here, the German Fuehrer shows his unbridled hatred of the Jewry of Europe ... a contempt that led to World War II, the death of over 50 million people and the systematic murder of an estimated 6 million people during the Holocaust. Hitler delivered this speech on the eve of Britain's entry into World War II.

' When on the evening of 30 January 1933, six years ago today, beneath the light of their torches the tens of thousands of National Socialist fighters passed through the Brandenberger Tor to express to me the newly nominated Chancellor of the Reich, their feelings of overflowing joy and their confession of loyalty as my followers, countless anxious eyes both here in Berlin and throughout Germany gazed at the beginning of a development the issue of which it appeared impossible to discern or to foresee. Some 13 million German voters, men and women then stood beside me. An imposing number, but yet only a little more than a third of the sum of the votes cast. It was true that the remaining twenty million were divided and split up between thirty five other parties and groups.

The one thing which united the opponents of National Socialism was their common hatred of the young movement, a hatred born of their guilty consciences and worse intentions. As is still does today in other parts of the world, this united the priests of the Centre Party and Communist atheists, the Socialist out to abolish private property and capitalists whose interests were bound up with the stock exchange, Conservatives who wished to destroy the State and Republicans whose aim was to destroy the Reich. During the long battle of National Socialism for the leadership of the country they had all come together in defense of their interests and made common cause with Jewry. The bishop politicians of the various Churches extended their hands in benediction over this union. And against this splitting up of the nation, united only in negation stood that third of German men and women, with their faith, those who had undertaken to raise anew the German people and Reich in the face of world internal and external opposition.

The whole picture of the greatness of the collapse of Germany at that time begins gradually to grow dim, but one thing even today is not forgotten. It seemed that only a miracle could save Germany at the twelfth hour. And we National Socialists believed in this miracle. Over the belief in this miracle our foes made merry. The thought that one should wish to redeem the nation from a ruin which now lasted a decade and a half simply through the force of a new idea appeared to those who were not National Socialists as the delusion of visionaries [phantasterei]; to the Jews and other enemies of the State it appeared as the last insignificant spasm of force within the national resistance, and when that was exhausted one might hope to be able finally to annihilate not only Germany but Europe.

A Germany sinking in Bolshevist chaos would at that time have hurled the whole West into a crisis of unimaginable gravity. Only the most limited of islanders could persuade themselves into believing that the Red plague would of its own accord have cried a halt before the sacredness of a democratic idea at the frontiers of States who had shown no interest in its advance. The rescue of Europe began at one end of the continent with Mussolini and Fascism. National Socialism continued this rescue in another part of Europe, and at the present moment we are witnessing in still a third country the same drama of a brave triumph over the Jewish international attempt to destroy

European civilization. The six years which now lie behind us are filled with the most stupendous events in the whole of our German history. On 30 January 1933 I entered the Wilhelmstrasse filled with profound anxiety for the future of my people. Today after six years I am able to speak before the Reichstag of Greater Germany. We are indeed perhaps better able than other generations to realise the full meaning of those pious words "What a change by the grace of God" ...

The German nation has no feeling of hatred towards England, America or France; all it wants is peace and quiet. But the other nations are continually being stirred up to hatred for Germany and the German people by Jewish and non-Jewish agitators. And so, should warmongers achieve what they are aiming at, our own people would be landed in a situation for which they would be psychologically quite unprepared and which they would thus fail to grasp. I therefore consider it necessary that from now on our propaganda and our press should always make a point of answering these attacks, and above all bring them to the notice of the German people. The German nation must know who the men are who want to bring about war by hook or crook. It is my conviction that these people are mistaken in their calculations, for when once National Socialist propaganda is devoted to the answering of the attacks, we shall succeed just as we succeeded inside Germany herself in overcoming, through the convincing power of our propaganda, the Jewish world-enemy. The nations will in a short time realise that National Socialist Germany wants no enmity with other nations; that all the assertions as to our intended attacks on other nations are lies, lies born of morbid hysteria, or of a mania for self-preservation on the part of certain politicians; but that in certain States these lies are being used by unscrupulous profiteers to salvage their own finances. That, above all, international Jewry may hope in this way to satisfy its thirst for revenge and gain, but that on the other hand this is the grossest defamation which can be brought to bear on a great and peace loving nation. Never, for instance, have German soldiers fought on American soil, unless it was in the cause of American independence and freedom; but American soldiers were brought to Europe to help strangle a great nation which was fighting for its freedom. Germany did not attack America, but America attacked Germany and as the Committee of Investigation of the American House of Representatives concluded: from purely capitalist motives, without any other cause. There is but one thing that everyone should realise: these attempts cannot influence Germany in the slightest as to the way in which she settles her Jewish problem. On the contrary, in connection with the Jewish question I have this to say: it is a shameful spectacle to see how the whole democratic world is oozing sympathy for the poor tormented Jewish people, but remains hard-hearted and obdurate when it comes to helping them—which is surely, in view of its attitude, an obvious duty. The arguments that are brought up as an excuse for not helping them actually speak for us Germans and Italians.

For this is what they say:

1. 'We', that is the democracies, 'are not in a position to take in the Jews'. Yet in these empires there are not 10 people to the square kilometre. While Germany, with her 135 inhabitants to the square kilometre, is supposed to have room for them!

2. They assure us: We cannot take them unless Germany is prepared to allow them a certain amount of capital to bring with them as immigrants.

For hundreds of years Germany was good enough to receive these elements, although they possessed nothing except infectious political and physical diseases. What they possess today, they have by a very large extent gained at the cost of the less astute German nation by the most reprehensible manipulations.

Today we are merely paying this people what it deserves. When the German nation was, thanks to the inflation instigated and carried through by Jews, deprived of the entire savings which it had accumulated in years of honest work, when the rest of the world took away the German nation's foreign investments, when we were divested of the whole of our colonial possessions, these philanthropic considerations evidently carried little noticeable weight with democratic statesmen.

Today I can only assure these gentlemen that, thanks to the brutal education with which the democracies favoured us for fifteen years, we are completely hardened to all attacks of sentiment. After more than 800 000 children of the nation had died of hunger and undernourishment at the close of the War, we witnessed almost one million head of milking cows being driven away from us in accordance with the cruel paragraphs of a dictate which the humane democratic apostles of the world forced upon us as a peace treaty. We witnessed over one million German prisoners of war being retained in confinement for no reason at all for a whole year after the War was ended. We witnessed over one and a half million Germans being torn away from all that they possessed in the territories lying on our frontiers, and being whipped out with practically only what they wore on their backs. We had to endure having millions of our fellow countrymen torn from us without their consent, and without their being afforded the slightest possibility of existence. I could supplement these examples with dozens of the most cruel kind. For this reason we ask to be spared all sentimental talk.

The German nation does not wish its interests to be determined and controlled by any foreign nation. France to the French, England to the English, America to the Americans, and Germany to the Germans. We are resolved to prevent the settlement in our country of a strange people which was capable of snatching for itself all the leading positions in the land, and to oust it. For it is our will to educate our own nation for these leading positions. We have hundreds of thousands of very intelligent children of peasants and of the working classes. We shall have them educated—in fact we have already begun—and we wish that one day they, and not the representatives of an alien race, may hold the leading positions in the State together with our educated classes. Above all, German culture, as its name alone shows, is German and not Jewish, and therefore its management and care will be entrusted to members of our own nation.

'... at the present moment we are witnessing in still a third country the same drama of a brave triumph over the Jewish international attempt to destroy European civilization.'

If the rest of the world cries out with a hypocritical mien against this barbaric expulsion from Germany of such an irreplaceable and culturally eminently valuable element, we can only be astonished at the conclusions they draw from this situation. For how thankful they must be that we are releasing these precious apostles of culture, and placing them at the disposal of the rest of the world. In accordance with their own declarations they cannot find a single reason to excuse themselves for refusing to receive this most valuable race in their own countries. Nor can I see a reason why the members of this race should be imposed upon the German nation, while in the States, which are so enthusiastic about these 'splendid people', their settlement should suddenly be refused with every imaginable excuse. I think that the sooner this problem is solved the better; for Europe cannot settle down until the Jewish question is cleared up. It may very well be possible that sooner or later an agreement on this problem may be reached in Europe, even between those nations which otherwise do not so easily come together.

The world has sufficient space for settlements, but we must once and for all get rid of the opinion that the Jewish race was only created by God for the purpose of being in a certain percentage a parasite living on the body and the productive work of other nations. The Jewish race will have to adapt itself to sound constructive activity as other nations do, or sooner or later it will succumb to a crisis of an inconceivable magnitude.

One thing I should like to say on this day which may be memorable for others as well as for us Germans. In the course of my life I have very often been a prophet, and have usually been ridiculed for it. During the time of my struggle for power it was in the first instance the Jewish race which only received my prophecies with laughter when I said that I would one day take over the leadership of the State, and with it that of the whole nation, and that I would then among many other things settle the Jewish problem. Their laughter was uproarious, but I think that for some time now they have been laughing on the other side of their face. Today I will once more be a prophet: If the international Jewish financiers in and outside Europe should succeed in plunging the nations once more into a world war, then the result will not be the Bolshevisation of the earth, and thus the victory of Jewry, but the annihilation of the Jewish race in Europe!

For the time when the non-Jewish nations had no propaganda is at an end. National Socialist Germany and Fascist Italy have institutions which enable them when necessary to enlighten the world about the nature of a question of which many nations are instinctively conscious, but which then have not yet clearly thought out. At the moment the Jews in certain countries may be fomenting hatred under the protection of the press, of the film, of wireless propaganda, of the theatre, of literature, etc., all of which they control. If this nation should once more succeed in inciting the millions which compose the nations into a conflict which is utterly senseless and only serves Jewish interests, then there will be revealed the effectiveness of an enlightenment which has completely routed the Jews of Germany in the space of a few years. The nations are no longer willing to die on the battlefield so that this unstable international race may profiteer from a war or satisfy its Old Testament vengeance. The Jewish watchword 'Workers of the world unite' will be conquered by a higher realisation, namely 'Workers of all classes and of all nations, recognise your common enemy!

'Today I will once more be a prophet: If the international Jewish financiers in and outside Europe should succeed in plunging the nations once more into a world war, then the result will not be the Bolshevisation of the earth, and thus the victory of Jewry, but the annihilation of the Jewish race in Europe!'

Born illegitimately in Braunau, Austria, Hitler enlisted in World War I where he achieved the modest rank of corporal. When the war ended in 1918, Hitler felt betrayed by the conditions set out in the Treaty of Versailles and found a platform for venting his anger and frustration against the federal government in one of the minor, post-war political parties—the National Socialist German Workers' Party (abbreviated to Nazi).

Hitler was appointed Chancellor in January 1933 when President Paul von Hindenberg was wrongly advised that the 'little corporal' could be more closely controlled inside the German Parliament. Hitler's followers burned the Reichstag to the ground that year—an act he blamed on the Communist Party— and after calling a general election and seizing power, he crushed rivals inside his own party in June 1934.

When von Hindenberg died in August, Hitler was named sole ruler of Germany and opposition parties were outlawed. In 1938 he created 'Greater Germany' by annexing Austria and then engineered events to present to an appeasing Britain and France an excuse to reclaim the German-populated borderland (Sudetenland) of neighbouring Czechoslovakia. On 1 September, 1939 German troops marched into Poland and precipitated the start of World War II (1939-45).

After almost six years of world conflict, Hitler's megalomania ended with a self-inflicted gunshot wound on 30 April 1945, as Russian troops attacked his Berlin bunker. Surrounded by his new wife, Eva Braun, his Minister of Propoganda, Joseph Goebbels and his family, and many of his closest associates—who calmly followed their Fuhrer's lead—Hitler's death drew to a close the most cataclysmic war known to mankind with the loss of an estimated 55 million lives.

Neville Chamberlain
'A Hint of War'

Speech to the House of Commons, 1 September 1939.

During the 1930s British Prime Minister Neville Chamberlain (1869-40) endeavoured to appease the nations of Germany and Italy in order to prevent another war in Europe. As a result, Britain stood by as Hitler's troops annexed Austria and threatened to wage war to 'liberate' the Sudeten Germans in neighbouring Czechoslovakia.

In 1938 Chamberlain was twice snubbed by Hitler before meeting him in Munich in September and securing an understanding from Germany that it could occupy the Sudetenland as long as it respected the sovereignty of its Czech neighbour. Arriving at Croydon Airport on 30 September 1938 Neville Chamberlain stood on the tarmac and spoke to the waiting media.

' I have in my hand a piece of paper, signed by Mr. Hitler, in which he assures us that there will be no war in Europe. '

The British Prime Minister was waving a statement that read:

' We, the German Fuehrer and Chancellor, and the British Prime Minister, have had a further meeting today and are agreed in recognising that the question of Anglo-German relations is of the first importance for two countries and for Europe.

We regard the agreement signed last night and the Anglo-German Naval Agreement as symbolic of the desire of our two peoples never to go to war with one another again.

We are resolved that the method of consultation shall be the method adopted to deal with any other questions that may concern our two countries, and we are determined to continue our efforts to remove possible sources of difference, and thus to contribute to assure the peace of Europe.'

Chamberlain then went to the Prime Minister's residence at 10 Downing Street and declared:

' My good friends, this is the second time in our history that there has come from Germany to Downing Street peace with honour. I believe it is peace for our time. We thank you from the bottom of our hearts. And now I recommend you to go home and sleep quietly in your beds. '

Neville Chamberlain's 'peace for our time' declaration proved prophetically short-lived. Within six months German troops marched into Prague. By 1939 it was clear to most international observers that Hitler was on the path to war and any further attempts to negotiate with Germany were fruitless. In August 1939 Hitler signed a 'non-aggression' pact with his sworn enemy, Josef Stalin, which guaranteed that Russia would not come to Poland's defence if attacked from the East. The Nazis then staged a fake raid on a German radio outpost along the German-Polish border as an excuse to invade Poland.

Just hours after Hitler's troops and dive bombers had invaded Poland, Prime Minister Neville Chamberlain gave this speech to the House of Commons, on 1 September 1939.

'I prayed that the responsibility might not fall upon me to ask this country to accept the awful arbitrament of war. I fear that I may not be able to avoid that responsibility.'

' I do not propose to say many words tonight. The time has come when action rather than speech is required. Eighteen months ago in this House I prayed that the responsibility might not fall upon me to ask this country to accept the awful arbitrament of war. I fear that I may not be able to avoid that responsibility.

But, at any rate, I cannot wish for conditions in which such a burden should fall upon me in which I should feel clearer than I do today as to where my duty lies.

No man can say that the Government could have done more to try to keep open the way for an honourable and equitable settlement of the dispute between Germany and Poland. Nor have we neglected any means of making it crystal clear to the German Government that if they insisted on using force again in the manner in which they had used it in the past we were resolved to oppose them by force.

'We shall enter [the war] with a clear conscience, with the support of the Dominions and the British Empire, and the moral approval of the greater part of the world.'

Now that all the relevant documents are being made public we shall stand at the bar of history knowing that the responsibility for this terrible catastrophe lies on the shoulders of one man, the German Chancellor, who has not hesitated to plunge the world into misery in order to serve his own senseless ambitions.

Only last night the Polish Ambassador did see the German Foreign Secretary, Herr von Ribbentrop. Once again he expressed to him what, indeed, the Polish Government had already said publicly, that they were willing to negotiate with Germany about their disputes on an equal basis.

What was the reply of the German Government? The reply was that without another word the German troops crossed the Polish frontier this morning at dawn and are since reported to be bombing open towns. In these circumstances there is only one course open to us.

His Majesty's Ambassador in Berlin and the French Ambassador have been instructed to hand to the German Government the following document:

"Early this morning the German Chancellor issued a proclamation to the German Army which indicated that he was about to attack Poland. Information which has reached His Majesty's Government in the United Kingdom and the French Government indicates that attacks upon Polish towns are proceeding. In these circumstances it appears to the Governments of the United Kingdom and France that by their action the German Government have created conditions, namely, an aggressive act of force against Poland threatening the independence of Poland, which call for the implementation by the Government of the

United Kingdom and France of the undertaking to Poland to come to her assistance. I am accordingly to inform your Excellency that unless the German Government are prepared to give His Majesty's Government satisfactory assurances that the German Government have suspended all aggressive action against Poland and are prepared promptly to withdraw their forces from Polish territory, His Majesty's Government in the United Kingdom will without hesitation fulfil their obligations to Poland."

If a reply to this last warning is unfavourable, and I do not suggest that it is likely to be otherwise, His Majesty's Ambassador is instructed to ask for his passports. In that case we are ready.

Yesterday, we took further steps towards the completion of our defensive preparation. This morning we ordered complete mobilisation of the whole of the Royal Navy, Army and Royal Air Force. We have also taken a number of other measures, both at home and abroad, which the House will not perhaps expect me to specify in detail. Briefly, they represent the final steps in accordance with pre-arranged plans. These last can be put into force rapidly, and are of such a nature that they can be deferred until war seems inevitable. Steps have also been taken under the powers conferred by the House last week to safeguard the position in regard to stocks of commodities of various kinds.

'How do we stand this time? The answer is that all three Services are ready, and that the situation in all directions is far more favourable and reassuring than in 1914.'

The thoughts of many of us must at this moment inevitably be turning back to 1914, and to a comparison of our position now with that which existed then. How do we stand this time? The answer is that all three Services are ready, and that the situation in all directions is far more favourable and reassuring than in 1914, while behind the fighting services we have built up a vast organisation of Civil Defence under our scheme of Air Raid Precautions.

As regards the immediate manpower requirements, the Royal Navy, the Army and the Air Force are in the fortunate position of having almost as many men as they can conveniently handle at this moment. There are, however, certain categories of service in which men are immediately required, both for Military and Civil Defence. These will be announced in detail through the press and the BBC.

The main and most satisfactory point to observe is that there is today no need to make an appeal in a general way for recruits such as was issued by Lord Kitchener 25 years ago. That appeal has been anticipated by many months, and the men are already available. So much for the immediate present. Now we must look to the future. It is essential in the face of the tremendous task which confronts us, more especially in view of our past experiences in this matter, to organise our manpower this time upon as methodical, equitable and economical a basis as possible.

We, therefore, propose immediately to introduce legislation directed to that end. A Bill will be laid before you which for all practical purposes will amount to an expansion of the Military Training Act. Under its operation all fit men between the ages of 18 and 41 will be rendered liable to military service if and when called upon. It is not intended at the outset that any considerable number of men other than those already liable shall be called up, and steps will be taken to ensure that the manpower essentially required by industry shall not be taken away.

There is one other allusion which I should like to make before I end my speech, and that is to record my satisfaction of His Majesty's Government, that throughout these last days of crisis Signor Mussolini also has been doing his best to reach a solution. It now only remains for us to set our teeth and to enter upon this struggle, which we ourselves earnestly endeavoured to avoid, with determination to see it through to the end.

We shall enter it with a clear conscience, with the support of the Dominions and the British Empire, and the moral approval of the greater part of the world.

We have no quarrel with the German people, except that they allow themselves to be governed by a Nazi Government. As long as that Government exists and pursues the methods it has so persistently followed during the last two years, there will be no peace in Europe. We shall merely pass from one crisis to another, and see one country after another attacked by methods which have now become familiar to us in their sickening technique.

We are resolved that these methods must come to an end. If out of the struggle we again re-establish in the world the rules of good faith and the renunciation of force, why, then even the sacrifices that will be entailed upon us will find their fullest justification.'

Just two days later on 3 September, Neville Chamberlain announced that a state of war existed between England and Germany. Chamberlain remained Prime Minister until May 1940 when criticism of his wartime leadership in the face of Hitler's invasion of Norway and Denmark saw him condemned by the hoots and jeers of his own supporters in the House of Commons. Announcing his resignation, he was replaced on 10 May 1940 by Winston Churchill. Neville Chamberlain died suddenly from stomach cancer later that same year.

War, Peace
and Freedom
1940-1949

Winston Churchill

'Our Finest Hour'

House of Commons, London, 18 June 1940.

Winston Leonard Spencer Churchill (1875-1965) is regarded as one of the most important statesmen of the twentieth century. The son of an aristocratic and politically influential father—Lord Randolph Churchill, the third son of the Duke of Marlborough—Winston appeared destined for high office from an early age.

The sound of World War II for a generation of people was Churchill's voice crackling over the radio across the Commonwealth. But the journey to his iconic status was by no means predictable. In 1900 he was elected to parliament as the Conservative MP for Oldham but his opposition to party leader Neville Chamberlain's policies saw him join the Liberal Party in 1904. Appointed Home Secretary in 1910, Churchill's political career suffered a major setback with his handling of the failed Dardanelles invasion at Gallipoli in 1915. Left out of the Conservative-Liberal coalition government, he resigned his seat and joined the army (serving in France) before returning to parliament as an independent member. However, Churchill's support of the Conservatives saw him serve in both Lloyd George and Stanley Baldwin's governments.

During the late 1930s Churchill again found himself an 'outcast' as a vocal opponent to Prime Minister Neville Chamberlain's seeming appeasement of Hitler during Germany's military build-up. When war broke out in September 1939 Chamberlain appointed Churchill First Lord of the Admiralty. After Chamberlain's resignation, Churchill was asked to lead the coalition government on 10 May 1940.

At the time of his appointment, Germany had begun massive attacks against Holland, Belgium, Luxembourg, and France and were experiencing stunning victories on all fronts. By the end of May, Holland, Luxembourg and Belgium had capitulated and the following month France fell. Britain now stood alone against the seemingly unstoppable German military juggernaut. As an island, the country's greatest threat was from the air—the Royal Air Force's 640 aircraft pitted against the German Luftwaffe's 2600. In this famous speech to the House of Commons, Prime Minister Winston Churchill inspired the nation to fight from the corner, and win.

'The disastrous military events which have happened during the past fortnight have not come to me with any sense of surprise. Indeed, I indicated a fortnight ago as clearly as I could to the House that the worst possibilities were open; and I made it perfectly clear then that whatever happened in France would make no difference to the resolve of Britain and the British Empire to fight on, if necessary for years, if necessary alone. This brings me, naturally, to the great question of invasion from the air, and of the impending struggle between the British and German Air Forces. It seems quite clear that no invasion on a scale beyond the capacity of our land forces to crush speedily is likely to take place from the air until our Air Force has been definitely overpowered. In the meantime, there may be raids by parachute troops and attempted descents of airborne soldiers. But the great question is: Can we break Hitler's air weapon?

Now, of course, it is a very great pity that we have not got an Air Force at least equal to that of the most powerful enemy within striking distance of these shores. But we have a very powerful Air Force which has proved itself far superior in quality, both in men and in many types of machine, to what we have met so far in the numerous and fierce air battles which have been fought with the Germans. In France, where we were at a considerable disadvantage and lost many machines on the ground when they were standing round the aerodromes, we were accustomed to inflict in the air losses of as much as two and two-and-a-half to one. In the fighting over Dunkirk, which was a sort of no-man's-land, we undoubtedly beat the German Air Force, and gained the mastery of the local air, inflicting here a loss of three or four to one day after day. Anyone who looks at the photographs which were

> **'I see great reason for intense vigilance and exertion, but none whatever for panic or despair.'**

published a week or so ago of the re-embarkation, showing the masses of troops assembled on the beach and forming an ideal target for hours at a time, must realize that this re-embarkation would not have been possible unless the enemy had resigned all hope of recovering air superiority at that time and at that place.

In the defence of this Island the advantages to the defenders will be much greater than they were in the fighting around Dunkirk. We hope to improve on the rate of three or four to one which was realized at Dunkirk; and in addition all our injured machines and their crews which get down safely—and, surprisingly, a very great many injured machines and men do get down safely in modern air fighting—all of these will fall, in an attack upon these Islands, on friendly soil and live to fight another day; whereas all the injured enemy machines and their complements will be total losses as far as the war is concerned.

During the great battle in France, we gave very powerful and continuous aid to the French Army, both by fighters and bombers; but in spite of every kind of pressure we never would allow the entire metropolitan fighter strength of the Air Force to be consumed. This decision was painful, but it was also right, because the fortunes of the battle in France could not have been decisively affected even if we had thrown in our entire fighter force. That battle was lost by the unfortunate strategical opening, by the extraordinary and unforseen power of the armoured columns, and by the great preponderance of the German Army in numbers. Our fighter Air Force might easily have been exhausted as a mere accident in that great struggle, and then we should have found ourselves at the present time in a very serious plight. But as it is, I am happy to inform the House that our fighter strength is stronger at the present time relatively to the Germans, who have suffered terrible losses, than it has ever been; and consequently we believe ourselves possessed of the capacity to continue the war in the air under better conditions than we have ever experienced before. I look forward confidently to the exploits of our fighter pilots—these splendid men, this brilliant youth—who will have the glory of saving their native land, their island home, and all they love, from the most deadly of all attacks.

There remains, of course, the danger of bombing attacks, which will certainly be made very soon upon us by the bomber forces of the enemy. It is true that the German bomber force is superior in numbers to ours; but we have a very large bomber force also, which we shall use to strike at military targets in Germany without intermission. I do not at all underrate the severity of the ordeal which lies before us; but I believe our countrymen will show themselves capable of standing up to it, like the brave men of Barcelona, and will be able to stand up to it, and carry on in spite of it, at least as well as any other people in the world. Much will depend upon this; every man and every woman will have the chance to show the finest qualities of their race, and render the highest service to their cause. For all of us, at this time, whatever our sphere, our station, our occupation or our duties, it will be a help to remember the famous lines:

'Let us brace ourselves to our duties, and bear ourselves that if the British Empire and its Commonwealth last for a thousand years, men will still say, "This was their finest hour."'

"He nothing common did or mean,
Upon that memorable scene."

I have thought it right upon this occasion to give the House and the country some indication of the solid, practical grounds upon which we base our inflexible resolve to continue the war. There are a good many people who say, "Never mind. Win or lose, sink or swim, better die than submit to tyranny—and such a tyranny." And I do not dissociate myself from them. But I can assure them that our professional advisers of the three Services unitedly advise that we should carry on the war, and that there are good and reasonable hopes of final victory. We have fully informed and consulted all the self-governing Dominions, and I have received from their Prime Ministers—Mr. Mackenzie King of Canada, Mr. Menzies of Australia, Mr. Fraser of New Zealand, and General Smuts of South Africa—I have received from all these eminent men, who all have Governments behind them elected on wide franchises, who are all there because they represent the will of their people, messages couched in the most moving terms in which they endorse our decision to fight on, and declare themselves ready to share our fortunes and to persevere to the end. That is what we are going to do.

We may now ask ourselves: In what way has our position worsened since the beginning of the war? It has worsened by the fact that the Germans have conquered a large part of the coast line of Western Europe, and many small countries have been overrun by them. This aggravates the possibilities of air attack and adds to our naval preoccupations. It in no way diminishes, but on the contrary definitely increases, the power of our long-distance blockade. Similarly, the entrance of Italy into the war increases the power of our long-distance blockade. We have stopped the worst leak by that. We do not know whether military resistance will come to an end in France or not, but should it do so, then of course the Germans will be able to concentrate their forces, both military and industrial, upon us. But for the reasons I have given to the House these will not be found so easy to apply. If invasion has become more imminent, as no doubt it has, we, being relieved from the task of maintaining a large army in France, have far larger and more efficient forces to meet it.

'If we fail, then the whole world, including all that we have known and cared for, will sink into the abyss of a new Dark Age made more sinister by the lights of perverted science.'

If Hitler can bring under his despotic control the industries of the countries he has conquered, this will add greatly to his already vast armament output. On the other hand, this will not happen immediately, and we are now assured of immense, continuous and increasing support in supplies and munitions of all kinds from the United States; and especially of aeroplanes and pilots from the Dominions and across the oceans coming from regions which are beyond the reach of enemy bombers.

I do not see how any of these factors can operate to our detriment on balance before the winter comes; and the winter will impose a strain upon the Nazi regime, with almost all Europe writhing and starving under its cruel heel, which, for all their ruthlessness, will run them very hard. We must not forget that from the moment when we declared war on the 3rd September it was always possible for Germany to turn all her Air Force upon this country, together with any other devices of invasion she might conceive, and that France could have done little or nothing to prevent her doing so. We have, therefore, lived under this danger, in principle and in a slightly modified form, during all these months. In the meanwhile, however, we have enormously improved our methods of defence, and we have learned what we had no right to assume at the beginning, namely, that the individual aircraft and the individual British pilot have a sure and definite superiority. Therefore, in casting up this dread balance sheet and contemplating our dangers with a disillusioned eye, I see great reason for intense vigilance and exertion, but none whatever for panic or despair.

We do not yet know what will happen in France or whether the French resistance will be prolonged, both in France and in the French Empire overseas. The French Government will be throwing away great opportunities and casting adrift their future if they do not continue the war in accordance with their treaty obligations, from which we have not felt able to release them. The House will have read the historic declaration in which, at the desire of many Frenchmen—and of our own hearts—we have proclaimed our willingness at the darkest hour in French history to conclude a union of common citizenship in this struggle. However matters may go in France or with the French Government, or other French Governments, we in this Island and in the British Empire will never lose our sense of comradeship with the French people. If we are now called upon to endure what they have been suffering, we shall emulate their courage, and if final victory rewards our toils they shall share the gains, aye, and freedom shall be restored to all. We abate nothing of our just demands; not one jot or tittle do we recede. Czechs, Poles, Norwegians, Dutch, Belgians have joined their causes to our own. All these shall be restored.

What General Weygand called the Battle of France is over. I expect that the Battle of Britain is about to begin. Upon this battle depends the survival of Christian civilization? Upon it depends our own British life, and the long continuity of our institutions and our Empire. The whole fury and might of the enemy must very soon be turned on us.

Hitler knows that he will have to break us in this Island or lose the war. If we can stand up to him, all Europe may be free and the life of the world may move forward into broad, sunlit uplands. But if we fail, then the whole world, including the United States, including all that we have known and cared for, will sink into the abyss of a new Dark Age made more sinister, and perhaps more protracted, by the lights of perverted science.

Let us therefore brace ourselves to our duties, and so bear ourselves that if the British Empire and its Commonwealth last for a thousand years, men will still say, 'This was their finest hour.'

Under Churchill's leadership, England weathered the 'Battle of Britain' during that summer before the RAF successfully repelled the German air attack by the end of October 1940. ('Never in the field of human conflict was so much owed by so many to so few', Churchill famously stated). The British Prime Minister worked tirelessly during the next five years to bring a successful end to the war; he travelled over 150 000 miles, took a hands-on approach in devising military strategy, attended meetings with Roosevelt and Stalin at Yalta and inspired England, occupied Europe and the world with the sound of his voice in constant radio broadcasts (it was later revealed after his death that Churchill often utilised the services of a 'voice actor' for some radio broadcasts). It was Churchill who announced the unconditional surrender of German troops on 8 May 1945.

With Japanese forces in retreat in the Pacific, Churchill dissolved the parliamentary coalition and sent the country to the polls. Tired and weary after the war, and looking to a new and brighter future, the people of Great Britain voted out his caretaker government in June 1945 in favour of Labour's Clement Atlee, who had served in Churchill's coalition cabinet as Deputy Prime Minister during the war.

Charles Lindbergh

'Neutrality and War'

Radio Broadcast on the United States Mutual Radio Network, 13 October, 1939.

Charles A Lindbergh (1902-1974), the son of a United States Congressman, became an instant hero to millions in May 1927 when he was the first to fly an aeroplane non-stop across the Atlantic Ocean. After a gruelling 33-hour flight from New York, the quietly-spoken, handsome young man landed his small plane, the Spirit of St Louis, in Paris. Tragically, the kidnapping and subsequent murder of his infant son in 1932 (German born carpenter Bruno Richard Hauptmann was executed for the crime, but there are many who still believe his innocence) and Lindbergh's anti-war stance (misrepresented as 'pro-Nazi' sympathies) changed the direction of his life.

In 1939, as Europe plunged into World War II and America wavered over its level of involvement, Charles Lindbergh spoke out against President Franklin Roosevelt's indirect military support of England and France and gave a voice to those Americans who wanted to keep their country out of war.

Two of Charles Lindbergh's most persuasive neutrality speeches were broadcast to the United States public over the Mutual Radio Network. This was the second of these, broadcast in October 1939.

'Tonight, I speak again to the people of this country who are opposed to the United States entering the war which is now going on in Europe. We are faced with the need of deciding on a policy of American neutrality. The future of our nation and of our civilization rests upon the wisdom and foresight we use. Much as peace is to be desired, we should realize that behind a successful policy of neutrality must stand a policy of war. It is essential to define clearly those principles and circumstances for which a nation will fight. Let us give no one the impression that America's love for peace means that she is afraid of war, of that we are not fully capable and willing to defend all that is vital to us. National life and influence depend upon national strength, both in character and in arms. A neutrality built on pacifism alone will eventually fail.

Before we can intelligently enact regulations for the control of our armaments, our credit, and our ships, we must draw a sharp dividing line between neutrality and war; there must be no gradual encroachment on the defenses of our nation. Up to this line we may adjust our affairs to gain the advantages of peace, but beyond it must lie all the armed might of America, coiled in readiness to spring if once this bond is cut. Let us make clear to all countries where this line lies. It must be both within our intent and our capabilities. There must be no question of trading or bluff in this hemisphere. Let us give no promises we cannot keep make no meaningless assurances to an Ethiopia, a Czechoslovakia, or a Poland. The policy we decide upon should be as clear cut as our shorelines, and as easily defended as our continent.

This western hemisphere is our domain. It is our right to trade freely within it. From Alaska to Labrador, from the Hawaiian Islands to Bermuda, from Canada to South America, we must allow no invading army to set foot. These are the outposts of the United States. They form the essential outline of our geographical defense. We must be ready to wage war with all the resources of our nation if they are ever seriously threatened. Their defense is the mission of our army, our navy, and our air corps the minimum requirement of our military strength. Around these places should lie our line between neutrality and war. Let there be no compromise about our right to defend or trade within this area. If it is challenged by any nation, the answer must be war. Our policy of neutrality should have this as its foundation.

We must protect our sister American nations from foreign invasion, both for their welfare and our own. But, in turn, they have a duty to us. They should not place us in the position of having to defend them in America while they engage in wars abroad. Can we rightfully permit any country in America to give bases to foreign warships, or to send its army abroad to fight while it remains secure in our protection at home? We desire the utmost friendship with the people of Canada. If their country is ever attacked, our Navy will be defending their seas, our soldiers will fight on their battlefields, our fliers will die in their skies. But have they the right to draw this hemisphere into a European war simply because they prefer the Crown of England to American independence?

'When the time came to pay us back, these [European] countries simply refused to do so. They seized all the German colonies and carved up Europe to suit their fancy. These were the 'fruits of war'. They took our money and they took our soldiers.'

Sooner or later we must demand the freedom of this continent and its surrounding islands from the dictates of European power. American history clearly indicates this need. As long as European powers maintain their influence in our hemisphere, we are likely to find ourselves involved in their troubles. And they will loose no opportunity to involve us.

Our congress is now assembled to decide upon the best policy for this country to maintain during the war which is going on in Europe. The legislation under discussion involves three major issues – the embargo of arms, the restriction of shipping, and the allowance of credit. The action we take in regard to these issues will be an important indication to ourselves, and to the nations of Europe, whether or not we are likely to enter the conflict eventually as we did in the last war. The entire world is watching us. The action we take in America may either stop or precipitate this war.

Let us take up these issues, one at a time, and examine them. First, the embargo of arms: It is argued that the repeal of this embargo would assist democracy in Europe, that it would let us make a profit for ourselves from the sale of munitions abroad, and, at the same time, help to build up our own arms industry.

I do not believe that repealing the arms embargo would assist democracy in Europe—because I do not believe this is a war for democracy. This is a war over the balance of power in Europe a war brought about by the desire for strength on the part of Germany and the fear of strength on the part of England and France. The [more] munitions the armies obtain, the longer the war goes on, and the more devastated Europe becomes, the less hope there is for democracy. That is a lesson we should have learned from participation in the last war. If democratic principles had been applied in Europe after that war, if the 'democracies' of Europe had been willing to make some sacrifice to help democracy in Europe while it was fighting for its life, if England and France had offered a hand to the struggling republic of Germany, there would be no war today.

If we repeal the arms embargo with the idea of assisting one of the warring sides to overcome the other, then why mislead ourselves by talk of neutrality? Those who advance this argument should admit openly that repeal is a step toward war. The next step would the extension of credit, and the next step would be the sending of American troops.

'Let us not dissipate our strength in these wars of politics and possession.'

To those who argue that we could make a profit and build up our own industry by selling munitions abroad, I reply that we in America have not yet reached a point where we wish to capitilize on the destruction and death of war. I do not believe that the material welfare of this country need, or that our spiritual welfare could withstand, such a policy. If our industry depends upon a commerce of arms for its strength, then our industrial system should be changed.

It is impossible for me to understand how America can contribute civilization and humanity by sending offensive instruments of destruction to European battlefields. This would not only implicate us in the war, but it would make us partly responsible for its devastation. The fallacy of helping to defend a political ideology, even though it be somewhat similar to our own, was clearly demonstrated to us in the last war. Through our help that war was won, but neither the democracy nor the justice for which we fought grew in the peace that followed our victory.

Our bond with Europe is a bond of race and not of political ideology. We had to fight a European army to establish democracy in this country. It is the European race we must preserve; political progress will follow. Racial strength is vital politics, a luxury. If the white race is ever seriously threatened, it may then be time for us to take our part in its protection, to fight side by side with the English, French, and Germans, but not with one against the other for our mutual destruction.

Let us not dissipate our strength, or help Europe to dissipate hers, in these wars of politics and possession. For the benefit of western civilization, we should continue our embargo on offensive armaments. As far as purely defensive arms are concerned, I, for one, am in favor of supplying European countries with as much as we can spare of the material that falls within this category. There are technicians who will argue that offensive and defensive arms cannot be separated completely. That is true, but it is no more difficult to make a list of defensive weapons than it is to separate munitions of war from semi-manufactured articles, and we are faced with that problem today. No one says that we should sell opium because it is difficult to make a list of narcotics. I would as soon see our country traffic in opium as in bombs. There are certain borderline cases, but there are plenty of clear cut examples: for instance, the bombing plane and the anti-aircraft cannon. I do not want to see American bombers dropping bombs which will kill and mutilate European children, even if they are not flown by American pilots. But I am perfectly willing to see American anti-aircraft guns shooting American shells at invading bombers over any European country. And I believe that most of you who are listening tonight will agree with me.

The second major issue for which we must create a policy concerns the restrictions to be placed on our shipping. Naval blockades have long been accepted as an element of warfare. They began on the surface of the sea, followed the submarine beneath it, and now reach up into the sky with aircraft. The laws and customs which were developed during the surface era were not satisfactory to the submarine. Now, aircraft bring up new and unknown factors for consideration. It is

> **'I do not believe this is a war for democracy. This is a war over the balance of power in Europe ... the desire for strength on the part of Germany and the fear of strength on the part of England and France.'**

simple enough for a battleship to identify the merchantman she captures. It is a more difficult problem for a submarine if that merchantman may carry cannon; it is safer to fire a torpedo than to come up and ask. For bombing planes flying at high altitudes and through conditions of poor visibility, identification of a surface vessel will be more difficult still.

In modern naval blockades and warfare, torpedoes will be fired and bombs dropped on probabilities rather than on certainties of identification. The only safe course for neutral shipping at this time is to stay away from the warring countries and dangerous waters of Europe.

The third issue to be decided relates to the extension of credit. Here again we may draw from our experience in the last war. After that war was over, we found ourselves in the position of having financed a large portion of European countries. And when the time came to pay us back, these countries simply refused to do so. They not only refused to pay the wartime loans we made, but they refused to pay back what we loaned them after the war was over. As is so frequently the case, we found that loaning money eventually created animosity instead of gratitude. European countries felt insulted when we asked to be repaid. They called us 'Uncle Shylock'. They were horror struck at the idea of turning over to us any of their islands in America to compensate for their debts, or for our help in winning their war. They seized all the German colonies and carved up Europe to suit their fancy. These were the 'fruits of war'. They took our money and they took our soldiers. But there was not the offer of one Caribbean island in return for the debts they 'could not afford to pay'.

The extension of credit to a belligerent country is a long step toward war, and it would leave us close to the edge. If American industry loans money to a belligerent country, many interests will feel that it is more important for that country to win than for our own to avoid the war. It is unfortunate but true that there are interests in America who would rather lose American lives than their own dollars. We should give them no opportunity.

I believe that we should adopt as our program of American neutrality—as our contribution to western civilization—the following policy:

1. An embargo on offensive weapons and munitions.
2. The unrestricted sale of purely defensive armaments.
3. The prohibition of American shipping from the belligerent countries of Europe and their danger zones.
4. The refusal of credit to belligerent nations or their agents.

Whether or not this program is adopted depends upon the support of those of us who believe in it. The United States of America is a democracy. The policy of our country is still controlled by our people. It is time for us to take action. There has never been a greater test for the democratic principle of government. '

The former hero of a nation was publicly denounced by President Roosevelt for his stance. He resigned his Army Air Corps officer's commission but when he tried to re-enlist after the Japanese attack on Pearl Harbour in December 1941, his request was refused. Lindbergh worked as at technical advisor and test pilot for the Ford Motor Company and the United Aircraft Corporation during the war. Although he remained in the private sector after the war, President Eisenhower restored Lindbergh's commission and appointed him a brigadier general in the air force. Lindbergh's book, Spirit of St Louis, won the Pulitzer Prize in 1954. Charles Lindbergh, who spoke out about conservation issues in latter life, died of cancer in 1974.

Cardinal Clement von Galen

'Against Aktion T4'

Sermon at Münster Cathedral, Germany, 3 August 1941.

Clement August von Galen (1878-1946) was the Catholic Bishop of Münster during the rise to power of the Nazi Party in the 1930s and was an outspoken opponent of the German government and its policies. He attacked the Gestapo for their raids on Jesuit houses in Münster and stated from the pulpit that no German citizen had any defence against the Nazis' power now 'they had replaced the courts and were above the law'.

The Nazi program to eliminate 'life unworthy of life', code-named 'Aktion T4', began in October 1939. It first focused on newborn and very young children, where midwives and doctors were required to register children up to age three who showed symptoms of mental retardation or physical deformity. On Hitler's orders, certain medical staff were granted the authority to name those who 'according to human judgment, are incurable ... (and) can, upon a most careful diagnosis of their condition of sickness, be accorded a mercy death.'

The Nazi euthanasia program expanded to include older disabled children and adults and was eventually taken over by the SS. Six 'killing centres' were established, including a well-known psychiatric clinic at Hadamar. A former prison at Brandenburg was converted into a killing centre where the first experimental gassings took place. Gas chambers were disguised as showers, but were sealed chambers connected by pipes to cylinders of carbon monoxide. Each killing centre also included a crematorium where the bodies were taken for disposal (families were informed the cause of death was purely medical, such as heart failure or pneumonia). This later became the blueprint for the extermination of Jewish people.

In 1941 the chaplain of a mental asylum briefed von Galen about the Nazi removal of patients to concentration camps for extermination because they were no longer 'productive'. On a Sunday, in Münster Cathedral, Cardinal Clement von Galen risked his life by openly condemning the Nazi euthanasia program.

Fellow Christians! In the pastoral letter of the German bishops of June 26 1941, which was read out in all the Catholic churches in Germany on July 6 1941, it states among other things: It is true that there are definite commandments in Catholic moral doctrine which are no longer applicable if their fulfilment involves too many difficulties.

However, there are sacred obligations of conscience from which no one has the power to release us and which we must fulfil even if it costs us our lives. Never under any circumstances may a human being kill an innocent person, apart from war and legitimate self-defence.

On July 6, I already had cause to add to the pastoral letter the following explanation: for some months we have been hearing reports that, on the orders of Berlin, patients from mental asylums who have been ill for a long time and may appear incurable, are being compulsorily removed. Then, after a short time, the relatives are regularly informed that the corpse has been burnt and the ashes can be delivered. There is a general suspicion verging on certainty, that these numerous unexpected deaths of mentally ill people do not occur of themselves but are deliberately brought about, that the doctrine is being followed, according to which one may destroy so-called "worthless life," that is, kill innocent people if one considers that their lives are of no further value for the nation and the state.

I am reliably informed that lists are also being drawn up in the asylums of the province of Westphalia as well of those patients who are to be taken away as so-called "unproductive national comrades" and shortly to be killed. The first transport left the Marienthal institution near Münster during this past week.

German men and women, section 211 of the Reich Penal Code is still valid. It states: "He who deliberately kills another person will be punished by death for murder if the killing is premeditated."

Those patients who are destined to be killed are transported away from home to a distant asylum presumably in order to protect those who deliberately kill those poor people, members of our families, from this legal punishment. Some illness is then given as the cause of death. Since the corpse has been burnt straight away, the relatives

> 'Who will be able to trust his doctor any more? He may report his patient as "unproductive" and receive instructions to kill him. It is impossible to imagine the degree of moral depravity, that would then spread if this dreadful doctrine is tolerated.'

and also the criminal police are unable to establish whether the illness really occurred and what the cause of death was.

However, I have been assured that the Reich Interior Ministry and the office of the Reich Doctors' Leader, Dr. Conti, make no bones about the fact that in reality a large number of mentally ill people in Germany have been deliberately killed and more will be killed in the future.

The Penal Code lays down in section 139: "He who receives credible information concerning the intention to commit a crime against life and neglects to alert the authorities or the person who is threatened in time ... will be punished."

When I learned of the intention to transport patients from Marienthal in order to kill them, I brought a formal charge at the State Court in Münster and with the Police President in Münster by means of a registered letter which read as follows: "According to information which I have received, in the course of this week a large number of patients from the Marienthal Provincial Asylum near Münster are to be transported to the Eichberg asylum as so-called "unproductive national comrades" and will then soon be deliberately killed, as is generally believed has occurred with such transports from other asylums. Since such an action is not only contrary to the moral laws of God and Nature but also is punishable with death as murder under section 211 of the Penal Code, I hereby bring a charge in accordance with my duty under section 139 of the Penal Code, and request you to provide immediate protection for the national comrades threatened in this way by taking action against those agencies who are intending their removal and murder, and that you inform me of the steps that have been taken."

I have received no news concerning intervention by the Prosecutor's Office or by the police ... Thus we must assume that the poor helpless patients will soon be killed.

For what reason? Not because they have committed a crime worthy of death. Not because they attacked their nurses or orderlies so that the latter had no other choice but to use legitimate force to defend their lives against their attackers. Those are cases where, in addition to the killing of an armed enemy in a just war, the use of force to the point of killing is allowed and is often required.

> 'None of our lives will be safe any more. No police force will protect us and no court will investigate our murder and give the murderer the punishment he deserves.'

No, it is not for such reasons that these unfortunate patients must die but rather because, in the opinion of some department, on the testimony of some commission, they have become "worthless life" because according to this testimony they are "unproductive national comrades." The argument goes: they can no longer produce commodities, they are like an old machine that no longer works, they are like an old horse which has become incurably lame, they are like a cow which no longer gives milk.

What does one do with such an old machine? It is thrown on the scrap heap. What does one do with a lame horse, with such an unproductive cow?

No, I do not want to continue the comparison to the end—however fearful the justification for it and the symbolic force of it are. We are not dealing with machines, horses and cows whose only function is to serve mankind, to produce goods for man. One may smash them, one may slaughter them as soon as they no longer fulfil this function.

No, we are dealing with human beings, our fellow human beings, our brothers and sisters. With poor people, sick people, if you like unproductive people.

But have they for that reason forfeited the right to life?

Have you, have I the right to live only so long as we are productive, so long as we are recognized by others as productive?

If you establish and apply the principle that you can kill "unproductive" fellow human beings then woe betide us all when we become old and frail! If one is allowed to kill the unproductive people then woe betide the invalids who have used up, sacrificed and lost their health and strength in the productive process. If one is allowed forcibly to remove one's unproductive fellow human beings then woe betide loyal soldiers who return to the homeland seriously disabled, as cripples, as invalids. If it is once accepted that people have the right to kill "unproductive" fellow humans—and even if initially it only affects the poor defenceless mentally ill—then as a matter of principle murder is permitted for all unproductive people, in other words for the incurably sick, the people who have become invalids through labour and war, for us all when we become old, frail and therefore unproductive.

Then, it is only necessary for some secret edict to order that the method developed for the mentally ill should be extended to other "unproductive" people ... to those suffering from incurable lung disease, to the elderly who are frail or invalids, to the severely disabled soldiers. Then none of our lives will be safe any more. Some commission can put us on the list of the "unproductive," who in their opinion have become worthless life. And no police force will protect us and no court will investigate our murder and give the murderer the punishment he deserves.

Who will be able to trust his doctor any more? He may report his patient as "unproductive" and receive instructions to kill him. It is impossible to imagine the degree of moral depravity, of general mistrust that would then spread even through families if this dreadful doctrine is tolerated, accepted and followed.

Woe to mankind, woe to our German nation if God's Holy Commandment "Thou shalt not kill," which God proclaimed on Mount Sinai amidst thunder and lightning, which God our Creator inscribed in the conscience of mankind from the very beginning, is not only broken, but if this transgression is actually tolerated and permitted to go unpunished.'

As a result of this sermon, Hitler momentarily suspended 'Aktion T4', however, the program quietly continued, but without the gassings. Drugs and starvation were used instead and doctors were encouraged to decide in favour of death whenever euthanasia was considered. A report published in 2005 stated that 200 000 mentally ill and handicapped German citizens were put to death under this program.

Although the Nazis left Bishop von Galen 'unharmed' to avoid making him into a martyr, persecution of priests continued with the arrest and then execution of three parish priests who had distributed von Galen's sermon. Hundreds of clergy were arrested, arraigned before Nazi courts and interned in concentration camps (in Dachau alone, 2770 priests, mainly Polish, were interned and some 4000 priests were put to death in concentration camps during the war). Ironically, the Cathedral in Münster was destroyed by allied bombs in October 1943.

In 1946 Pope Pius XII announced that Bishop von Galen would be one of thirty new cardinals ordained in Rome and the man who had defied Hitler, was warmly greeted by crowds outside St Peters. The following month, on 22 March, Cardinal von Galen died from a burst appendix upon his return to Germany. Calls for his beatification—the first step on road to sainthood—began in 1956 and were finally answered by Pope John Paul II in 2004.

Mohandas K Gandhi

'Quit India'

Address to All India Congress Committee, Bombay, 8 August 1942

Mohandas Gandhi proved in his lifetime that non-violent defiance of unjust laws could change the world. He used this effectively both against the British and in an attempt to broker peace between Muslim and Hindu factions in his own country. It was a message as old as the time of Jesus and one subsequently used in protest movements throughout the world.

'Mahatma' (which means 'Great Soul') Gandhi's belief in the injustice of British colonialism in India saw him imprisoned several times, where he used fasting as an act of defiance and protest. In 1931 Gandhi was released from prison and, after brokering a truce between the National Congress and the British, travelled to London to attend the Round Table Conference on Indian constitutional reform. Returning to India, his pattern of civil disobedience and arrest continued but he also threatened to fast 'unto death' to placate warring religious factions. Finally Britain allowed Indian Congress ministers to hold office in provincial legislatures in 1937.

After the outbreak of World War II in September 1939, Gandhi stepped up his campaign for Indian home rule, arguing that an independent India could best serve Britain in her fight against fascism. In August 1942 Gandhi outlined his plan of action to the All India Congress Committee in Bombay, which was the formal vehicle being used to communicate with Britain. The following extract is part of the concluding portion of Gandhi's speech which was delivered in English.

'I have taken such an inordinately long time over pouring out what was agitating my soul, to those whom I had just now the privilege of serving. I have been called their leader or, in the military language, their commander. But I do not look at my position in that light. I have no weapon but love to wield my authority over anyone. I do sport a stick which you can break into bits without the slightest exertion. It is simply my staff with the help of which I walk. Such a cripple is not elated, when he has been called upon to bear the greatest burden. You can share that burden only when I appear before you not as your commander but as a humble servant. And he who serves best is the chief among equals.

I want to declare to the world. Although I may forfeit the regard of many friends in the West and I must bow my head low; but even for their friendship or love I must not suppress the voice of conscience—promoting my inner basic nature today. There is something within me impelling me to cry out my agony. I have known humanity. I have studied something of psychology. Such a man knows exactly what it is. I do not mind how you describe it. That voice within tells me, 'You have to stand against the whole world although you may have to stand alone. You have to stare in the face the whole world although the world may look at you with bloodshot eyes. Do not fear. Trust the little voice residing within your heart. It says : "Forsake friends, wife and all; but testify to that for which you have lived and for which you have to die. I want to live my full span of life. And for me I put my span of life at 120 years. By that time India will be free, the world will be free."

Let me tell you that I do not regard England or for that matter America as free countries. They are free after their own fashion, free to hold in bondage coloured races of the earth. Are England and America fighting for the liberty of these races today? If not, do not ask me to wait until after the war. You shall not limit my concept of freedom.

Unconsciously from its very foundations long ago, this Congress has been building on non-violence known as constitutional methods. I trust the whole of India today to launch upon a non-violent struggle. I trust, because of my nature to rely upon the innate goodness of human nature which

'And even when India is met with such angry opposition, she says, "We won't hit below the belt, we have learnt sufficient gentlemanliness. We are pledged to non-violence."'

perceives the truth and prevails during the crisis as if by instinct. But even if I am deceived in this I shall not swerve. I shall not flinch. From its very inception the Congress based its policy on peaceful methods, included Swaraj and the subsequent generations added non-violence. When Dadabhai entered the British Parliament, Salisbury dubbed him as a black man; but the English people defeated Salisbury and Dadabhai went to the Parliament by their vote. India was delirious with joy. These things however India has outgrown.

It is, however, with all these things as the background that I want Englishmen, Europeans and all the United Nations to examine in their hearts what crime has India committed in demanding Independence. I ask, is it right for you to distrust such an organization with all its background, tradition and record of over half a century and misrepresent its endeavours before all the world by every means at your command? Is it right that by hook or by crook, aided by the foreign press, aided by the President of the USA, or even by the Generalissimo of China [Chiang Kai-shek] who has yet to win his laurels, you should present India's struggle in shocking caricature? I have met the Generalissimo. I have known him through Madame Shek who was my interpreter; and though he seemed inscrutable to me, not so Madame Shek; and he allowed me to read his mind through her. There is a chorus of disapproval and righteous protest all over the world against us. They say we are erring, the move is inopportune. I used to have great regard for British diplomacy which has enabled them to hold the Empire so long. Now it stinks in my nostrils, and others have studied that diplomacy and are putting it into practice. They may succeed in getting, through these methods, world opinion on their side for a time; but India will speak against that world opinion. She will raise her voice against all the organized propaganda. I will speak against it. Even if all the United Nations opposed me, even if the whole of India forsakes me, I will say, "You are wrong. India will wrench with non-violence her liberty from unwilling hands."

I will go ahead not for India's sake alone, but for the sake of the world. Even if my eyes close before there is freedom, non-violence will not end. They will be dealing a mortal blow to China and to Russia if they oppose the freedom of non-violent India which is pleading with bended knees for the fulfilment of debt along overdue. Does a creditor ever go to debtor like that? And even when India is met with such angry opposition, she says, "We won't hit below

the belt, we have learnt sufficient gentlemanliness. We are pledged to non-violence." I have been the author of the non-embarrassment policy of the Congress and yet today you find me talking this strong language. I say it is consistent with our honour. If a man holds me by the neck and wants to drawn me, may I not struggle to free myself directly? There is no inconsistency in our position today.

There are representatives of the foreign press assembled here today. Through them I wish to say to the world that the United Powers who somehow or other say that they have need for India, have the opportunity now to declare India free and prove their bona fides. If they miss it, they will be missing the opportunity of their lifetime, and history will record that they did not discharge their obligations to India in time, and lost the battle. I want the blessings of the whole world so that I may succeed with them. I do not want the United Powers to go beyond their obvious limitations. I do not want them to accept non-violence and disarm today. There is a fundamental difference between fascism and this imperialism which I am fighting. Do the British get from India which they hold in bondage? Think what difference it would make if India was to participate as a free ally. That freedom, if it is to come, must come today. It will have no taste left in it today if you who have the power to help cannot exercise it. If you can exercise it, under the glow of freedom what seems impossible, today, will become possible tomorrow.

If India feels that freedom, she will command that freedom for China. The road for running to Russia's help will be open. The Englishmen did not die in Malaya or on Burma soil. What shall enable us to retrieve the situation? Where shall I go, and where shall

I take the forty crores of India? How is this vast mass of humanity to be aglow in the cause of world deliverance, unless and until it has touched and felt freedom. Today they have no touch of life left. It has been crushed out of them. It lustre is to be put into their eyes, freedom has to come not tomorrow, but today.'

Mohandas Karamchand Gandhi was born in 1869 in Poorbandar, West India. The son of the chief minister of the province and his fourth wife, a deeply religious Hindu, Gandhi was unable to find suitable work as a barrister and so accepted a contract to work in Natal, South Africa. There he came face to face with institutionalised racial discrimination and for the next 20 years opposed legislation that sought to deprive Indians and other minorities of their rights. Gandhi's non-violent defiance of unfair laws focused attention on his civil activities for the first time and his establishment of a volunteer Ambulance Corps during the Boer War (1899-1902) won him the English War Medal.

Returning to India in 1914, Gandhi became an advocate for 'home rule'—the complete withdrawal of English Imperial interests. He became the dominant figure of the National Congress movement but never wavered from his policies of non-violent, non co-operation in achieving Indian independence despite the threat of arrest and jail.

In the 1920s, with Hindu and Muslim members of the National Congress unable to find common ground, warring factions aligned to the two religious groups led to bloodshed. Unable to reason with either side Gandhi undertook a three-week fast that not only restored the non-violent aims of the 'home rule' campaign but also promoted his personal act of spiritual cleansing.

Gandhi famously described a British proposal for a new constitution after the war as 'a post-dated cheque on a crashing bank.' In 1942 he was jailed for civil disobedience designed to 'obstruct the war effort' and was not released until 1944. Gandhi then negotiated with the British Cabinet Mission in India which ultimately recommended a new constitutional structure for home rule in India.

However, divisions between Muslim and Hindu factions within the National Congress ultimately led to the formation of separate nations, India and Pakistan, and the dream of a country united in its freedom was lost. Britain effectively relinquished 163 years of empirial rule in India on 15 August, 1947—an act Gandhi described as 'the noblest act of the British nation.'

The final months of Gandhi's life were spent shaming the instigators of community and religious violence by fasting. Just as his fasting looked set to avert the country from plummeting into complete anarchy, Mohandas Gandhi was assassinated in Delhi on 30 January, 1948 by Hindu fanatic Nathuram Godse while walking in a garden with his grandchildren.

General George S Patton

'D-Day Address'

Enniskillen Manor Grounds, England, 17 May 1944.

George Smith Patton Jnr (1885-1945) was one of the most outspoken, complicated and ultimately controversial American generals in military history. Educated at West Point, he competed in the modern pentathlon during the 1912 Stockholm Olympics—an event originally open only to military personnel—but lost his chance for a medal when he used his favoured .38 revolver for the pistol shooting event instead of the smaller .22 calibre pistol. In World War I Patton became the first member of the newly formed US Tank Corps and saw tanks as the future of modern warfare. In World War II, Patton played an important role in the Allied invasion of North Africa (1942) and led the US 7th Army's sweep of Sicily before being put in charge of the US 3rd Army in preparation of the liberation of France.

Three weeks before the D-Day invasion of Normandy—the straight-talking General gave his US troops a pep-talk at Enniskillen Manor Grounds, England where they were preparing for the liberation of France.

'Men, this stuff some sources sling around about America wanting to stay out of the war and not wanting to fight is a lot of baloney! Americans love to fight, traditionally. All real Americans love the sting and clash of battle. America loves a winner. America will not tolerate a loser. Americans despise a coward; Americans play to win. That's why America has never lost and never will lose a war.

You are not all going to die. Only two percent of you, right here today, would be killed in a major battle.

Death must not be feared. Death, in time, comes to all of us. And every man is scared in his first action. If he says he's not, he's a goddamn liar. Some men are cowards, yes, but they fight just the same, or get the hell slammed out of them.

The real hero is the man who fights even though he's scared. Some get over their fright in a minute, under fire; others take an hour; for some it takes days; but a real man will never let the fear of death overpower his honor, his sense of duty, to his country and to his manhood.

'When you're sitting around the fireside with your grandson on your knee and he asks you what you did in the war, you won't have to shift him to the other knee, cough, and say, "I shovelled shit in Louisiana".'

All through your Army careers, you've been bitching about what you call "chicken-shit drills". That, like everything else in the Army, has a definite purpose. That purpose is instant obedience to orders and to create and maintain constant alertness! This must be bred into every soldier. A man must be alert all the time if he expects to stay alive. If not, some German son-of-a-bitch will sneak up behind him with a sock full of shit! There are four hundred neatly marked graves somewhere in Sicily, all because one man went to sleep on his job—but they are German graves, because we caught the bastards asleep!

An Army is a team; lives, sleeps, fights, and eats as a team. This individual hero stuff is a lot of horse shit! The bilious bastards who write that kind of stuff for the Saturday Evening Post don't know any more about real fighting under fire than they know about fucking! Every single man in the Army plays a vital role. Every man has his job to do and must do it. What if every truck driver decided that he didn't like the whine of a shell overhead, turned yellow and jumped headlong into a ditch? What if every man thought, "They won't miss me, just one in millions?" Where in Hell would we be now? Where would our country, our loved ones, our homes, even the world, be?

No, thank God, Americans don't think like that. Every man does his job, serves the whole. Ordnance men supply and maintain the guns and vast machinery of this war, to keep us rolling. Quartermasters bring up clothes and food, for where we're going, there isn't a hell of a lot to steal. Every last man on K.P. has a job to do, even the guy who boils the water to keep us from getting the G.I. shits!

> **'A man must be alert all the time if he expects to stay alive. If not, some German son-of-a-bitch will sneak up behind him with a sock full of shit!'**

Remember, men, you don't know I'm here. No mention of that is to be made in any letters. The USA is supposed to be wondering what the hell has happened to me. I'm not supposed to be commanding this Army, I'm not supposed even to be in England. Let the first bastards to find out be the goddamn Germans. I want them to look up and howl, "Ach, it's the goddamn Third Army and that son-of-a-bitch Patton again!"

We want to get this thing over and get the hell out of here, and get at those purple-pissin' Japs! The shortest road home is through Berlin and Tokyo! We'll win this war, but we'll win it only by showing the enemy we have more guts than they have or ever will have!

There's one great thing you men can say when it's all over and you're home once more. You can thank God that twenty years from now, when you're sitting around the fireside with your grandson on your knee and he asks you what you did in the war, you won't have to shift him to the other knee, cough, and say, "I shovelled shit in Louisiana".'

This speech was never meant to be published and a request to Patton's widow after the War to have an audio recording of Patton's address published was politely refused. Mrs Patton took the position that the speech was made by the General only for the men who were going to fight and die with him—it was not a speech for posterity, and somewhat embarrassed by the frank language, not one for public consumption.

George Patton's single-mindedness, and lack of political and personal tact, often brought him into conflict with military hierarchy but there was no denying his brilliance as a tactician (Patton also had a strong moral character; when his Third Army liberated the Buchenwald concentration camp he made local Germans tour the camp—a policy adopted by other generals). On 9 December 1945 he was fatally injured in a car accident in occupied Germany and died 12 days later. Patton was buried in Hamm, Germany alongside his men who had died in the Battle of the Bulge.

It is easy to see why Patton was regarded as a man of the people when you compare his rhetoric with the then Supreme Commander General Dwight D. 'Ike' Eisenhower's. Ike's actual D-Day order on 6 June was understated, dispassionate and historic—it was later broadcast to the world:

'Soldiers, Sailors, and Airmen of the Allied Expeditionary Force! You are about to embark upon the Great Crusade, toward which we have striven these many months. The eyes of liberty loving people everywhere march with you. In company with our brave Allies and brothers in arms on other fronts, you will bring about the destruction of the German war machine, the elimination of Nazi tyranny over the oppressed peoples of Europe, and security for ourselves in a free world.

Your task will not be an easy one. Your enemy is well trained, well equipped, and battle-hardened. He will fight savagely.

But this is the year 1944. Much has happened since the Nazi triumphs of 1940-41.

The United Nations have inflicted upon the Germans great defeat in open battle man to man. Our air offensive has seriously reduced their strength in the air and their capacity to wage war on the ground.

Our home fronts have given us an overwhelming superiority in weapons and munitions of war and placed at our disposal great reserves of trained fighting men.

The tide has turned.

The free men of the world are marching together to victory. I have full confidence in your courage, devotion to duty, and skill in battle.

We will accept nothing less than full victory.

Good luck, and let us all beseech the blessings of Almighty God upon this great and noble undertaking. '

Golda Meir

'The Struggle for a Jewish State'

Council of Jewish Federations, Chicago, 2 January 1948.

I srael's third Prime Minister, Golda Meir (1898-1978) was born in Kiev in Russia and emigrated with her family to Milwaukee, Wisconsin, in the United States in 1906. She joined the Labor Zionist Organization (Poalei Zion) in 1915 and moved to Palestine with her husband Morris Myerson. A leading socialist Zionist during the 1930s, she was also an International Zionist representative and spent 1932 working in America. After the end of World War II, Golda adopted the Hebrew name 'Meir' (which means 'to burn brightly') and became president of the political bureau of the Jewish Agency as thousands of Palestinian Jews and European refugees agitated for the formation of an official Jewish State in the traditional Holy Land region.

In February 1947 Britain ceded control of occupied Palestine to the United Nations which passed the seemingly impossible resolution to partition Palestine into Jewish and Arab states. Britain was ordered to leave Palestine by August 1948 but could do little to prepare either Jewish or Arab communities for independence. By the end of 1947, Palestinian and resettled Jewry were fighting both Arab terrorist and British peace-keeping forces.

In January 1948, Golda Meir flew to the United States to raise funds for weapons that were urgently needed to defend the 700 000 Jews in Palestine being threatened by Arab attacks. She made an unscheduled appearance before the Council of Jewish Federations and gave this heartfelt speech that moved thousands of people to give moral and financial support to the fledgling nation of Israel.

'I have had the privilege of representing Palestine Jewry in this country and in other countries when the problems that we faced were those of building more kibbutzim, of bringing in more Jews in spite of political obstacles and Arab riots.

We always had faith that in the end we would win, that everything we were doing in the country led to the independence of the Jewish people and to a Jewish state.

Long before we had dared pronounce that word, we knew what was in store for us.

Today we have reached a point when the nations of the world have given us their decision—the establishment of a Jewish state in a part of Palestine. Now in Palestine we are fighting to make this resolution of the United Nations a reality, not because we wanted to fight. If we had the choice, we would have chosen peace to build in peace.

We have no alternative.

Friends, we have no alternative in Palestine. The Mufti and his men have declared war upon us. We have to fight for our lives, for our safety, and for what we have accomplished in Palestine, and perhaps above all, we must fight for Jewish honour and Jewish independence. Without exaggeration, I can tell you that the Jewish community in Palestine is doing this well. Many of you have visited Palestine; all of you have read about our young people and have a notion as to what our youth is like. I have known this generation for the last twenty-seven years. I thought I knew them. I realize now that even I did not.

These young boys and girls, many in their teens, are bearing the burden of what is happening in the country with a spirit that no words can describe. You see these youngsters in open cars—not armoured cars—in convoys going from Tel Aviv to Jerusalem, knowing that every time they start out from Tel Aviv or from Jerusalem there are probably Arabs behind the orange groves or the hills, waiting to ambush the convoy.

These boys and girls have accepted the task of bringing Jews over these roads in safety as naturally as though they were going out to their daily work or to their classes in the university.

We must ask the Jews the world over to see us as the front line.

All we ask of Jews the world over, and mainly of the Jews in the United States, is to give us the possibility of going on with the struggle.

When trouble started, we asked young people from the age of seventeen to twenty-five who were not members of Haganah, to volunteer. Up to the day that I left home on Thursday morning, when the registration of this age group was still going on, over 20 000 young men and women had signed up. As of now we have about 9 000 people mobilized in the various parts of the country. We must triple this number within the next few days.

We have to maintain these men. No government sends its soldiers to the front and expects them to take along from their homes the most elementary requirements—blankets, bedding, clothing.

A people that is fighting for its very life knows how to supply the men they send to the front lines. We too must do the same.

Thirty-five of our boys, unable to go by car on the road to besieged Kfar Etzion to bring help, set out by foot through the hills; they knew the road, the Arab villages on that road, and the danger they would have to face. Some of the finest youngsters we have in the country were in that group, and they were all killed, every one of them. We have a description from an Arab of how they fought to the end for over seven hours against hundreds of Arabs. According to this Arab, the last boy killed, with no more ammunition left, died with a stone in his hand.

I want to say to you, friends, that the Jewish community in Palestine is going to fight to the very end. If we have arms to fight with, we will fight with those, and if not, we will fight with stones in our hands.

I want you to believe me when I say that I came on this special mission to the United States today not to save 700 000 Jews. During the last few years the Jewish people lost 6 million Jews, and it would be audacity on our part to worry the Jewish people throughout the world because a few hundred thousand more Jews were in danger. That is not the issue.

The issue is that if these 700 000 Jews in Palestine can remain alive, then the Jewish people as such is alive and Jewish independence is assured. If these 700 000 people are killed off, then for many centuries, we are through with this dream of a Jewish people and a Jewish homeland.

My friends, we are at war. There is no Jew in Palestine who does not believe that finally we will be victorious. That is the spirit of the country. And every Jew in the country also knows that within a few months a Jewish state in Palestine will be established.

We knew that the price we would have to pay would be the best of our people. There are over 300 killed by now. There will be more. There is no doubt that there will be more. But there is also no doubt that the spirit of our young people is such that no matter how many Arabs invade the country, their spirit will not falter. However, this valiant spirit alone cannot face rifles and machine guns. Rifles and machine guns without spirit are not worth very much, but spirit without arms can in time be broken with the body.

I have come to the United States, and I hope you will understand me if I say that it is not an easy matter for any of us to leave home at present—to my sorrow I am not in the front line. I am not with my daughter in the Negev or with other sons and daughters in the trenches. But I have a job to do.

> 'I have come here to try to impress Jews in the United States with the fact that within a very short period, a couple of weeks, we must have in cash between 25 and 30 million dollars.'

I have come here to try to impress Jews in the United States with the fact that within a very short period, a couple of weeks, we must have in cash between 25 and 30 million dollars. In the next two or three weeks we can establish ourselves. Of that we are convinced, and you must have faith; we are sure that we can carry on.

I said before that the Yishuv will give, is giving of its means. But please remember that even while shooting is going on, we must carry on so that our economy remains intact. Our factories must go on. Our settlements must not be broken up.

We know that this battle is being waged for those not yet in the country.

There are 30 000 Jews detained right next door to Palestine in Cyprus. I believe that within a very short period, within the next two or three months at most, these 30 000 will be with us, among them thousands of infants and young children. We must now think of preparing means of absorbing them. We know that within the very near future, hundreds of thousands more will be coming in. We must see that our economy is intact.

I want you to understand that there is no despair in the Yishuv. When you go to Tel Aviv now, you will find the city full of life; only the shooting that you hear on the outskirts of Tel Aviv and Jaffa reminds one that the situation in the country is not normal. But it would be a crime on my part not to describe the situation to you exactly as it is.

Merely with our ten fingers and merely with spirit and sacrifice, we cannot carry on this battle, and the only hinterland that we have is you. The Mufti has the Arab states—not all so enthusiastic about helping him but states with government budgets. The Egyptian government can vote a budget to aid our antagonists. The Syrian government can do the same.

We have no government. But we have millions of Jews in the Diaspora, and exactly as we have faith in our youngsters in Palestine I have faith in Jews in the United States; I believe that they will realize the peril of our situation and will do what they have to do.

I know that we are not asking for something easy. I myself have sometimes been active in various campaigns and fund collections, and I know that collecting at once a sum such as I ask is not simple.

But I have seen our people at home. I have seen them come from the offices to the clinics when we called the community to give their blood for a blood bank to treat the wounded. I have seen them lined up for hours, waiting so that some of their blood can be added to this bank.

It is blood plus money that is being given in Palestine.

We are not a better breed; we are not the best Jews of the Jewish people. It so happened that we are there and you are here. I am certain that if you were in Palestine and we were in the United States, you would be doing what we are doing there, and you would ask us here to do what you will have to do.

I want to close with paraphrasing one of the greatest speeches that was made during the Second World War—the words of Churchill. I am not exaggerating when I say that the Yishuv in Palestine will fight in the Negev and will fight in Galilee and will fight on the outskirts of Jerusalem until the very end.

> 'The Jewish community in Palestine is going to fight to the very end. If we have arms to fight with, we will fight with those, and if not, we will fight with stones in our hands.'

You cannot decide whether we should fight or not. We will. The Jewish community in Palestine will raise no white flag for the Mufti. That decision is taken. Nobody can change it. You can only decide one thing: whether we shall be victorious in this fight or whether the Mufti will be victorious. That decision American Jews can make. It has to be made quickly within hours, within days.

And I beg of you—don't be too late. Don't be bitterly sorry three months from now for what you failed to do today. The time is now.

I have spoken to you without a grain of exaggeration. I have not tried to paint the picture in false colours. It consists of spirit and certainty of our victory on the one hand, and dire necessity for carrying on the battle on the other.

I want to thank you again for having given me the opportunity at a conference that I am certain has a full agenda to say these few words to you. I leave the platform without any doubt in my mind or my heart that the decision that will be taken by American Jewry will be the same as that which was taken by the Jewish community in Palestine, so that within a few months from now we will all be able to participate not only in the joy of resolving to establish a Jewish state, but in the joy of laying the cornerstone of the Jewish state.'

The State of Israel was proclaimed on 14 May 1948, but the fight against Egypt, Transjordan, Iraq, Syria and Lebanon for ultimate survival began the next day. Thousands of Israeli and Arab soldiers died in the ensuing fighting with 600 000 Palestinian refugees fleeing their homeland—a problem that continues today. Foundation Prime Minister, David Ben-Gurion, later stated:

'Someday, when history will be written, it will be said that there was a Jewish woman who got the money which made the state possible.'

In 1966 Golda Meir became secretary general of the Israeli Workers Party (Mapai) and following its incorporation into the Israeli Labor Party, she was chosen as its secretary. Upon the death of Levi Eshkol in 1969 the respective party factions chose Meir as Prime Minister. Her first challenge as Israeli leader was during the victorious Six-Day War in June 1967 in which neighbouring Arab States of Egypt, Syria and Jordan attempted to exact revenge for territories lost in disputes in 1948 and 1956.

In 1972 Palestinian terrorists killed 11 Israeli athletes competing in the Munich Olympics. The following year, Israel was involved in another conflict—the 'Yom Kippur War'—in which Egyptian leader Anwar el-Sadat attempted to enforce the United Nations 'Resolution 242'—Israel's total withdrawal from territories taken in 1967. Although Meir was able to form a government following the end of the conflict in the December 1973 elections, she had lost the control of her cabinet and resigned as Prime Minister in April 1974.

Golda Meir died in Jerusalem on 8 December, 1978, aged 80.

The Cold War
1950-1959

Joseph R McCarthy

'Wheeling Speech'

Delivered in Wheeling and repeated to US Congress,
20 February 1950.

I n the 1950s, US Wisconsin Republican Senator Joseph R McCarthy (1908-1957) did more than any other individual to turn post-war concerns about domestic security into national hysteria. His highly-publicised witch-hunts threatened to expose anyone remotely suspected of being a subversive influence in government or public institutions, including Hollywood and created a new term in the English language—'McCarthyism'.

McCarthy had entered the Senate in 1946 and with his first term coming to an end he desperately searched for an issue to increase his national profile before re-election. As the mid-term Congressional election year got underway in 1946, Alger Hiss, a former State Department official suspected of espionage, was convicted of perjury. Following the Communist Party victory in China, the successful explosion of an A-bomb by the Soviet Union and the 'Alger Hiss' investigation, the Republican Party was on the attack in an atmosphere of growing paranoia about the spread of communism.

Democratic President Harry Truman seemed to buckle to political pressure and established a 'loyalty program' for all federal employees and asked the Justice Department to compile an official list of subversive organisations in America.

On February 9 1950, Senator McCarthy spoke at the Ohio County Women's Republican Club in Wheeling, West Virginia and attacked President Truman's foreign policy, stating that the State Department and its Secretary, Dean Acheson, were harbouring 'traitorous' communists.

According to press reports of the speech, McCarthy said that he had in his hand a list of 205 members of the Communist Party and members of a spy ring who were 'shaping the policy of the State Department.' When later challenged to produce his evidence, McCarthy maintained that he was actually referring to communist 'party loyalists' in the State Department.

In this moderated version of that 'Wheeling' speech, repeated in Congress on February 20, he reduced the number of alleged communists to 57. In fact, McCarthy had no such list at all, but the damage was done. Those he named and accused lost their jobs as they were branded communists, but their guilt was never proved.

'Tonight as we celebrate the 141st birthday of one of the great men in American history, I would like to be able to talk about what a glorious day today is in the history of the world. As we celebrate the birth of this man, who with his whole heart and soul hated war, I would like to be able to speak of peace in our time, of war being outlawed, and of worldwide disarmament. These would be truly appropriate things to be able to mention as we celebrate the birthday of Abraham Lincoln.

Five years after a world war has been won, men's hearts should anticipate a long peace, and men's minds should be free from the heavy weight that comes with war. But this is not such a period—for this is not a period of peace. This is a time of the Cold War. This is a time when all the world is split into two vast, increasingly hostile armed camps—a time of a great armaments race. Today we can almost physically hear the mutterings and rumblings of an invigorated god of war. You can see it, feel it, and hear it all the way from the hills of Indochina, from the shores of Formosa right over into the very heart of Europe itself ...

Today we are engaged in a final, all-out battle between communistic atheism and Christianity. The modern champions of communism have selected this as the time. And, ladies and gentlemen, the chips are down—they are truly down.

Lest there be any doubt that the time has been chosen, let us go directly to the leader of communism today—Joseph Stalin. Here is what he said—not back in 1928, not

'When [the Secretary of State] this pompous diplomat in striped pants, with a phony British accent, proclaimed to the American people that Christ on the Mount endorsed communism, high treason, and betrayal of a sacred trust, the blasphemy was so great that it awakened the dormant indignation of the American people.'

before the war, not during the war—but two years after the last war was ended: 'To think that the communist revolution can be carried out peacefully, within the framework of a Christian democracy, means one has either gone out of one's mind and lost all normal understanding, or has grossly and openly repudiated the communist revolution.'

And this is what was said by Lenin in 1919, which was also quoted with approval by Stalin in 1947: 'We are living', said Lenin, 'not merely in a state but in a system of states, and the existence of the Soviet Republic side by side with Christian states for a long time is unthinkable. One or the other must triumph in the end. And before that end supervenes, a series of frightful collisions between the Soviet Republic and the bourgeois states will be inevitable.'

Ladies and gentlemen, can there be anyone here tonight who is so blind as to say that the war is not on? Can there be anyone who fails to realize that the communist world has said, 'The time is now'— that this is the time for the showdown between the democratic Christian world and the communist atheistic world? Unless we face this fact, we shall pay the price that must be paid by those who wait too long.

Six years ago, at the time of the first conference to map out peace— Dumbarton Oaks—there was within the Soviet orbit 180 million people. Lined up on the anti-totalitarian side there were in the world at that time roughly 1.625 billion people. Today, only six years later, there are 800 million people under the absolute domination of Soviet Russia—an increase of over 400 percent. On our side, the figure has shrunk to around 500 million. In other words, in less than six years the odds have changed from 9 to 1 in our favor to 8 to 5 against us. This indicates the swiftness of the tempo of communist victories and American defeats in the Cold War. As one of our outstanding historical figures once said, "When a great democracy is destroyed, it will not be because of enemies from without but rather because of enemies from within." The truth of this statement is becoming terrifyingly clear as we see this country each day losing on every front.

At war's end we were physically the strongest nation on Earth and, at least potentially, the most powerful intellectually and morally. Ours could have been the honor of being a beacon in the desert of destruction, a shining, living proof that civilization was not yet ready to destroy itself. Unfortunately, we have failed miserably and tragically to arise to the opportunity.

The reason why we find ourselves in a position of impotency is not because our only powerful, potential enemy has sent men to invade our shores, but rather because of the traitorous actions of those who have been treated so well by this nation. It has not been the less fortunate or members of minority groups who have been selling this nation out, but rather those who have had all the benefits that the wealthiest nation on earth has had to offer—the finest homes, the finest college education, and the finest jobs in government we can give.

This is glaringly true in the State Department. There the bright young men who are born with silver spoons in their mouths are the ones who have been worst.

Now I know it is very easy for anyone to condemn a particular bureau or department in general terms. Therefore, I would like to cite one rather unusual case—the case of a man who has done much to shape our foreign policy.

When Chiang Kai-shek was fighting our war, the State Department had in China a young man named John S. Service. His task, obviously, was not to work for the communization of China. Strangely, however, he sent official reports back to the State Department urging that we torpedo our ally Chiang Kai-shek and stating, in effect, that communism was the best hope of China.

Later, this man—John Service—was picked up by the Federal Bureau of Investigation for turning over to the communists' secret State Department information. Strangely, however, he was never prosecuted. However, Joseph Grew, the undersecretary of state, who insisted on his prosecution, was forced to resign. Two days after, Grew's successor, Dean Acheson, took over as undersecretary of state, this man—John Service—who had been picked up by the FBI and who had previously urged that communism was the best hope of China, was not only reinstated in the State Department but promoted; and finally, under Acheson, placed in charge of all placements and promotions. Today, ladies and gentlemen, this man Service is on his way to represent the State Department and Acheson in Calcutta—by far and away the most important listening post in the Far East.

Now, let's see what happens when individuals with communist connections are forced out of the State Department. Gustave Duran, who was labeled as, I quote, "a notorious international communist," was made assistant Secretary of State in charge of Latin American affairs. He was taken into the State Department from his job as a lieutenant colonel in the Communist International Brigade. Finally, after intense congressional pressure and criticism, he resigned in 1946 from the State Department—and, ladies and gentlemen, where do you think he is now? He took over a high-salaried job as chief of Cultural Activities Section in the office of the assistant secretary-general of the United Nations.

This, ladies and gentlemen, gives you somewhat of a picture of the type of individuals who have been helping to shape our foreign policy. In my opinion the State Department, which is one of the most important government departments, is thoroughly infested with communists.

I have in my hand 57 cases of individuals who would appear to be either card-carrying members or certainly loyal to the Communist Party, but who nevertheless are still helping to shape our foreign policy.

One thing to remember in discussing the communists in our government is that we are not dealing with spies who get 30 pieces of silver to steal the blueprints of new weapons. We are dealing with a far more sinister type of activity because it permits the enemy to guide and shape our policy.

This brings us down to the case of one Alger Hiss, who is important not as an individual anymore but rather because he is so representative of a group in the State Department. It is unnecessary to go over the sordid events showing how he sold out the nation which had given him so much. Those are rather fresh in all of our minds. However, it should be remembered that the facts in regard to his connection with this international communist spy ring were made known to the then-Under Secretary of State Berle three days after Hitler and Stalin signed the

Russo-German Alliance Pact. At that time one Whittaker Chambers—who was also part of the spy ring—apparently decided that with Russia on Hitler's side, he could no longer betray our nation to Russia. He gave Under Secretary of State Berle—and this is all a matter of record—practically all, if not more, of the facts upon which Hiss' conviction was based.

'As one of our outstanding historical figures once said, "When a great democracy is destroyed, it will not be because of enemies from without but rather because of enemies from within".'

Under Secretary Berle promptly contacted Dean Acheson and received word in return that Acheson, and I quote, "could vouch for Hiss absolutely"—at which time the matter was dropped. And this, you understand, was at a time when Russia was an ally of Germany. This condition existed while Russia and Germany were invading and dismembering Poland, and while the communist groups here were screaming "warmonger" at the United States for their support of the Allied nations.

Again in 1943, the FBI had occasion to investigate the facts surrounding Hiss' contacts with the Russian spy ring. But even after that FBI report was submitted, nothing was done.

Then, late in 1948—on August 5—when the Un-American Activities Committee called Alger Hiss to give an accounting, President Truman at once issued a presidential directive ordering all government agencies to refuse to turn over any information whatsoever in regard to the communist activities of any government employee to a congressional committee.

Incidentally, even after Hiss was convicted, it is interesting to note that the president still labeled the expose of Hiss as a "red herring."

If time permitted, it might be well to go into detail about the fact that Hiss was Roosevelt's chief adviser at Yalta when Roosevelt was admittedly in ill health and tired physically and mentally ... and when, according to the Secretary of State, Hiss and Gromyko drafted the report on the conference.

According to the then-Secretary of State Stettinius, here are some of the things that Hiss helped to decide at Yalta: 1) the establishment of a European High Commission; 2) the treatment of Germany—this you will recall was the conference at which it was decided that we would occupy Berlin with Russia occupying an area completely encircling the city, which as you know, resulted in the Berlin airlift which cost 31 American lives; 3) the Polish question; 4) the relationship between UNRRA and the Soviet; 5) the rights of Americans on control commissions of Rumania, Bulgaria and Hungary; 6) Iran; 7) China—here's where we gave away Manchuria; 8) Turkish Straits question; 9) international trusteeships; 10) Korea.

Of the results of this conference, Arthur Bliss Lane of the State Department had this to say: "As I glanced over the document, I could not believe my eyes. To me, almost every line spoke of a surrender to Stalin."

As you hear this story of high treason, I know that you are saying to yourself, "Well, why doesn't the Congress do something about it?" Actually, ladies and gentlemen, one of the important reasons for the graft, the corruption, the dishonesty, the disloyalty, the treason in high government positions—one of the most important reasons why this continues—is a lack of moral uprising on the part of the 140 million American people. In the light of history, however, this is not hard to explain.

It is the result of an emotional hangover and a temporary moral lapse which follows every war. It is the apathy to evil which people who have been subjected to the tremendous evils of war feel. As the people of the world see mass murder, the destruction of defenseless and innocent people, and all of the crime and lack of morals which go with war, they become numb and apathetic. It has always been thus after war. However, the morals of our people have not been destroyed. They still exist. This cloak of numbness and apathy has only needed a spark to rekindle them. Happily, this spark has finally been supplied.

As you know, very recently the Secretary of State proclaimed his loyalty to a man guilty of what has always been considered as the most abominable of all crimes—of being a traitor to the people who gave him a position of great trust.

The Secretary of State, in attempting to justify his continued devotion to the man who sold out the Christian world to the atheistic world, referred to Christ's Sermon on the Mount as a justification and reason therefore, and the reaction of the American people to this would have made the heart of Abraham Lincoln happy. When this pompous diplomat in striped pants, with a phony British accent, proclaimed to the American people that Christ on the Mount endorsed communism, high treason, and betrayal of a sacred trust, the blasphemy was so great that it awakened the dormant indignation of the American people. He has lighted the spark which is resulting in a moral uprising and will end only when the whole sorry mess of twisted warped thinkers are swept from the national scene so that we may have a new birth of national honesty and decency in government. '

President Truman responded to these charges in a news conference the following month and stated that McCarthy's attacks were sabotaging the nation's bipartisan foreign policy agenda and were actually advancing the cause of communism. With the outbreak of war in Korea in April that year the Republican Party finally had a weapon to attack the Democrats and 'Tail-gunner' Joe McCarthy had finally achieved national—and international—notoriety. 'McCarthyism' raged out of control for the next four years, even after Truman had been voted out of office.

Edward Murrow's CBS program in 1954 exposed McCarthy's fanaticism and saw his ratings in the Gallup polls drop substantially. When the Senator lost further 'face' against Army Chief Counsel Joseph Welch in the 'Senate-Army' hearings in June, his political career was over. McCarthy was condemned by his own party for his unsubstantiated allegations and later lost his seat in the Senate and died, a broken alcoholic, in 1957 aged just 49.

Margaret Chase Smith

'Declaration of Conscience'

Speech to the US Senate, 1 June 1950.

Margaret Madeline Chase (1897-1995) was the only woman elected to serve both houses of the United States Congress. After establishing the Maine chapter of the Business and Professional Women's Club in 1922 she married newspaper publisher Clyde Smith, who was elected to Congress in 1936. When Smith died suddenly, she succeeded him in the House of Representatives and began 33 years of Congressional service.

Although a Republican, she often opposed her party and voted with her conscience in the best interests of the people of Maine.

In 1948 Mrs Chase Smith was elected to the US Senate without the support of her party with the greatest majority total vote in the history of Maine—70 per cent—which she maintained in election victories in 1954, 1960 and 1966. In June 1950 she was one of the first elected representatives to speak out against Joseph McCarthy—a fellow Republican—and denounce the smear and bullying tactics used by the Senator in his anti-communist campaign.

' Mr. President. I would like to speak briefly and simply about a serious national condition. It is a national feeling of fear and frustration that could result in national suicide and the end of everything that we Americans hold dear. It is a condition that comes from the lack of effective leadership in either the Legislative Branch or the Executive Branch of our Government.

That leadership is so lacking that serious and responsible proposals are being made that national advisory commissions be appointed to provide such critically needed leadership.

I speak as briefly as possible because too much harm has already been done with irresponsible words of bitterness and selfish political opportunism. I speak as briefly as possible because the issue is too great to be obscured by eloquence. I speak simply and briefly in the hope that my words will be taken to heart.

I speak as a Republican. I speak as a woman. I speak as a United States Senator. I speak as an American.

> 'I think that it is high time that we remembered that the Constitution, as amended, speaks not only of the freedom of speech but also of trial by jury instead of trial by accusation.'

The United States Senate has long enjoyed worldwide respect as the greatest deliberative body in the world. But recently that deliberative character has too often been debased to the level of a forum of hate and character assassination sheltered by the shield of congressional immunity.

It is ironical that we Senators can in debate in the Senate directly or indirectly, by any form of words, impute to any American who is not a Senator any conduct or motive unworthy or unbecoming an American—and without that non-Senator American having any legal redress against us—yet if we say the same thing in the Senate about our colleagues we can be stopped on the grounds of being out of order.

It is strange that we can verbally attack anyone else without restraint and with full protection and yet we hold ourselves above the same type of criticism here on the Senate Floor. Surely the United States Senate is big enough to take self-criticism and self-appraisal. Surely we should be able to take the same kind of character attacks that we "dish out" to outsiders.

I think that it is high time for the United States Senate and its members to do some soul-searching—for us to weigh our consciences—on the manner in which we are performing our duty to the people of America—on the manner in which we are using or abusing our individual powers and privileges.

I think that it is high time that we remembered that we have sworn to uphold and defend the Constitution. I think that it is high time that we remembered that the Constitution, as amended, speaks not only of the freedom of speech but also of trial by jury instead of trial by accusation.

Whether it be a criminal prosecution in court or a character prosecution in the Senate, there is little practical distinction when the life of a person has been ruined.

Those of us who shout the loudest about Americanism—in making character assassinations—are all too frequently those who—by our own words and acts—ignore some of the basic principles of Americanism:

The right to criticize;
The right to hold unpopular beliefs;
The right to protest;
The right of independent thought.

The exercise of these rights should not cost one single American citizen his reputation or his right to a livelihood nor should he be in danger of losing his reputation or livelihood merely because he happens to know someone who holds unpopular beliefs. Who of us doesn't? Otherwise none of us could call our souls our own. Otherwise thought control would have set in.

The American people are sick and tired of being afraid to speak their minds lest they be politically smeared as "communists" or "fascists" by their opponents. Freedom of speech is not what it used to be in America. It has been so abused by some that it is not exercised by others.

The American people are sick and tired of seeing innocent people smeared and guilty people whitewashed. But there have been enough proved cases, such as the 'Amerasia' case, the Hiss case, the Coplon case, the Gold case, to cause the nationwide distrust and strong suspicion that there may be something to the unproved, sensational accusations.

As a Republican, I say to my colleagues on this side of the aisle that the Republican Party faces a challenge today that is not unlike the challenge that it faced back in Lincoln's day. The Republican Party so successfully met that challenge that it emerged from the Civil War as the champion of a united nation—in addition to being a Party that unrelentingly fought loose spending and loose programs.

Today our country is being psychologically divided by the confusion and the suspicions that are bred in the United States Senate to spread like cancerous tentacles of "know nothing, suspect everything" attitudes. Today we have a Democratic Administration that has developed a mania for loose spending and loose programs. History is repeating itself—and the Republican Party again has the opportunity to emerge as the champion of unity and prudence.

'Today our country is being psychologically divided by the confusion and the suspicions that are bred in the United States Senate to spread like cancerous tentacles of "know nothing, suspect everything" attitudes.'

The record of the present Democratic Administration has provided us with sufficient campaign issues without the necessity of resorting to political smears. America is rapidly losing its position as leader of the world simply because the Democratic Administration has pitifully failed to provide effective leadership.

The Democratic Administration has completely confused the American people by its daily contradictory grave warnings and optimistic assurances—that show the people that our Democratic Administration has no idea of where it is going.

The Democratic Administration has greatly lost the confidence of the American people by its complacency to the threat of communism here at home and the leak of vital secrets to Russia though key officials of the Democratic Administration. There are enough proved cases to make this point without diluting our criticism with unproved charges.

Surely these are sufficient reasons to make it clear to the American people that it is time for a change and that a Republican victory is necessary to the security of this country. Surely it is clear that this nation will continue to suffer as long as it is governed by

> **'The nation sorely needs a Republican victory. But I don't want to see the Republican Party ride to political victory on the Four Horsemen of Calumny—Fear, Ignorance, Bigotry, and Smear.'**

the present ineffective Democratic Administration.

Yet to displace it with a Republican regime embracing a philosophy that lacks political integrity or intellectual honesty would prove equally disastrous to this nation. The nation sorely needs a Republican victory. But I don't want to see the Republican Party ride to political victory on the Four Horsemen of Calumny—Fear, Ignorance, Bigotry, and Smear.

I doubt if the Republican Party could—simply because I don't believe the American people will uphold any political party that puts political exploitation above national interest. Surely we Republicans aren't that desperate for victory.

I don't want to see the Republican Party win that way. While it might be a fleeting victory for the Republican Party, it would be a more lasting defeat for the American people. Surely it would ultimately be suicide for the Republican Party and the two-party system that has protected our American liberties from the dictatorship of a one party system.

As members of the Minority Party, we do not have the primary authority to formulate the policy of our Government. But we do have the responsibility of rendering constructive criticism, of clarifying issues, of allaying fears by acting as responsible citizens.

As a woman, I wonder how mothers, wives, sisters, and daughters feel about the way in which members of their families have been politically mangled in the Senate debate—and I use the word "debate" advisedly.

As a United States Senator, I am not proud of the way in which the Senate has been made a publicity platform for irresponsible sensationalism. I am not proud of the reckless abandon in which unproved charges have been hurled from the side of the aisle. I am not proud of the obviously staged, undignified counter-charges that have been attempted in retaliation from the other side of the aisle.

I don't like the way the Senate has been made a rendezvous for vilification, for selfish political gain at the sacrifice of individual reputations and national unity. I am not proud of the way we smear outsiders from the Floor of the Senate and hide behind the cloak of congressional immunity and still place ourselves beyond criticism on the Floor of the Senate.

As an American, I am shocked at the way Republicans and Democrats alike are playing directly into the Communist design of "confuse, divide, and conquer." As an American, I don't want a Democratic Administration "whitewash" or "cover-up" any more than I want a Republican smear or witch hunt.

As an American, I condemn a Republican "Fascist" just as much I condemn a Democratic "Communist." I condemn a Democrat "Fascist" just as much as I condemn a Republican "Communist." They are equally dangerous to you and me and to our country. As an American, I want to see our nation recapture the strength and unity it once had when we fought the enemy instead of ourselves.

It is with these thoughts that I have drafted what I call a "Declaration of Conscience." I am gratified that Senator Tobey, Senator Aiken, Senator Morse, Senator Ives, Senator Thye, and Senator Hendrickson have concurred in that declaration and have authorized me to announce their concurrence.'

Although she didn't mention her Republican colleague by name, Smith's 15-minute speech earned McCarthy's ire—and the admiration of her president, Harry S Truman. McCarthy removed Mrs Chase Smith as a member of the Permanent Subcommittee on Investigations and gave her place to the junior senator from California—Richard M Nixon.

In 1964 Margaret Chase Smith became the first woman to be nominated by a major party as a Presidential candidate and received 27 nominating votes at the Republican National Convention. In 1973, after serving in the Senate for 24 years, Chase Smith lost her seat. After leaving the Senate, Smith lectured at colleges and conducted public policy seminars. She wrote for newspapers and magazines and authored Gallant Women (biographies of twelve American women) and Declaration of Conscience, about her time serving the American people.

Chase Smith continued to champion women's rights and oppose bigotry and injustice long after she left office. She received innumerable awards during her lifetime and was one of the original inductees of the National Women's Hall of Fame (1973). She received more than 85 honorary degrees and was named 'Woman of the Year' by the Associated Press in 1948, 1949, 1950 and 1957. In 1989 she received the Presidential Medal of Freedom from President Bill Clinton. Margaret Chase Smith died in Skowhegan, Maine in 1995.

Douglas MacArthur

'Old Soldiers Never Die'

Address to US Congress, Washington DC, 20 April 1951.

D ouglas MacArthur (1880-1964), the hero of the Pacific during World War II, fell spectacularly from grace during the Korean War. Despite being relieved of his command, he was given a hero's homecoming, and is today remembered as a modern military icon.

After serving in the Philippines and France in World War I, he became Commander in Chief of US army forces in the Pacific theatre of World War II. Forced to retreat from the Philippines in March 1942, he conducted the liberation of the southwest Pacific from his Australian base during the next three years. In September 1945, MacArthur formally accepted the Japanese surrender aboard the USS Missouri and as the head of occupied forces in Japan earned the unflattering empirical mantle of 'Viceroy of Japan' for his superior single-mindedness in doing things his own way. MacArthur was even considered as a Republican presidential candidate but his defeat in the Wisconsin primary in 1948 eroded his support base.

During World War II, Korea had been divided into two states along the invisible 38th Parallel, with Russia protecting the northern section and America the southern. Both sections held 'elections' in the late 1940s but North Korea had become dominated by communists and unification with the (southern-based) 'Republic of Korea' seemed as far as away as ever. In June 1950, 80 000 North Korean troops backed by Russian tanks launched a surprise invasion of South Korea. US President Harry S Truman immediately dispatched American troops based in Japan and was able to garner support from the United Nations to undertake a 'police action' under the control of General Douglas MacArthur to recapture Seoul.

After early success pushing North Korean troops back past the 38th Parallel, MacArthur rashly pressed on towards the northern capital Pyongyang. Sure that Russian and Chinese troops would not support the North Koreans,

MacArthur bombed bridges on the Yula, which prompted China's Chairman Mao to send 300 000 troops to support the North Koreans. United Nations forces were then forced to retreat.

The hero of World War II was determined to pursue this conflict and openly criticised President Truman, his own military superiors and America's allies for their lack of support in the face of Chinese aggression. He made his intentions clear in the press: blockade the Chinese mainland, use atomic weapons to suppress the enemy and invade both China and Korea with the help of Chiang Kai-shek's Nationalist forces. When he independently invited the Chinese leadership to meet with him in April 1951, Truman removed MacArthur from his command.

On his return to the United States, General Douglas MacArthur was invited to address a joint session of Congress. He condemned America's 'blackmail of appeasement' and ended with one of the most-quoted epitaphs of the twentieth century—old soldiers never die; they just fade away.

'
I stand on this rostrum with a sense of deep humility and great pride—humility in the wake of those great architects of our history who have stood here before me, pride in the reflection that this home of legislative debate represents human liberty in the purest form yet devised.

Here are centered the hopes and aspirations and faith of the entire human race.

I do not stand here as advocate for any partisan cause, for the issues are fundamental and reach quite beyond the realm of partisan considerations. They must be resolved on the highest plane of national interest, if our course is to prove sound and our future protected.

I trust, therefore, that you will do me the justice of receiving that which I have to say as solely expressing the considered viewpoint of a fellow American.

I address you with neither rancor nor bitterness in the fading twilight of life, with but one purpose in mind:

To serve my country.

The issues are global, and so interlocked that to consider the problems of one sector oblivious to those of another is to court disaster for the whole. While Asia is commonly referred to as the gateway to Europe, it is no less true that Europe is the gateway to Asia, and the broad influence of the one cannot fail to have its impact upon the other.

There are those who claim our strength is inadequate to protect on both fronts, that we cannot divide our effort. I can think of no greater expression of defeatism.

'The Communist threat is a global one. Its successful advance in one sector threatens the destruction of every other sector.'

If a potential enemy can divide his strength on two fronts, it is for us to counter his efforts. The Communist threat is a global one. Its successful advance in one sector threatens the destruction of every other sector. You cannot appease or otherwise surrender to Communism in Asia without simultaneously undermining our efforts to halt its advance in Europe.

Beyond pointing out these general truisms, I shall confine my discussion to the general areas of Asia.

While I was not consulted prior to the President's decision to intervene in support of the Republic of Korea, that decision, from a military standpoint, proved a sound one. As I say, it proved a sound one, as we hurled back the invader and decimated his forces. Our victory was complete, and our objectives within reach, when Red China intervened with numerically superior ground forces.

This created a new war and an entirely new situation, a situation not contemplated when our forces were committed against the North Korean invaders; a situation which called for new decisions in the diplomatic sphere to permit the realistic adjustment of military strategy. Such decisions have not been forthcoming.

While no man in his right mind would advocate sending our ground forces into continental China, and such was never given a thought, the new situation did urgently demand a drastic revision of strategic planning, if our political aim was to defeat this new enemy as we had defeated the old.

Apart from the military need, as I saw it, to neutralize the sanctuary protection given the enemy north of the Yalu, I felt that military necessity in the conduct of the war made necessary:

1. The intensification of our economic blockade against China.
2. The imposition of a naval blockade against the China coast.
3. Removal of restrictions on air reconnaissance of China's coastal area and of Manchuria.
4. Removal of restrictions on the forces of the Republic of China on Formosa, with logistical support to contribute to their effective operations against the Chinese mainland.

For entertaining these views, all professionally designed to support our forces committed to Korea and to bring hostilities to an end with the least possible delay and at a saving of countless American and Allied lives, I have been severely criticized in lay circles, principally abroad, despite my understanding that, from a military standpoint, the above views have been fully shared in the past by practically every military leader concerned with the Korean campaign, including our own Joint Chiefs of Staff.

I called for reinforcements, but was informed that reinforcements were not available. I made clear that if not permitted to destroy the enemy built-up bases north of the Yalu, if not permitted to utilize the friendly Chinese force of some 600 000 men on Formosa, if not permitted to blockade the China coast to prevent the Chinese Reds from getting succor from without, and if there were to be no hope of major reinforcements, the position of the command from the military standpoint forbade victory.

We could hold in Korea by constant manoeuvre and at an approximate area where our supply-line advantages were in balance with the supply-line disadvantages of the enemy, but we could hope at best for only an indecisive campaign with its terrible and constant attrition upon our forces if the enemy utilized his full military potential.

I have constantly called for the new political decisions essential to a solution. Efforts have been made to distort my position. It has been said, in effect, that I was a warmonger. Nothing could be further from the truth.

I know war as few other men now living know it, and nothing to me is more revolting! I have long advocated its complete abolition, as its very destructiveness on both friend and foe has rendered it useless as a means of settling international disputes.

'It has been said, in effect, that I was a warmonger. Nothing could be further from the truth. I know war as few other men now living know it, and nothing to me is more revolting!'

Indeed, on the second day of September, 1945, just following the surrender of the Japanese nation on the battleship Missouri, I formally cautioned as follows:

"Men since the beginning of time have sought peace. Various methods through the ages have been attempted to devise an international process to prevent or settle disputes between nations. From the very start, workable methods were found in so far as individual citizens were concerned, but the mechanics of an instrumentality of larger international scope have never been successful.

Military alliances, balances of power, leagues of nations, all in turn failed, leaving the only path to be by way of the crucible of war. The utter destructiveness of war now blocks out this alternative. We have had our last chance. If we will not devise some greater and more equitable system, our Armageddon will be at our door. The problem basically is theological and involves a spiritual recrudescence, an improvement of human character that will synchronize with our almost matchless advances in science, art, literature, and all material and cultural developments of the past two thousand years. It must be of the spirit if we are to save the flesh.

But once war is forced upon us, there is no other alternative than to apply every available means to bring it to a swift end. War's very object is victory, not prolonged indecision. In war, there is no substitute for victory."

There are some who, for varying reasons, would appease Red China. They are blind to history's clear lesson, for history teaches with

'In war, there is no substitute for victory.' unmistakable emphasis that appeasement but begets new and bloodier war. It points to no single instance where this end has justified that means, where appeasement has led to more than a sham peace. Like blackmail, it lays the basis for new and successively greater demands until, as in blackmail, violence becomes the only other alternative.

Why, my soldiers asked of me, surrender military advantages to an enemy in the field? I could not answer.

Some may say to avoid spread of the conflict into an all-out war with China. Others, to avoid Soviet intervention. Neither explanation seems valid, for China is already engaging with the maximum power it can commit, and the Soviet [Union] will not necessarily mesh its actions with our moves. Like a cobra, any new enemy will more likely strike whenever it feels that the relativity in military or other potential is in its favor on a world-wide basis.

The tragedy of Korea is further heightened by the fact that its military action is confined to its territorial limits. It condemns that nation, which it is our purpose to save, to suffer the devastating impact of full naval and air bombardment, while the enemy's sanctuaries are fully protected from such attack and devastation.

Of the nations of the world Korea alone, up to now, is the sole one which has risked its all against communism. The magnificence of the courage and fortitude of the Korean people defies description. They have chosen to risk death rather than slavery. Their last words to me were: "Don't scuttle the Pacific."

I have just left your fighting sons in Korea. They have met all tests there, and I can report to you without reservation that they are splendid in every way. It was my constant effort to preserve them and end this savage conflict honorably and with the least loss of time and a minimum sacrifice of life. Its growing bloodshed has caused me the deepest anguish and anxiety. Those gallant men will remain often in my thoughts and in my prayers always.

I am closing my 52 years of military service. When I joined the army, even before the turn of the century, it was the fulfillment of all of my boyish hopes and dreams.

The world has turned over many times since I took the oath on the plain at West Point, and the hopes and dreams have long since vanished, but I still remember the refrain of one of the most popular barracks ballads of that day which proclaimed most proudly that 'old soldiers never die; they just fade away.' And like the old soldier of that ballad, I now close my military career and just fade away, an old soldier who tried to do his duty as God gave him the light to see that duty. Good-bye. '

General MacArthur retired to private life when he was defeated by another war hero—Dwight D.Eisenhower—for the Republican nomination for the 1952 presidential race. MacArthur later worked on the boards of several companies before passing away in Washington DC on 5 April, 1964, aged 84.

Bertrand Russell

'Russell-Einstein Manifesto'

BBC Broadcast, London, 9 July 1955.

A long-standing collaboration between pacifist Bertrand Russell and atomic scientist Albert Einstein resulted in the publication of the 'Russell-Einstein' Manifesto in 1955. The two men came from very different backgrounds, yet their powerful union laid the foundations for the modern peace movement—especially the Campaign for Nuclear Disarmament.

Albert Einstein was born in Ulm, Germany, in 1879. A professed pacifist, he took Swiss nationality in 1901 as a protest against increasing German nationalism. In 1905 he published his theory of relativity and obtained his PhD in Zurich before returning to Berlin as director of the Kaiser Wilhelm Physical Institute in 1914. He won the Nobel Prize for Physics in 1921 but his increasingly pacifist views—and the fact that he was a Jew—made his position in Berlin untenable after the rise of Nazism. When Hitler assumed power in 1933 Einstein was touring California and realised that to return to Germany would mean certain death. He decided to stay in the United States and warned President Roosevelt that German scientists were in a position to develop a 'super-weapon'—the atomic bomb.

While this information encouraged Roosevelt to undertake the 'Manhattan Project'—the development of an atomic bomb, which would ultimately be used against Japan—Einstein urged the world to control the development of atomic weapons after World War II. 'This weapon was delivered into the hands of the American and British nations in their roles as trustees of all mankind, and as fighters for peace and liberty,' he stated in New York in 1945, 'The war is won, but the peace is not'.

Bertrand Russell, philosopher, author and mathematician (1872-1970) lost his fellowship at Trinity College and served six months imprisonment in 1918 for his pacifist views. He renounced pacifism in the face of fascist aggression in Europe in 1939 and became a champion of nuclear disarmament at the end of World War II. A Nobel Prize winner in Literature in 1950, Russell corresponded with world leaders and important figures of his time in an effort to bring about greater understanding about the dangers of the unchecked expansion of nuclear weapons.

Working from England, Russell communicated by mail with Albert Einstein, where he was teaching at Princeton, New Jersey. They discussed publishing a document signed by leading scientists of the time. In 1955, Einstein wrote to Russell.

Dear Bertrand Russell,

Thank you for your letter of April 5. I am gladly willing to sign your excellent statement. I also agree with your choice of the prospective signers.

With kind regards,
A. Einstein

A few days later Einstein died aged 76, but he had already sent Russell his final letter confirming his support for their manifesto. It was published in England the July after Einstein's death. It laid the foundations for the modern peace movement and became the credo of the Pugwash Conferences on Science and World Affairs—the Nobel Peace Prize-winning organisation dedicated to eliminating nuclear weapons and war. Russell used the following manifesto as the basis for several BBC broadcasts and lectures.

' In the tragic situation which confronts humanity, we feel that scientists should assemble in conference to appraise the perils that have arisen as a result of the development of weapons of mass destruction, and to discuss a resolution in the spirit of the appended draft.

We are speaking on this occasion, not as members of this or that nation, continent or creed, but as human beings, members of the species man, whose continued existence is in doubt. The world is full of conflicts; and overshadowing all minor conflicts, the titanic struggle between Communism and anti-Communism.

Almost everybody who is not politically conscious has strong feelings about one or more of these issue; but we want you, if you can, to set aside such feelings and consider yourselves only as members of a biological species which has had a remarkable history, and whose disappearance none of us can desire.

We shall try to say no single word which should appeal to one group rather than to another. All, equally, are in peril, and, if the peril is understood, there is hope that we may collectively avert it.

We have to learn to think in a new way. We have to learn to ask ourselves, not what steps can be taken to give military victory to whatever military group we prefer, for there no longer are such steps; the question we have to ask ourselves is: What steps can be taken to prevent a military contest of which the issue must be disastrous to all parties?

The general public, and even many men in positions of authority, have not realized what would be involved in a war with nuclear bombs. The general public still thinks in terms of the obliteration of cities. It is understood that new bombs are more powerful than the old, and that, while one A-bomb could obliterate Hiroshima, one H-bomb could obliterate the largest cities, such as London, New York and Moscow.

No doubt in an H-bomb war great cities would be obliterated. But this is one of the minor disasters that would have to be faced. If everybody in London, New York and Moscow were exterminated, the world might, in the course of a few centuries, recover from the blow. But we now know, especially from the Bikini test, that nuclear bombs can gradually spread destruction over a very much wider area than had been supposed.

It is stated on very good authority that a bomb can now be manufactured which will be 2 500 times as powerful as that which destroyed Hiroshima.

Such a bomb, if exploded near the ground or underwater, sends radioactive particles into the upper air. They sink gradually and reach the surface of the earth in a form of a deadly dust or rain. It was this dust which infected the Japanese fishermen and their catch of fish.

> **'Agreements reached in a time of peace ... would no longer be binding in a time of war.'**

No one knows how widely such lethal radioactive particles might be diffused, but the best authorities are unanimous in saying that a war with H-bombs might quite possibly put an end to the human race. It is feared that if many H-bombs are used there will be universal death—sudden only for a minority, but for the majority a slow torture of disease and disintegration.

Many warnings have been uttered by eminent men of science and by authorities in military strategy. None of them will say that the worst results are certain. What they do say is that these results are possible, and that no one can be sure that they will not be realized.

We have not yet found that the views of experts depend in any way upon their politics or prejudices. They depend only, so far as our researches have revealed, upon the extent of the particular expert's knowledge. We have found that the men who know most are the most gloomy.

Here, then is the problem which we present to you, stark and dreadful, and inescapable: shall we put an end to the human race, or shall mankind renounce war? People will not face this alternative because it is so difficult to abolish war.

The abolition of war will demand distasteful limitations of national sovereignty. But what perhaps impedes understanding of the situation more than anything else, is that the term mankind feels vague and abstract. People scarcely realize in imagination that the danger is to themselves and their children and grandchildren, and not only to their dimly apprehended humanity. They can scarcely bring themselves to grasp that they, individually, and those whom they love are in imminent danger of perishing agonizingly. And so they hope that perhaps war may be allowed to continue provided modern weapons are prohibited.

BERTRAND RUSSELL   139

This hope is illusory.

Whatever agreements not to use the H-bombs had been reached in time of peace, they would no longer be considered binding in time of war, and both sides would set to work to manufacture H-bombs as soon as war broke out, for, if one side manufactured H-bombs and the other did not, the side that manufactured them would inevitably be victorious.

Although an agreement to renounce nuclear weapons as part of a general reduction of armaments would not afford an ultimate solution, it would serve certain important purposes.

First: Any agreement between East and West is to the good because it serves to diminish tension. Second: The abolition of thermonuclear weapons, if each side believed that the other had carried it out sincerely, would lessen fear of a sudden attack in the style of Pearl Harbour, which at present keeps both sides in a state of nervous apprehension. We should therefore, welcome such an agreement, though only as a first step.

Most of us are not neutral in feelings, but, as human beings, we have to remember that, if the issues between East and West are to be decided in any manner that can give any possible satisfaction to anybody, whether Communist or anti-Communist, whether Asian or European or American, whether white of black, then these issues must not be decided by war. We should wish this to be understood both in the East and in the West.

There lies before us, if we choose, continual progress in happiness, knowledge and wisdom. Shall we, instead, choose death, because we cannot forget our quarrels? We appeal, as human beings, to human beings: Remember your humanity and forget the rest. If you can do so, the way lies open to a new paradise; if you cannot, there lies before you the risk of universal death.

RESOLUTION

We invite the congress [to be convened], and through it, the scientists of the world and the general public, to subscribe to the following resolution:

In view of the fact that in any future world war, nuclear weapons will certainly be employed, and that such weapons threaten the continued existence of mankind, we urge governments of the world to realize, and to acknowledge publicly that their purposes cannot be furthered by a world war, and we urge them consequently, to find peaceful means for the settlement of all matters of dispute between them.

Professor Max Born (Professor of Theoretical Physics at Berlin, Frankfurt, and Gottingen, and of Natural Philosophy, Edinburgh; Nobel Prize in physics)

Professor P.W. Bridgman (Professor of Physics, Harvard University; Nobel Prize in physics)

Professor Albert Einstein

Professor L. Infeld (Professor of Theoretical Physics, University of Warsaw)

Professor J. F. Joliot-Curie (Professor of Physics, College de France; Nobel Prize in chemistry)

Professor H. J. Muller (Professor of Zoology at the University of Indiana; Nobel Prize in physiology and medicine)

Professor Linus Pauling (Professor of Chemistry, California Institute of Technology; Nobel Prize in chemistry)

Professor J. Rotblat (Professor of Physics, University of London; Medical College of St. Bartholomew's Hospital)

Bertrand Russell

Professor Hideki Yukawa (Professor of Theoretical Physics, Kyoto University; Nobel Prize in physics).'

The Russell-Einstein Manifesto was endorsed by thousands of scientists from many countries. As a direct result of this statement, Bertrand Russell acted as a mediator with President Kennedy on behalf of Nikita Khrushchev during the Cuban Missile Crisis in 1962. Russell passed away in 1972, aged 98, and is regarded as one of the foremost philosophers of the twentieth century.

Half a century after Albert Einstein's death, the ideals which he promoted throughout his life are admired by millions and are gradually being implemented by an ever-increasing number of scientists and politicians.

Nikita Khrushchev
'The Cult of the Individual'

Twentieth Congress of the Communist Party of the Soviet Union, 24 February 1956.

N ikita Khrushchev (1894-1971) joined the Bolshevik Party in 1918 and by World War II, was serving under Josef Stalin in the Politburo and the Presidium of the Supreme Soviet. Upon Stalin's death in 1953, Khrushchev emerged as the undisputed leader of the Soviet Union. The first secretary of the USSR Communist Party, Khrushchev had Stalin's remains removed from the Kremlin. In 1956, three years after Stalin's death, Khrushchev addressed the Party Congress and denounced the excesses of 'Stalinism', criticising the 'cult of personality' that had corrupted Stalin's terrifying shift from idealist to tyrant.

'Comrades!

Quite a lot has been said about the cult of the individual and about its harmful consequences. After Stalin's death the Central Committee began to implement a policy of explaining concisely and consistently that it is impermissible and foreign to the spirit of Marxism-Leninism to elevate one person, to transform him into a superman possessing supernatural characteristics akin to those of a god.

Such a belief about a man, and specifically about Stalin, was cultivated among us for many years.

The objective of the present report is not a thorough evaluation of Stalin's life and activity. Concerning Stalin's merits an entirely sufficient number of books, pamphlets and studies have already been written ... [Khrushchev then reports the positions of Marx, Engels and Lenin in relation to collective leadership, the role of the party and the working class, etc, and introduces the delegates to the documents relating to Lenin's Testament, in which he warns against Stalin, concluding with a reading of a letter from Lenin to Stalin].

When socialism in our country was fundamentally constructed, when the exploiting classes were generally liquidated, when the Soviet social structure had radically changed, when the social basis for political movements and groups hostile to the party had violently contracted, when the ideological opponents of the party had long since been defeated politically—then the repression directed against them began. ... We must assert that, in regard to those persons who in their time had opposed the party line, there were often no sufficiently serious reasons for their physical annihilation. The formula "enemy of the people" was specifically introduced for the purpose of physically annihilating such individuals. ...

Had Leninist principles been observed ... we certainly would not have had such a brutal violation of revolutionary legality and many thousands of people would not have fallen victim to the method of terror. [Khrushchev then recalls the incident of Kamenev and Zinoviev's betrayal of the Revolution in October 1917, and their subsequent reinstatement to the leadership.]

> 'Had Leninist principles been observed ... we certainly would not have had such a brutal violation of revolutionary legality and many thousands of people would not have fallen victim to the method of terror.'

As facts prove, Stalin, using his unlimited power, allowed himself many abuses, acting in the name of the Central Committee, not asking for the opinion of the Committee members nor even the members of the Politburo, or even informing them ... During Lenin's lifetime, Party Congresses were convened regularly ... It should be sufficient to mention that during all the years of the Great Patriotic War, not a single Central Committee plenum took place ...

NIKITA KRUSHCHEV   143

A party commission was [recently] charged with investigating what made possible the mass repressions against the majority of the Central Committee members and candidates elected at the Seventeenth Congress ... many party activists who were branded in 1937-38 as "enemies" were actually never enemies, spies, wreckers, etc but were always honest communists ... and often, no longer able to bear barbaric tortures, they charged themselves with all kinds of grave and unlikely crimes.

...of the 139 members and candidates of the party's Central Committee who were elected at the Seventeenth Congress, 98 persons, i.e., 70 per cent, were arrested and shot! [There is consternation in the hall.] What was the composition of the delegates? 80 per cent joined the party during the years of illegality before the Revolution and during the Civil War before 1921. By social origin the basic mass of the delegates were workers (60 per cent of the voting members).

For this reason, it is inconceivable that a congress so composed would have elected a Central Committee a majority of whom would prove to be enemies of the people ... The same fate met not only the Central Committee members but also the majority of the delegates to the Seventeenth Congress. Of 1,966 delegates, 1,108 persons were arrested ... This very fact shows how absurd, wild and contrary to common sense were the charges of counter-revolutionary crimes ... [indignation in the hall].

... repression increased after the congress... after the complete liquidation of the Trotskyites, Zinovievites and Bukharinites, when as a result of that fight the party achieved unity, Stalin ceased to an even greater degree to consider members of the Central Committee or Politburo.

After the criminal murder of S M Kirov, mass repressions and brutal acts of violation of socialist legality began. ... the circumstances surrounding Kirov's murder hide many things which are inexplicable and mysterious ...top functionaries of the NKVD were shot presumably to cover up ...

Mass repressions grew tremendously from the end of 1936 ... the mass repressions at this time were made under the slogan of a fight against the Trotskyites ... but ... Trotskyism was completely disarmed ... it was clear that there was no basis for mass terror in the country. This terror was actually directed not at the remnants of the exploiting classes but against the honest workers. ...

> 'Where were the members of the Politburo? Why did they not assert themselves against the cult of the individual in time? And why is this being done only now?'

Using Stalin's formulation, namely, that the closer we are to socialism the more enemies we will have ... the number of arrests based on charges of counter-revolutionary crimes grew 10 times between 1936 and 1937. ... Confessions of guilt were gained with the help of cruel and inhuman tortures ... when they retracted their confessions before the military tribunal [no one was told] ...

[Khrushchev cites at length the testimony of Eikhe, a member since 1905, tortured and shot in February 1940, and details the cases other well-known veterans denounced by Stalin, to consternation in the hall. Khrushchev moves on to talk of Stalin's role in World War II.]

... Stalin put forward the thesis that the tragedy which our nation experienced in the first part of the war was the result of the "unexpected" attack of the Germans against the Soviet Union. But, comrades, this is completely untrue. As soon as Hitler came to power in Germany he assigned to himself the task of liquidating Communism. The fascists were saying this openly; they did not hide their plans. ...

Churchill personally warned Stalin [and] ... stressed this repeatedly in his despatches of 18 April and in the following days. However, Stalin took no notice of these warnings ... information of this sort ... was coming from our own military and diplomatic sources ...

[Stalin ordered that] no preparatory defensive work should be undertaken at the borders, that the Germans were not to be given any pretext ... when the fascist armies actually invaded Soviet territory and military operations had begun, Stalin issued the order that the German

NIKITA KRUSHCHEV   145

fire was not to be returned. Why? It was because Stalin, despite evident facts, thought that the war had not yet started ...

Very grievous consequences followed Stalin's annihilation of many military commanders and political workers during 1937-41 because of his suspiciousness and through slanderous accusations ... during this time the cadre of leaders who had gained military experience in Spain and the Far East was almost completely liquidated ... large scale repression against the military cadres led also to undermined military discipline ... after the first severe disaster and defeats at the front, Stalin thought that this was the end. In one of his speeches he said: "All that which Lenin created we have lost forever". After this Stalin for a long time did not direct the military operations and ceased to do anything whatever. ... when he returned to active leadership ... the nervousness and hysteria which Stalin demonstrated, interfering with actual military operations, caused our Army serious damage. ... during the whole Patriotic War, he never visited any section of the front or any liberated city ...

[Laughter begins to break out in the hall from time to time as Khrushchev ridicules Stalin's exaggeration of his role after the war, and he concludes ...]

...All the more monstrous are the acts whose initiator was Stalin .. we refer to the mass deportations from their native places, of whole nations .. not dictated by any military considerations ... the Ukrainians avoided this fate only because there were too many of them and there was no place to deport them [laughter]. [Khrushchev then tells of the 'Leningrad affair' in which eminent military leaders were denounced and shot].

Stalin became even more capricious, irritable and brutal; in particular his suspicion grew. His persecution mania reached unbelievable dimensions ...

[Khrushchev then delivers a prolonged attack on the role of Beria. He then explains how Stalin personally edited the biographies and histories lauding his role to ensure that his own role was presented in terms of the most extreme glorification, receiving applause as he suggests that Stalin's name be removed from the national anthem, which should praise instead the role of the party, and loud, prolonged applause follows. As Khrushchev turns to the theme of how Stalin elevated himself above Lenin, even in the period of the Revolution, and denounced Stalin for this, he is greeted by repeated bursts of applause].

Comrades! If we sharply criticise today the cult of the individual which was so widespread during Stalin's life, and if we speak about so many negative phenomena generated by this cult which is so alien to the spirit of Marxism-Leninism, various persons may ask: How could it be? Stalin headed the party and the country for 30 years and many victories were gained during his lifetime. Can we deny that?

The Socialist Revolution was attained by the working class and by the poor peasantry with the partial support of middle-class peasants. It was attained by the people under the leadership of the Bolshevik Party. Lenin's great service consisted in the fact that he created a militant party of the working class, but he was armed with Marxist understanding of the laws of social development and with the science of proletarian victory in the fight with capitalism, and he steeled this party in the crucible of revolutionary struggle of the masses of the people. ... Our historical victories were attained thanks to the organisational work of the party, ...and to the self-sacrificing work of our great nation.

... during the last years of Stalin's life he became a serious obstacle ... During Stalin's leadership our peaceful relations with other nations were often threatened, ... In recent years we managed to free ourselves of the harmful practice of the cult of the individual ...

Some comrades may ask us: Where were the members of the Politburo? Why did they not assert themselves against the cult of the individual in time? And why is this being done only now? ...

Initially many of them backed Stalin actively because Stalin was one of the strongest Marxists and his logic, his strength and his will greatly influenced the cadres and party work. ...

At that time Stalin gained great popularity, sympathy and support. The party had to fight those who attempted to lead the country away from the correct Leninist path; it had to fight Trotskyites,

Zinovievites, and Rightists, and Bourgeois Nationalists. This fight was indispensable.

Later, however, Stalin, abusing his power more and more, began to fight eminent party leaders and to use terroristic methods against honest Soviet people. ...

Bulganin once said: "It has happened sometimes that a man goes to Stalin on his invitation as a friend. And, when he sits with Stalin, he does not know where he will be sent next—home or jail".

It is clear that such conditions put every member of the Political Bureau in a very difficult situation ...

... had Stalin remained at the helm for another few months, Comrades Molotov and Mikoyan would probably not have delivered any speeches at this Congress. Stalin had plans to finish off the old members of the Political Bureau. ...

We consider that Stalin was excessively extolled. However, in the past, Stalin doubtless performed great services to the party, to the working class and to the international workers' movement....

Stalin was convinced that [these things he did] were necessary .. He saw this from the position of the interest of the working class, of the interest of the laboring people, of the interests of the victory of Socialism and Communism. We cannot say that these were the deeds of a giddy despot. ... In this lies the whole tragedy!

[Khrushchev then suggests that Stalin's name, and also those of other leaders be removed from towns etc bearing their names, but] this should be done calmly and slowly. ... if we begin to remove the signs everywhere and to change names, people will think that these comrades in whose honour the given enterprises, kolkhozes or cities are named have met some bad fate and that they have also been arrested. ...

We should in all seriousness consider the question of the cult of the individual. We cannot let this matter get out of the party, especially not to the press. It is for this reason that we are considering it here at a closed Congress session. We should know the limits; we should not give ammunition to the enemy; we should not wash our dirty linen before their eyes. I think that the delegates to the Congress will understand and assess properly all these proposals.

We are absolutely certain that our party, armed with the historical resolutions of the Twentieth Congress, will lead the Soviet people along the Leninist path to new successes, to new victories. Long live the victorious banner of our Party—Leninism! '

'Long live the victorious banner of our Party—Leninism!'

Nikita Khrushchev was Soviet Prime Minister from 1958 to 1964 and figured prominently in Cold War rhetoric with two American Presidents, Eisenhower and Kennedy. At times boorish and dramatic in his gestures, he once famously banged his shoe on the podium during a speech to the United Nations General Assembly. Khrushchev was deposed by Brezhnev in 1964, largely over the fallout over the Cuban Missile Crisis, but it was a bloodless transition. Forced into retirement (the only Soviet leader before Mikhail Gorbachev not to die in office) Khrushchev passed away in 1971. Because of his fall from power, he was the only Soviet leader not to be buried in the Kremlin wall.

Women's rights campaigner Emmeline Pankhurst in the Battery area of New York, after her release from Ellis Island Immigration Station in 1913. The English barrister drafted the first women's suffrage bill in Britain and founded the Women's Franchise League in 1899.

Above left: Adolf Hitler played on people's insecurities and demonstrated his unbridled hatred of Jews in his 1939 speech—delivered on the eve of World War II.

Above right: In his famous speech to the British people during the 'Battle of Britain', Winston Churchill inspired the nation to fight and win. It altered the course of the war.

Russian leader Vladimir Ilyich Ulianov—better known as Lenin (left)—poses in Gorki, Soviet Union, with Iosif Vissarionovich Dzhugashvili—Joseph Stalin (right)—in 1922.

Above left: In June 1950, Margaret Madeline Chase Smith was one of the first American elected representatives to speak out against Joseph McCarthy—a fellow Republican—and denounce the smear and bullying tactics used in his anti-communist campaign.

Above right: One of the most controversial generals in American history, George Patton Jnr spoke to his troops on 17 May 1944—three weeks before the D-Day invasion of Normandy and the liberation of France—during World War II.

Nobel Prize winner and influential anti-nuclear campaigner Bertrand Russell addresses a peace meeting in 1955. The *Russell-Einstein Manifesto* laid the foundations for the modern peace movement—especially the Campaign for Nuclear Disarmament.

In 1959 Harold MacMillan addressed British voters and won a general election. A year later he told the South African Parliament that his government's responsibility was to uphold the rights of individuals, signalling a major shift in attitude towards the colonial past and especially towards apartheid.

Martin Luther King waves from the steps of the Lincoln Memorial in Washington DC, before his famous 'I have a dream' speech in 1963.

A thoroughly disgraced American President Nixon announces his resignation in August 1974, when he finally realised that impeachment was unavoidable.

Egyptian President Anwar Sadat and American President Jimmy Carter share a happy moment during the signing ceremony of the historic peace settlement with Israel that returned the Sinai Peninsula to Egypt in 1979.

Above left: Indira Gandhi broke the mould for Indian women, She converted to Islam from caste-bound Hinduism and became Prime Minister and mother to a Prime Minister. She outlined her concept of women's liberation in a March 1980 speech in New Delhi.

Above right: Jesse Jackson was the first African-American presidential candidate in American history and accepted the vice-presidential place on the 1988 Democratic ticket.

British Prime Minisister Margaret Thatcher confirmed her 'Iron Lady' status during the 1982 Falklands war. She sent a formidable military task force to restore British sovereignty over the disputed 'Malvinas' islands, without United Nations approval.

Mikhail Gorbachev, the Soviet Union's last leader, resigned in 1991. His policies of *glasnost* and *perestroika* modernised the communist state, but also led to its demise.

Nelson Mandela (centre) with South African president F W de Klerk (left) who released him from life imprisonment in 1990. Mandela defeated de Klerk in the 1994 general election that brought majority rule to South Africa and the African National Congress to power. Mandela made de Klerk vice president in a government of national unity. Thabo Mbeki (right) succeeded Mandela as President in 1999.

Indian writer, 1997 Booker Prize winner and social activist Arundhati Roy addresses the opening ceremony of the 2004 World Social Forum. Roy was controversially awarded the Sydney Peace Prize in November 2004 and delivered a stinging critique of the West's response to the World Trade Centre attack and the invasion of Iraq.

Revolution
1960-1969

Harold MacMillan

'The Wind of Change'

Address to the South African Parliament in Cape Town, 3 February 1960.

H arold MacMillan (1894-1986) was British Prime Minister from 1957 to 1963 at a time when the black independence movement was sweeping the African continent. In 1960 MacMillan visited the African Commonwealth states of Ghana and Nigeria and addressed the South African Parliament. Acknowledging the rights of African nations to rule their own affairs, he stated that it was his government's responsibility to promote the creation of societies that upheld the rights of individuals. This was the first public statement by a British government in this vein and signalled a major shift in attitude not only towards the Commonwealth's colonial past, but towards the apartheid regime in South Africa.

'As I've travelled around the Union I have found everywhere, as I expected, a deep preoccupation with what is happening in the rest of the African continent. I understand and sympathise with your interests in these events and your anxiety about them.

Ever since the break-up of the Roman Empire one of the constant facts of political life in Europe has been the emergence of independent nations. They have come into existence over the centuries in different forms, with different kinds of Government, but all have been inspired by a deep, keen feeling of nationalism, which has grown as the nations have grown.

In the twentieth century, and especially since the end of the war, the processes which gave birth to the nation states of Europe have been repeated all over the world. We have seen the awakening of national consciousness in peoples who have for centuries lived in dependence upon some other power. Fifteen years ago this movement spread through Asia. Many countries there of different races and civilizations pressed their claim to an

independent national life. Today the same thing is happening in Africa, and the most striking of all the impressions I have formed is of the strength of this African national consciousness. In different places it takes different forms, but it is happening everywhere. The wind of change is blowing through this continent, and, whether we like it or not, this growth of national consciousness is a political fact. We must all accept it as a fact, and our national policies must take account of it.

Of course, you understand this better than anyone. You are sprung from Europe, the home of nationalism, and here in Africa you have yourselves created a new nation. Indeed, in the history of our times yours will be recorded as the first of the African nationalisms, and this tide of national consciousness which is now rising in Africa is a fact for which you and we and the other nations of the Western World are ultimately responsible. For its causes are to be found in the achievements of Western civilization, in the pushing forward of the frontiers of knowledge, in the applying of science in the service of human needs, in the expanding of food production, in the speeding and multiplying of the means of communication, and perhaps, above all, the spread of education ...

As I see it the great issue in this second half of the twentieth century is whether the uncommitted peoples of Asia and Africa will swing to the East or to the West. Will they be drawn into the Communist camp? Or will the great experiments in self-government that are now being made in Asia and Africa, especially within the Commonwealth, prove so successful, and by their example so compelling, that the balance will come down in favour of freedom and order and justice?

The struggle is joined, and it is a struggle for the minds of men. What is now on trial is much more than our military strength or our diplomatic and administrative skill. It is our way of life. The uncommitted nations want to see before they choose.

HAROLD MACMILLAN 153

What can we show them to help them choose right? Each of the independent members of the Commonwealth must answer that question for itself. It is a basic principle of our modern Commonwealth that we respect each other's sovereignty in matters of internal policy. At the same time we must recognise that in this shrinking world in which we live today the internal policies of one nation may have effects outside it. We may sometimes be tempted to say to each other, 'Mind your own business,' but in these days I would myself expand the old saying so that it runs: 'Mind your own business, but mind how it affects my business, too.'

Let me be very, frank with you, my friends. What governments and Parliaments in the United Kingdom have done since the war in according independence to India, Pakistan, Ceylon, Malaya and Ghana, and what they will do for Nigeria and other countries now nearing independence, all this, though we take full and sole responsibility for it, we do in the belief that it is the only way to establish the future of the Commonwealth and of the Free World on sound foundations. All this of course is also of deep and close concern to you for nothing we do in this small world can be done in a corner or remain hidden. What we do today in West, Central and East Africa becomes known tomorrow to everyone in the Union, whatever his language, colour or traditions. Let me assure you, in all friendliness, that we are well aware of this and that we have acted and will act with full knowledge of the responsibility we have to all our friends.

Nevertheless I am sure you will agree that in our own areas of responsibility we must each do what we think right. What we think right derives from a long experience both of failure and success in the management of our own affairs. We have tried to learn and apply the lessons of our judgement of right and wrong. Our justice is rooted in the same soil as yours—in Christianity and in the rule of law as the basis of a free society. This experience of our own explains why it has been our aim in the countries for which we have borne responsibility, not only to raise the material standards of living, but also to create a society which respects the rights of individuals, a society in which men are given the opportunity to grow to their full stature—and that must in our view include the opportunity to have an increasing share in political power and responsibility, a society in which individual merit and individual merit alone is the criterion for a man's advancement, whether political or economic ...

'Our justice is rooted in the same soil as yours.'

The attitude of the United Kingdom towards this problem was clearly expressed by the Foreign Secretary, Mr Selwyn Lloyd, speaking at the United Nations General Assembly on 17 September 1959. These were his words:

"In those territories where different races or tribes live side by side the task is to ensure that all the people may enjoy security and freedom and the chance to contribute as individuals to the progress and well being of these countries. We reject the idea of any inherent superiority of one race over another. Our policy therefore is non-racial. It offers a future in which Africans, Europeans, Asians, the peoples of the Pacific and others with whom we are concerned, will all play their full part as citizens in the countries where they live, and in which feelings of race will be submerged in loyalty to new nations.

I have thought you would wish me to state plainly and with full candour the policy for which we in Britain stand. It may well be that in trying to do our duty as we see it we shall sometimes make difficulties for you. If this proves to be so we shall regret it. But I know that even so you would not ask us to flinch from doing our duty.

As a fellow member of the Commonwealth it is our earnest desire to give South Africa our support and encouragement, but I hope you won't mind my saying frankly that there are some aspects of your policies which make it impossible for us to do this without being false to our own deep convictions about the political destinies of free men to which in our own territories we are trying to give effect. I think we ought, as friends, to face together, without seeking to apportion credit or blame, the fact that in the world of today this difference of outlook lies between us ..."

The fact is that in this modern world no country, not even the greatest, can live for itself alone. Nearly two thousand years ago, when the whole of the civilized world was comprised within the confines of

HAROLD MACMILLAN   155

the Roman Empire, St Paul proclaimed one of the great truths of history—we are all members one of another. During this twentieth century that eternal truth has taken on a new and exciting significance. It has always been impossible for the individual man to live in isolation from his fellows, in the home, the tribe, the village, or the city. Today it is impossible for nations to live in isolation from one another. What Dr John Donne said of individual men three hundred years ago is true today of my country, your country, and all the countries of the world:

"Any man's death diminishes me, because I am involved in Mankind. And therefore never send to know for whom the bell tolls; it tolls for thee."

All nations now are interdependent one upon another, and this is generally realised throughout the Western World ... Those of us who by grace of the electorate are temporarily in charge of affairs in your country and in mine, we fleeting transient phantoms on the great stage of history, we have no right to sweep aside on this account the friendship that exists between our countries, for that is the legacy of history. It is not ours alone to deal with as we wish. To adapt a famous phrase, it belongs to those who are living, but it also belongs to those who are dead and to those who are yet unborn. We must face the differences, but let us try to see beyond them down the long vista of the future.

I hope—indeed, I am confident—that in another 50 years we shall look back on the differences that exist between us now as matters of historical interest, for as time passes and one generation yields to another, human problems change and fade. Let us remember these truths. Let us resolve to build, not to destroy, and let us remember always that weakness comes from division, strength from unity.'

The great fear of the British and other Western governments was that newly-independent African nations would align themselves with the Communist East and upset the balance of power during the Cold War. A fortnight after this historic speech, Britain announced a power-sharing agreement with

Kenyan nationalists before that country's independence in 1963. By 1961 Nigeria, Somalia, Sierra Leone and Tanzania would also gain their independence.

However, South African Prime Minister Hendrik Verwoerd responded to McMillan's speech by stating that 'justice to all, does not only mean being just to the black man of Africa, but also to the white man of Africa' because it was the white man who 'historically brought civilisation to a bare continent'.

On 31 May, 1961—largely in response to domestic civil unrest and the fear of political interference from Britain—the white South African regime pushed through its declaration of independence and created a republic founded on systemic apartheid.

In 1964 several high-profile black nationalists (including Nelson Mandela) were jailed for treason, Prime Minister Verwoerd was assassinated by a mentally disturbed white parliamentary clerk in 1966, and South Africa gradually became the pariah of western democracies during the next three decades.

After the finest moment of his political career, Harold MacMillan resigned his position as Prime Minister because of ill health in 1963 and left parliament the following year. He was made an Earl on his 90th birthday in 1984, two years before his death.

John F Kennedy

'The Cuban Missile Crisis'

National television broadcast, 22 October 1962.

John F. Kennedy (1917-63) was regarded as the 'new generation' of US leader—young, charismatic and a powerful communicator. The second son of a former US Ambassador to England, JFK was a Harvard graduate, a war hero, a Democratic Representative (1947) and Senator (1952), whose book, *Profiles in Courage*, won the 1956 Pulitzer Prize for Literature.

It is hard to believe that Kennedy was the underdog to Republican Party candidate, Vice-President Richard Nixon, in the 1960 presidential race. But Kennedy's charisma translated well on television and the medium became an important factor in his election victory when he outpointed the more-experienced Richard Nixon in the first televised series of debates.

Nixon looked decidedly nervous—and untrustworthy—next to the debonair Senator from Massachusetts (interestingly, television viewers thought Kennedy had easily won the debates while radio listeners put Nixon ahead).

On a cold January morning in 1961, John F. Kennedy took the oath of office and became the 35th President of the United States of America. His inauguration speech—with a bold challenge for all Americans and the 'citizens of the world'—signalled the birth of one of the most historic, controversial and mythical periods in American politics. Kennedy's time as president, barely 1000 days, was known as 'Camelot'.

On 16 October 1962, President Kennedy was shown aerial photos taken by an American U-2 spy plane over Cuba—just ninety miles off the coast of Florida—of the Soviet installation of offensive nuclear missiles.

Four days later he summoned the Soviet Minister of Foreign Affairs, Andrei Gromyko, who informed him that the weapons were for defensive purposes only.

The President then met with top military aides—and his brother, Attorney General Robert Kennedy—to discuss America's response. On Sunday October 21, Kennedy and his advisors spent the entire day considering two main military options—an air strike against the bases or a naval blockade of Cuba. The President chose the latter option, which would be referred to by the less provocative term 'quarantine', and forced a stand-off with the Russians.

At 7 pm (EST) on 22 October 1962, President Kennedy informed the American people on national television of the recently discovered Soviet military build-up in Cuba.

'This Government, as promised, has maintained the closest surveillance of the Soviet Military build-up on the island of Cuba. Within the past week, unmistakable evidence has established the fact that a series of offensive missile sites is now in preparation on that imprisoned island. The purpose of these bases can be none other than to provide a nuclear strike capability against the Western Hemisphere.

Upon receiving the first preliminary hard information of this nature last Tuesday morning at 9 am, I directed that our surveillance be stepped up. And having now confirmed and completed our evaluation of the evidence and our decision on a course of action, this Government feels obliged to report this new crisis to you in fullest detail.

The characteristics of these new missile sites indicate two distinct types of installations. Several of them include medium range ballistic missiles capable of carrying a nuclear warhead for a distance of more than 1 000 nautical miles. Each of these missiles, in short, is capable of striking Washington, DC, the Panama Canal, Cape Canaveral, Mexico City, or any other city in the south-eastern part of the United States, in Central America, or in the Caribbean area.

Additional sites not yet completed appear to be designed for intermediate range ballistic missiles—capable of traveling more than twice as far—and thus capable of striking most of the major cities in the Western Hemisphere, ranging as far north as Hudson Bay, Canada, and as far south as Lima, Peru. In addition, jet bombers, capable of carrying nuclear weapons, are now being uncrated and assembled in Cuba, while the necessary air bases are being prepared.

This urgent transformation of Cuba into an important strategic base—by the presence of these large, long range, and clearly offensive weapons of sudden mass destruction—constitutes an explicit threat to the peace and security of all the Americas, in flagrant and deliberate defiance of the Rio Pact of 1947, the traditions of this Nation and hemisphere, the joint resolution of the 87th Congress, the Charter of the United Nations, and my own public warnings to the Soviets on September 4 and 13. This action also contradicts the repeated assurances of Soviet spokesmen, both publicly and privately delivered, that the arms build-up in Cuba would retain its original defensive character, and that the Soviet Union had no need or desire to station strategic missiles on the territory of any other nation.

The size of this undertaking makes clear that it has been planned for some months. Yet only last month, after I had made clear the distinction between any introduction of ground-to-ground missiles and the existence of defensive antiaircraft missiles, the Soviet Government publicly stated on September 11, and I quote, "the armaments and military equipment sent to Cuba are designed exclusively for defensive purposes," that, and I quote the Soviet Government, "there is no need for the Soviet Government to shift its weapons . . . for a retaliatory blow to any other country, for instance Cuba," and that, and I quote their government, "the Soviet Union has no powerful rockets to carry these nuclear warheads that there is no need to search for sites for them beyond the boundaries of the Soviet Union." That statement was false.

Only last Thursday, as evidence of this rapid offensive build-up was already in my hand, Soviet Foreign Minister Gromyko told me in my office that he was instructed to make it clear once again, as he said his government had already done, that Soviet assistance to Cuba, and I quote, "pursued solely the purpose of contributing to the defense capabilities of Cuba," that, and I quote him, "training by Soviet specialists of Cuban nationals in handling defensive armaments was by no means offensive, and if it were otherwise," Mr. Gromyko went on, "the Soviet Government would never become involved in rendering such assistance." That statement also was false.

Neither the United States of America nor the world community of nations can tolerate deliberate deception and offensive threats on the part of any nation, large or small. We no longer live in a world where only the actual firing of weapons represents a

'To the captive people of Cuba ... Now your leaders are no longer Cuban leaders inspired by Cuban ideals. They are puppets and agents of an international conspiracy.'

sufficient challenge to a nation's security to constitute maximum peril. Nuclear weapons are so destructive and ballistic missiles are so swift, that any substantially increased possibility of their use or any sudden change in their deployment may well be regarded as a definite threat to peace.

For many years both the Soviet Union and the United States, recognising this fact, have deployed strategic nuclear weapons with great care, never upsetting the precarious status quo which insured that these weapons would not be used in the absence of some vital challenge. Our own strategic missiles have never been transferred to the territory of any other nation under a cloak of secrecy and deception; and our history—unlike that of the Soviets since the end of World War II—demonstrates that we have no desire to dominate or conquer any other nation or impose our system upon its people. Nevertheless, American citizens have become adjusted to living daily on the bull's-eye of Soviet missiles located inside the USSR or in submarines.

In that sense, missiles in Cuba add to an already clear and present danger—although it should be noted the nations of Latin America have never previously been subjected to a potential nuclear threat.

But this secret, swift, and extraordinary build-up of Communist missiles—in an area well known to have a special and historical relationship to the United States and the nations of the Western Hemisphere, in violation of Soviet assurances, and in defiance of American and hemispheric policy—this sudden, clandestine decision to station strategic weapons for the first time outside of Soviet

> 'Our goal is not the victory of might, but the vindication of right—not peace at the expense of freedom, but both peace and freedom, here in this hemisphere, and, we hope, around the world.'

soil—is a deliberately provocative and unjustified change in the status quo which cannot be accepted by this country, if our courage and our commitments are ever to be trusted again by either friend or foe.

The 1930's taught us a clear lesson: aggressive conduct, if allowed to go unchecked and unchallenged ultimately leads to war. This nation is opposed to war. We are also true to our word. Our unswerving objective, therefore, must be to prevent the use of these missiles against this or any other country, and to secure their withdrawal or elimination from the Western Hemisphere.

Our policy has been one of patience and restraint, as befits a peaceful and powerful nation, which leads a worldwide alliance. We have been determined not to be diverted from our central concerns by mere irritants and fanatics. But now further action is required—and it is under way; and these actions may only be the beginning. We will not prematurely or unnecessarily risk the costs of worldwide nuclear war in which even the fruits of victory would be ashes in our mouth— but neither will we shrink from that risk at any time it must be faced.

Acting, therefore, in the defense of our own security and of the entire Western Hemisphere, and under the authority entrusted to me by the Constitution as endorsed by the resolution of the Congress, I have directed that the following initial steps be taken immediately:

First: To halt this offensive build-up, a strict quarantine on all offensive military equipment under shipment to Cuba is being initiated. All ships of any kind bound for Cuba from whatever nation or port will, if found to contain cargoes of offensive weapons, be turned back. This quarantine will be extended, if needed, to other types of cargo and carriers. We are not at this time, however, denying the necessities of life as the Soviets attempted to do in their Berlin blockade of 1948.

Second: I have directed the continued and increased close surveillance of Cuba and its military build-up. The foreign ministers of the OAS, in their communique of 6 October, rejected secrecy in such matters in this hemisphere. Should these offensive military preparations continue, thus increasing the threat to the hemisphere, further action will be justified. I have directed the Armed Forces to prepare for any eventualities; and I trust that in the interest of both the Cuban people and the Soviet technicians at the sites, the hazards to all concerned in continuing this threat will be recognised.

Third: It shall be the policy of this Nation to regard any nuclear missile launched from Cuba against any nation in the Western Hemisphere as an attack by the Soviet Union on the United States, requiring a full retaliatory response upon the Soviet Union.

Fourth: As a necessary military precaution, I have reinforced our base at Guantanamo, evacuated today the dependents of our personnel there, and ordered additional military units to be on a standby alert basis.

Fifth: We are calling tonight for an immediate meeting of the Organ of Consultation under the Organization of American States, to consider this threat to hemispheric security and to invoke articles 6 and 8 of the Rio Treaty in support of all necessary action. The United Nations Charter allows for regional security arrangements— and the nations of this hemisphere decided long ago against the military presence of outside powers. Our other allies around the world have also been alerted.

Sixth: Under the Charter of the United Nations, we are asking tonight that an emergency meeting of the Security Council be convoked without delay to take action against this latest Soviet threat to world peace. Our resolution will call for the prompt dismantling and withdrawal of all offensive weapons in Cuba, under the supervision of U.N. observers, before the quarantine can be lifted.

Seventh and finally: I call upon Chairman Khrushchev to halt and eliminate this clandestine, reckless and provocative threat to world peace and to stable relations between our two nations. I call upon him further to abandon this course of world domination, and to join in an historic effort to end the perilous arms race and to transform the history of man. He has an opportunity now to move the world back from the abyss of destruction—by returning to his government's own words that it had no need to station missiles outside its own territory, and withdrawing these weapons from Cuba—by refraining from any action which will widen or deepen the present crisis—and then by participating in a search for peaceful and permanent solutions.

This Nation is prepared to present its case against the Soviet threat to peace, and our own proposals for a peaceful world, at any time and in any forum—in the OAS, in the United Nations, or in any other meeting that could be useful—without limiting our freedom of action. We have in the past made strenuous efforts to limit the spread of nuclear weapons. We have proposed the elimination of all arms and military bases in a fair and effective disarmament treaty. We are prepared to discuss new proposals for the removal of tensions on both sides—including the possibility of a genuinely independent Cuba, free to determine its own destiny. We have no wish to war with the Soviet Union—for we are a peaceful people who desire to live in peace with all other peoples.

But it is difficult to settle or even discuss these problems in an atmosphere of intimidation. That is why this latest Soviet threat—or any other threat which is made independently or in response to our actions this week—must and will be met with determination. Any hostile move anywhere in the world against the safety and freedom of peoples to whom we are committed—including in particular the brave people of West Berlin—will be met by whatever action is needed.

Finally, I want to say a few words to the captive people of Cuba, to whom this speech is being directly carried by special radio facilities. I speak to you as a friend, as one who knows of your deep attachment to your fatherland, as one who shares your aspirations for liberty and justice for all. And I have watched and the American people have watched with deep sorrow how your nationalist revolution was betrayed—and how your fatherland fell under foreign domination. Now your leaders are no longer Cuban leaders inspired by Cuban ideals. They are puppets and agents of an international conspiracy which has turned Cuba against your friends and neighbors in the Americas—and turned it into the first Latin American country to become a target for nuclear war—the first Latin American country to have these weapons on its soil.

These new weapons are not in your interest. They contribute nothing to your peace and well-being. They can only undermine it. But this country has no wish to cause you to suffer or to impose any system upon you. We know that your lives and land are being used as pawns by those who deny your freedom.

Many times in the past, the Cuban people have risen to throw out tyrants who destroyed their liberty. And I have no doubt that most Cubans today look forward to the time when they will be truly free—free from foreign domination, free to choose their own leaders, free to select their own system, free to own their own land, free to speak and write and worship without fear or degradation. And then shall Cuba be welcomed back to the society of free nations and to the associations of this hemisphere.

My fellow citizens: let no one doubt that this is a difficult and dangerous effort on which we have set out. No one can see precisely what course it will take or what costs or casualties will be incurred. Many months of sacrifice and self-discipline lie ahead -months in which our patience and our will be tested—months in which many threats and denunciations will keep us aware of our dangers. But the greatest danger of all would be to do nothing.

The path we have chosen for the present is full of hazards, as all paths are—but it is the one most consistent with our character and courage as a nation and our commitments around the world. The cost of freedom is always high—and Americans have always paid it. And one path we shall never choose, and that is the path of surrender or submission.

Our goal is not the victory of might, but the vindication of right—not peace at the expense of freedom, but both peace and freedom, here in this hemisphere, and, we hope, around the world. God willing, that goal will be achieved.

Thank you and good night. '

The 'Missiles of October' brought the world to the brink of nuclear war, but Kennedy's steel will and unequivocal diplomacy forced the USSR's mighty hand. TheSoviets backed down and removed the missiles.

Although his legislative career during his time as President was not extensive, John Kennedy can be seen as a leader for his time—a man who was able divine the mood of the people, synthesise the major issues of the day and move government policy towards an ideal—especially regarding civil rights.

On Friday, 22 November 1963 JFK was killed by an assassin's bullet as he rode in a motorcade through Dallas, Texas. Later that afternoon, Lee Harvey Oswald was implicated in the President's death when he was arrested in a theatre and charged with the murder of a Dallas policeman (see Lyndon Johnson, 'Let Us Continue', p 215).

Martin Luther King

'I Have a Dream'

Lincoln Memorial, Washington DC, 28 August 1963.

Atlanta-born Martin Luther King Jnr (1929-68) is rightly regarded by historians as one of the most significant civil rights leaders of the 20th Century—arguably the most significant in the modern history of the United States—and one whose lifetime achievements and lasting impact ranks him alongside that of Mohandas Gandhi.

King graduated from Crozer Theological Seminary in Chester, Pennsylvania in 1953 and was granted his doctorate two years later after completing his dissertation. That same year, he became pastor of the Dexter Avenue Baptist Church in Montgomery, Alabama, at a time when the local black community had a formed a boycott of local bus companies because of the South's strict code of racial segregation. The boycott lasted 382 days, King was arrested and his home was bombed but ultimately, the Supreme Court declared bus segregation unconstitutional and outlawed racial segregation on public transport.

In August 1963, the Reverend Martin Luther King Jnr led a march to Washington DC to demonstrate the commitment of the American people—of all creeds and religions—to seek equal rights in every facet of American society. King's speech, delivered before hundreds of thousands of followers assembled on the steps of the Lincoln Memorial, is one of the greatest speeches of the twentieth century.

‘ I am happy to join with you today in what will go down in history as the greatest demonstration for freedom in the history of our nation.

Five score years ago, a great American, in whose symbolic shadow we stand today, signed the Emancipation Proclamation. This momentous decree came as a great beacon light of hope to millions

> **'We refuse to believe that the bank of justice is bankrupt.'**

of Negro slaves, who had been seared in the flames of withering injustice. It came as a joyous daybreak to end the long night of their captivity.

But one hundred years later, the Negro still is not free. One hundred years later, the life of the Negro is still sadly crippled by the manacles of segregation and the chains of discrimination. One hundred years later, the Negro lives on a lonely island of poverty in the midst of a vast ocean of material prosperity. One hundred years later, the Negro still languishes in the corners of American society and finds himself an exile in his own land.

So we've come here today to dramatise a shameful condition. In a sense, we've come to our nation's capital to cash a check. When the architects of our Republic wrote the magnificent words of the Constitution and the Declaration of Independence, they were signing a promissory note to which every American was to fall heir. This note was a promise that all men—yes, black men as well as white men—would be guaranteed the unalienable rights of life, liberty, and the pursuit of happiness.

It is obvious today that America has defaulted on this promissory note insofar as her citizens of colour are concerned. Instead of honoring this sacred obligation, America has given the Negro people a bad check, a check which has come back marked "insufficient funds." But we refuse to believe that the bank of justice is bankrupt. We refuse to believe that there are insufficient funds in the great vaults of opportunity of this nation. So we've come to cash this check—a check that will give us upon demand the riches of freedom and the security of justice.

We have also come to this hallowed spot to remind America of the fierce urgency of "now." This is no time to engage in the luxury of cooling off or to take the tranquilising drug of gradualism. Now is the time to make real the promises of democracy. Now is the time to rise from the dark and desolate valley of segregation to the sunlit path of racial justice. Now is the time to lift our nation from the quicksand of racial injustice to the solid rock of brotherhood.

Now is the time to make justice a reality for all of God's children.

It would be fatal for the nation to overlook the urgency of the moment. This sweltering summer of the Negro's legitimate discontent will not pass until there is an invigorating autumn of freedom and equality. Nineteen sixty-three is not an end, but a beginning. Those who hope that the Negro needed to blow off steam and will now be content will have a rude awakening if the nation returns to business as usual. There will be neither rest nor tranquillity in America until the Negro is granted his citizenship rights. The whirlwinds of revolt will continue to shake the foundations of our nation until the bright day of justice emerges.

But that is something that I must say to my people who stand on the warm threshold which leads into the palace of justice. In the process of gaining our rightful place we must not be guilty of wrongful deeds. Let us not seek to satisfy our thirst for freedom by drinking from the cup of bitterness and hatred.

We must forever conduct our struggle on the high plane of dignity and discipline. We must not allow our creative protest to degenerate into physical violence. Again and again we must rise to the majestic heights of meeting physical force with soul force. The marvelous new militancy which has engulfed the Negro community must not lead us to a distrust of all white people, for many of our white brothers, as evidenced by their presence here today, have come to realise that their destiny is tied up with our destiny. And they have come to realise that their freedom is inextricably bound to our freedom. We cannot walk alone.

As we walk, we must make the pledge that we shall always march ahead. We cannot turn back.

There are those who are asking the devotees of civil rights, "When will you be satisfied?" We can never be satisfied as long as the Negro is the victim of the unspeakable horrors of police brutality. We can never be satisfied as long as our bodies, heavy with the fatigue of travel, cannot gain lodging in the motels of the highways and the hotels of the

'We will not be satisfied until justice rolls down like waters and righteousness like a mighty stream!'

cities. We cannot be satisfied as long as the Negro's basic mobility is from a smaller ghetto to a larger one. We can never be satisfied as long as our children are stripped of their selfhood and robbed of their dignity by signs stating "For Whites Only." We cannot be satisfied as long as a Negro in Mississippi cannot vote and a Negro in New York believes he has nothing for which to vote. No, no, we are not satisfied, and we will not be satisfied until justice rolls down like waters and righteousness like a mighty stream!

'We will be able to join hands and sing in the words of the old Negro spiritual, "Free at last! Free at last! Thank God Almighty, we are free at last!"'

I am not unmindful that some of you have come here out of great trials and tribulations. Some of you have come fresh from narrow jail cells. Some of you have come from areas where your quest for freedom left you battered by the storms of persecution and staggered by the winds of police brutality. You have been the veterans of creative suffering. Continue to work with the faith that unearned suffering is redemptive.

Go back to Mississippi, go back to Alabama, go back to South Carolina, go back to Georgia, go back to Louisiana, go back to the slums and ghettos of our Northern cities, knowing that somehow this situation can and will be changed. Let us not wallow in the valley of despair.

I say to you today, my friends, so even though we face the difficulties of today and tomorrow, I still have a dream. It is a dream deeply rooted in the American dream.

I have a dream that one day this nation will rise up and live out the true meaning of its creed: "We hold these truths to be self-evident; that all men are created equal."

I have a dream that one day on the red hills of Georgia the sons of former slaves and the sons of former slave owners will be able to sit down together at the table of brotherhood.

I have a dream that one day even the state of Mississippi, a state sweltering with the heat of injustice, sweltering with the heat of oppression, will be transformed into an oasis of freedom and justice.

I have a dream that my four little children will one day live in a nation where they will not be judged by the colour of their skin but by the content of their character.

I have a dream today!

I have a dream that one day, down in Alabama, with its vicious racists, with its governor having his lips dripping with the words of interposition and nullification, one day right there in Alabama little black boys and black girls will be able to join hands with little white boys and white girls as sisters and brothers ... I have a dream today!

I have a dream that one day every valley shall be exalted, every hill and mountain shall be made low, the rough places will be made plain and the crooked places will be made straight, and the glory of the Lord shall be revealed, and all flesh shall see it together!

This is our hope. This is the faith that I go back to the South with. With this faith, we will be able to hew out of the mountain of despair a stone of hope. With this faith we will be able to transform the jangling discords of our nation into a beautiful symphony of brotherhood. With this faith we will be able to work together, to pray together, to struggle together, to go to jail together, to stand up for freedom together, knowing that we will be free one day!

This will be the day ... this will be the day when all of God's children will be able to sing with new meaning. "My country 'tis of thee, sweet land of liberty, of thee I sing. Land where my fathers died, land of the Pilgrims' pride, from every mountainside, let freedom ring," and if America is to be a great nation, this must become true.

So let freedom ring! From the prodigious hilltops of New Hampshire, let freedom ring. From the mighty mountains of New York, let freedom ring, from the heightening Alleghenies of Pennsylvania!

Let freedom ring from the snow-capped Rockies of Colorado!

Let freedom ring from the curvaceous slopes of California! But not only that.

Let freedom ring from Stone Mountain of Georgia!

Let freedom ring from Lookout Mountain in Tennessee!

Let freedom ring from every hill and mole hill of Mississippi. From every mountainside, let freedom ring, and when this happens ... when we allow freedom to ring, when we let it ring from every village and every hamlet, from every state and every city, we will be able to speed up that day when all of God's children, black men and white men, Jews and Gentiles, Protestants and Catholics, will be able to join hands and sing in the words of the old Negro spiritual, "Free at last! Free at last! Thank God Almighty, we are free at last!"'

Dr Martin Luther King Jnr was named Time Magazine's 'Person of the Year' in 1963 and, a few months later, received the 1964 Nobel Peace Prize— at the time the youngest man to be so honoured. On his return from Norway, King threw himself into a new cause—voter registration in Selma Alabama.

In 1965, President Johnson asked Congress to ratify a tough voting rights bill in his State of the Union speech. When Congress stalled, King and over 500 supporters marched from Selma to Montgomery to register African-Americans to vote. Alabama police attacked the marchers and the violence shown on national television shocked the country.

It took government intervention—the 'federalising' of the Alabama National Guard and the addition of another 2000 guards—to allow a second, 3000 strong, march to Montgomery to begin on March 21, 1965. Congress finally passed the bill (known as the Civil Rights Act of 1965 or the Voting Rights Act of 1965) on 5 August 1965.

Dr King went on to battle other issues—domestic poverty, Chicago slums and the war in Vietnam—as well as factions within the equal rights movement in the remaining years of his short life.

In 1968 King was planning another massive march on Washington—'a demonstration of such intensity and size' that Congress would have to finally take notice of the nation's poor—when he was invited to Memphis, Tennessee to support striking sanitation workers. He gave his famous 'I have seen the Promised Land' speech at the Mason Temple in Memphis on the evening of 3 April, 1968.

The following day Martin Luther King Jnr was shot and killed as he stood on the balcony of the black-owned Lorraine Hotel, just off Beale Street. He was talking to Ralph Abernathy and Jesse Jackson when he was struck in the neck and died at the scene soon after.

For a man of peace, Martin Luther King Jnr died a violent death and his passing caused a wave of destruction in major cities across the United States.

Robert F Kennedy

'Announcement of Martin Luther King's Death'

Rally for presidential votes, Indianapolis, Indiana, 4 April 1968.

Robert Francis Kennedy (1925-68) served on the Select Committee for Improper Activities in the late 1950s—taking on Teamster Union boss Jimmy Hoffa—before being appointed Attorney General during the presidency of his older brother, John F Kennedy. After John Kennedy's death in 1963, Bobby Kennedy left the White House in 1964 and became the Democratic Senator for New York the following year. When President Lyndon Johnson announced that he would not seek re-election in March 1968, the younger Kennedy stepped up his bid for the Democratic Party nomination and began a hectic schedule of campaigning—largely on an anti-Vietnam war platform.

On 4 April, 1968 Bobby Kennedy arrived by plane into Indianapolis, Indiana, to address a largely black rally to promote 'RFK for President'. On that same day Dr Martin Luther King Jnr had been murdered in Memphis. On his arrival Kennedy asked the rally organiser, 'Do they know about Martin Luther King?' The man responded by saying, 'No. We've left that up to you.' Kennedy asked the crowd to lower their pro-Kennedy placards and then addressed them in this heartfelt, spontaneous speech that evoked the memory of his own slain brother.

' I have bad news for you, for all of our fellow citizens and people who love peace all over the world—and that is that Martin Luther King was shot and killed tonight.

Martin Luther King dedicated his life to love and to justice for his fellow human beings, and he died because of that effort.

In this difficult day, in this difficult time for the United States, it is perhaps well to ask what kind of a nation we are and what direction we want to move in. For those of you who are black—considering the evidence there evidently is, that there were white people who were responsible—you can be filled with bitterness, with hatred, and a desire for revenge. We can move in that direction as a country, in great polarisation—black people amongst black, white people amongst white, filled with hatred toward one another.

Or we can make an effort, as Martin Luther King did, to understand and to comprehend, and to replace that violence, that stain of blood shed that has spread across our land, with an effort to understand with compassion and love.

For those of you who are black and are tempted to be filled with hatred and distrust at the injustice of such an act, against all white people, I can only say that I feel in my own heart that same kind of feeling. I had a member of my family killed, but he was killed by a white man. But we have to make an effort in the United States, we have to make an effort to understand, to go beyond these rather difficult times.

My favorite poet was Aeschylus. He wrote: "In our sleep, pain which cannot forget falls drop by drop upon the heart until, in our own despair, against our will, comes wisdom through the awful grace of God."

What we need in the United States is not division; what we need in the United States is not hatred; what we need in the United States is not violence or lawlessness; but love and wisdom, and compassion toward one another, and a feeling of justice toward those who still suffer within our country, whether they be white or they be black.

So I shall ask you tonight to return home, to say a prayer for the family of Martin Luther King, that's true, but more importantly, to say a prayer for our own country, which all of us love—a prayer for understanding and that compassion of which I spoke.

'The vast majority of black people in this country want to live together, want to improve the quality of our life, and want justice for all human beings who abide in our land.'

ROBERT F KENNEDY   175

'We can make an effort, as Martin Luther King did, to understand and to comprehend, and to replace that violence, that stain of bloodshed that has spread across our land, with an effort to understand with compassion and love.'

We can do well in this country. We will have difficult times; we've had difficult times in the past; we will have difficult times in the future. It is not the end of violence; it is not the end of lawlessness; it is not the end of disorder.

But the vast majority of white people and the vast majority of black people in this country want to live together, want to improve the quality of our life, and want justice for all human beings who abide in our land.

Let us dedicate ourselves to what the Greeks wrote so many years ago: to tame the savageness of man and make gentle the life of this world.

Let us dedicate ourselves to that, and say a prayer for our country and for our people.'

Ten weeks later, on 4 June 1968, Robert F.Kennedy won the California Primary for the Democratic nomination and pulled away from his closest rivals, Eugene McCarthy and Hubert Humphrey. His short victory speech, delivered at the Ambassador Hotel's Embassy Ballroom just before midnight, constituted his final public appearance:

'
I think we can end the divisions within the United States. What I think is quite clear is that we can work together in the last analysis. And that what has been going on with the United States over the period of that last three years, the divisions, the violence, the disenchantment with our society, the divisions—whether it's between blacks and whites, between the poor and the more affluent, or between age groups, or in the war in Vietnam—that we can work together. We are a great country, an unselfish country and a compassionate country. And I intend to make that my basis for running.'

Kennedy then left the rostrum, behind a curtain, taking a back route to the press room via the hotel kitchen. There, at 12:23 am on the morning of 5 June, Kennedy was shot in the head by Jordanian immigrant Sirhan Sirhan.

The 24-year-old assassin was allegedly upset by Kennedy's support of Israel during the Six-Day War the previous year, but as was the case with the death of John Kennedy and Martin Luther King, Sirhan's crime started a conspiracy industry (Sirhan was sentenced to death but this was commuted to life imprisonment).

Robert Kennedy was taken to the nearby Good Samaritan Hospital where—on the fifth floor, surrounded by family and friends—Kennedy, and his unfulfilled potential, died the following day.

Edward 'Teddy' Kennedy

'Eulogy for Robert F Kennedy'

St. Patrick's Cathedral, New York, 8 June 1968.

E dward Moore 'Teddy' Kennedy was born in 1932, the youngest of four sons and five daughters born to Joseph and Rose Kennedy. After studying at Harvard and the Virginia University Law School, he was admitted to the bar in 1959. Teddy Kennedy was elected Democratic Senator for Massachusetts in 1962—the position vacated by his brother John F. Kennedy when he became President in 1961—at the young age of 30. The youngest Kennedy was an important part of the mythical Kennedy political 'dynasty' but even more pressure was placed on the last of the family line following the assassinations of his brothers in 1963 and 1968. (The Kennedy's oldest brother, Joe Jnr, was killed in World War II while another sister, Kathleen, died in a plane accident).

Senator Teddy Kennedy delivered the eulogy for his brother Bobby at St Patrick's Cathedral, New York, on 8 June 1968. Towards the end of this speech Kennedy's voice strained under the emotion—highlighting the poignancy of the occasion.

‘ On behalf of Mrs Robert Kennedy, her children and the parents and sisters of Robert Kennedy, I want to express what we feel to those who mourn with us today in this cathedral and around the world. We loved him as a brother and father and son. From his parents, and from his older brothers and sisters—Joe, Kathleen and Jack—he received inspiration which he passed on to all of us. He gave us strength in time of trouble, wisdom in time of uncertainty, and sharing in time of happiness. He was always by our side.

Love is not an easy feeling to put into words. Nor is loyalty, or trust or joy. But he was all of these. He loved life completely and lived it intensely.

A few years back, Robert Kennedy wrote some words about his own father and they expressed the way we in his family feel about him. He said of what his father meant to him:

'Each time a man stands up for an ideal, or acts to improve the lot of others, or strikes out against injustice, he sends forth a tiny ripple of hope.'

What it really all adds up to is love—not love as it is described with such facility in popular magazines, but the kind of love that is affection and respect, order, encouragement, and support. Our awareness of this was an incalculable source of strength, and because real love is something unselfish and involves sacrifice and giving, we could not help but profit from it.

Beneath it all, he has tried to engender a social conscience. There were wrongs which needed attention. There were people who were poor and who needed help. And we have a responsibility to them and to this country. Through no virtues and accomplishments of our own, we have been fortunate enough to be born in the United States under the most comfortable conditions. We, therefore, have a responsibility to others who are less well off.

This is what Robert Kennedy was given. What he leaves us is what he said, what he did and what he stood for. A speech he made to the young people of South Africa on their Day of Affirmation in 1966 sums it up best, and I would read it now:

There is discrimination in this world, and slavery and slaughter and starvation. Governments repress their people; and millions are trapped in poverty while the nation grows rich; and wealth is lavished on armaments everywhere.

These are differing evils, but they are common works of man. They reflect the imperfection of human justice, the inadequacy of human compassion, our lack of sensibility toward the sufferings of our fellows.

But we can perhaps remember—even if only for a time—that those who live with us are our brothers; that they share with us the same

> 'What it all adds up to is love—not love as it is described in popular magazines, but the kind of love that is affection and respect, order, encouragement and support.'

short moment of life; that they seek—as we do—nothing but the chance to live out their lives in purpose and happiness, winning what satisfaction and fulfillment they can.

Surely this bond of common faith, this bond of common goal, can begin to teach us something. Surely, we can learn, at least, to look at those around us as fellow men. And surely we can begin to work a little harder to bind up the wounds among us and to become in our own hearts brothers and countrymen once again.

Our answer is to rely on youth—not a time of life but a state of mind, a temper of the will, a quality of imagination, a predominance of courage over timidity, of the appetite for adventure over the love of ease. The cruelties and obstacles of this swiftly changing planet will not yield to obsolete dogmas and outworn slogans. They cannot be moved by those who cling to a present that is already dying, who prefer the illusion of security to the excitement and danger that come with even the most peaceful progress. It is a revolutionary world we live in; and this generation, at home and around the world, has had thrust upon it a greater burden of responsibility than any generation that has ever lived.

Some believe there is nothing one man or one woman can do against the enormous array of the world's ills. Yet many of the world's great movements, of thought and action, have flowed from the work of a single man. A young monk began the Protestant reformation, a young general extended an empire from Macedonia to the borders of the earth, and a young woman reclaimed the territory of France. It was a young Italian explorer who discovered the New World, and the thirty-two-year-old Thomas Jefferson who proclaimed that all men are created equal.

These men moved the world, and so can we all. Few will have the greatness to bend history itself, but each of us can work to change a small portion of events, and in the total of all those acts will be written the history of this generation. It is from numberless diverse acts of courage and belief that human history is shaped. Each time a man stands up for an ideal, or acts to improve the lot of others, or strikes out against injustice, he sends forth a tiny ripple of hope, and crossing each other from a million different centers of energy and daring, those ripples build a current that can sweep down the mightiest walls of oppression and resistance.

'As he said many times: "Some men see things as they are and say why not. I dream things that never were and say why not".'

Few are willing to brave the disapproval of their fellows, the censure of their colleagues, the wrath of their society. Moral courage is a rarer commodity than bravery in battle or great intelligence. Yet it is the one essential, vital quality for those who seek to change a world that yields most painfully to change. And I believe that in this generation those with the courage to enter the moral conflict will find themselves with companions in every corner of the globe.

For the fortunate among us, there is the temptation to follow the easy and familiar paths of personal ambition and financial success so grandly spread before those who enjoy the privilege of education. But that is not the road history has marked out for us. Like it or not, we live in times of danger and uncertainty. But they are also more open to the creative energy of men than any other time in history. All of us will ultimately be judged, and as the years pass, we will surely judge ourselves on the effort we have contributed to building a new world society and the extent to which our ideals and goals have shaped that effort.

The future does not belong to those who are content with today, apathetic toward common problems and their fellow man alike, timid and fearful in the face of new ideas and bold projects. Rather it will belong to those who can blend vision, reason and courage in a personal commitment to the ideals and great enterprises of American society.

Our future may lie beyond our vision, but it is not completely beyond our control. It is the shaping impulse of America that neither fate nor nature nor the irresistible tides of history, but the work of our own hands, matched to reason and principle, that will determine our destiny. There is pride in that, even arrogance, but there is also experience and truth. In any event, it is the only way we can live."

EDWARD 'TEDDY' KENNEDY   181

This is the way he lived. My brother need not be idealised, or enlarged in death beyond what he was in life, to be remembered simply as a good and decent man, who saw wrong and tried to right it, saw suffering and tried to heal it, saw war and tried to stop it.

Those of us who loved him and who take him to his rest today, pray that what he was to us and what he wished for others will some day come to pass for all the world. As he said many times, in many parts of this nation, to those he touched and who sought to touch him:

"Some men see things as they are and say why.

I dream things that never were and say why not."'

Within a year, Teddy Kennedy's dream of following his slain brothers into the White House disappeared in the murky waters off Chappaquiddick Island. Kennedy's conduct regarding the death of party secretary Mary Jo Kopechne in a submerged car after a night of partying at Martha's Vineyard did not endear him to the American public. He ultimately ran for President in 1980, but his loss to Jimmy Carter at the Democratic National Convention in New York in August 1980 confirmed what the American public already knew—Teddy Kennedy would never become President. It was the end of the dream of a 'Kennedy dynasty'.

In 1999 Teddy Kennedy—still the Democratic Senator for Massachusetts but promoted by fate from kid brother to family patriarch and eulogiser—was again called upon after his nephew, 38 year-old John Kennedy Jnr, his wife Carolyn and sister-in-law Lauren Bessette, were killed in a light plane crash off the coast of Massachusetts.

Absolute
Power
1970-1979

John Kerry

'Against the War in Vietnam'

House Foreign Relations Committee, Washington DC, 22 April 1971.

J ohn F Kerry was the Democratic presidential candidate against George W Bush in 2004. During that campaign, at a time when America was fighting an unpopular war in Iraq, Kerry's Vietnam War experiences became a major issue in his bid to become president. Kerry was both lauded by ex-comrades and publicly vilified by his Republican opponents about his war record. (He accepted the Democratic nomination in July 2004 by stating 'I'm John Kerry ... reporting for duty' as he saluted the party faithful.) President George Bush ultimately won the November elections, but the Vietnam veteran pushed Bush to the narrowest margin of primary votes by any sitting president in American history.

Kerry was born on 11 December, 1943 in Colorado, the son of an Army Air Corps test pilot who flew DC-3s and B-29s during World War II. Kerry's father, Richard, was a Foreign Service Officer in the Eisenhower administration. After graduating from Yale University, Kerry—a liberal, well-to-do Catholic with a military heritage—volunteered to serve in Vietnam because he felt it was 'the right thing to do'. Kerry completed two tours of duty and on the latter, volunteered to serve on a patrol boat scouring the Vietnamese river deltas. His leadership and courage under fire earned him a Silver Star, a Bronze Star with Combat V, and three Purple Hearts.

Along with many Vietnam veterans, Kerry's wartime experience led him to speak out against the war. He joined Vietnam Veterans Against the War (VVAW) and was later co-founded Vietnam Veterans of America. In April 1971, the then 27 year-old testified before the House Foreign Relations Committee and openly questioned America's involvement in the civil war in Vietnam.

' I would like to say for the record, and also for the men sitting behind me who are also wearing the uniforms and their medals, that my sitting here is really symbolic. I am not here as John Kerry. I am here as one member of a group of 1,000, which is a small representation of a very much larger group of veterans in this country, and were it possible for all of them to sit at this table, they would be here and have the same kind of testimony. I would simply like to speak in general terms. I apologise if my statement is general because I received notification [only] yesterday that you would hear me, and, I am afraid, because of the injunction I was up most of the night and haven't had a great deal of chance to prepare.

I would like to talk, representing all those veterans, and say that several months ago, in Detroit, we had an investigation at which over 150 honorably discharged, and many very highly decorated, veterans testified to war crimes committed in Southeast Asia. These were not isolated incidents, but crimes committed on a day-to-day basis, with the full awareness of officers at all levels of command. It is impossible to describe to you exactly what did happen in Detroit—the emotions in the room, and the feelings of the men who were reliving their experiences in Vietnam. They relived the absolute horror of what this country, in a sense, made them do.

They told stories that, at times, they had personally raped, cut off ears, cut off heads, taped wires from portable telephones to human genitals and turned up the power, cut off limbs, blown up bodies, randomly shot at civilians, razed villages in fashion reminiscent of Ghengis Khan, shot cattle and dogs for fun, poisoned food stocks, and generally ravaged the countryside of South Vietnam, in addition to the normal ravage of war and the normal and very particular ravaging which is done by the applied bombing power of this country.

We call this investigation the Winter Soldier Investigation. The term "winter soldier" is a play on words of Thomas Paine's in 1776, when he spoke of the "sunshine patriots," and "summertime soldiers" who deserted at Valley Forge because the going was rough.

'We cannot consider ourselves America's best men when we are ashamed of and hated what we were called on to do in Southeast Asia.'

We who have come here to Washington have come here because we feel we have to be winter soldiers now. We could come back to this country, we could be quiet, we could hold our silence, we could not tell what went on in Vietnam, but we feel, because of what threatens this country, not the reds, but the crimes which we are committing that threaten it, that we have to speak out.

I would like to talk to you a little bit about what the result is of the feelings these men carry with them after coming back from Vietnam. The country doesn't know it yet, but it has created a monster, a monster in the form of millions of men who have been taught to deal and to trade in violence, and who are given the chance to die for the biggest nothing in history; men who have returned with a sense of anger and a sense of betrayal which no one has yet grasped.

As a veteran and one who felt this anger, I would like to talk about it. We are angry because we feel we have been used in the worst fashion by the administration of this country.

In 1970, at West Point, Vice President Agnew said, "some glamorise the criminal misfits of society while our best men die in Asian rice paddies to preserve the freedom which most of those misfits abuse," and this was used as a rallying point for our effort in Vietnam.

But for us, as boys in Asia whom the country was supposed to support, his statement is a terrible distortion from which we can only draw a very deep sense of revulsion. Hence the anger of some of the men who are here in Washington today. It is a distortion because we in no way consider ourselves the best men of this country, because those he calls misfits were standing up for us in a way that nobody else in this country dared to, because so many who have died would have returned to this country to join the misfits in their efforts to ask for an immediate withdrawal from South Vietnam, because so many of those best men have returned as quadriplegics and amputees, and they lie forgotten in Veterans' Administration hospitals in this country which fly the flag which so many have chosen as their own personal symbol. And we cannot consider ourselves America's best men when we are ashamed of and hated what we were called on to do in Southeast Asia.

In our opinion, and from our experience, there is nothing in South Vietnam which could happen that realistically threatens the United States of America. And to attempt to justify the loss of one American life in Vietnam, Cambodia, or Laos by linking such loss to the preservation of freedom, which those misfits supposedly abuse, is to us the height of criminal hypocrisy, and it is that kind of hypocrisy which we feel has torn this country apart.

'The country doesn't know it yet, but it has created a monster, a monster in the form of millions of men who have been taught to deal and to trade in violence, and who are given the chance to die for the biggest nothing in history.'

We found that not only was it a civil war, an effort by a people who had for years been seeking their liberation from any colonial influence whatsoever, but, also, we found that the Vietnamese, whom we had enthusiastically molded after our own image, were hard-put to take up the fight against the threat we were supposedly saving them from.

We found most people didn't even know the difference between communism and democracy. They only wanted to work in rice paddies without helicopters strafing them and bombs with napalm burning their villages and tearing their country apart. They wanted everything to do with the war, particularly with this foreign presence of the United States of America, to leave them alone in peace, and they practiced the art of survival by siding with whichever military force was present at a particular time, be it Viet Cong, North Vietnamese or American.

We found also that, all too often, American men were dying in those rice paddies for want of support from their allies. We saw first hand how monies from American taxes were used for a corrupt dictatorial regime. We saw that many people in this country had a one-sided idea of who was kept free by the flag, and blacks provided the highest percentage of casualties. We saw Vietnam ravaged equally by American bombs and search-and-destroy missions as well as by Viet Cong terrorism—and yet we listened while this country tried to blame all of the havoc on the Viet Cong.

We rationalised destroying villages in order to save them. We saw America lose her sense of morality as she accepted very coolly a My Lai, and refused to give up the image of American soldiers who hand out chocolate bars and chewing gum.

We learned the meaning of free-fire zones—shooting anything that moves—and we watched while America placed a cheapness on the lives of Orientals.

We watched the United States falsification of body counts, in fact the glorification of body counts. We listened while, month after month, we were told the back of the enemy was about to break. We fought using weapons against "Oriental human beings" with quotation marks around that. We fought using weapons against those people which I do not believe this country would dream of using, were we fighting in the European theater. We watched while men charged up hills because a general said that hill has to be taken, and, after losing one platoon, or two platoons, they marched away to leave the hill for reoccupation by the North Vietnamese. We watched pride allow the most unimportant battles to be blown into extravaganzas, because we couldn't lose, and we couldn't retreat, and because it didn't matter how many American bodies were lost to prove that point, and so there were Hamburger Hills and Khe Sanhs and Hill 81s and Fire Base 6s, and so many others.

'When, thirty years from now, our brothers go down the street without a leg, without an arm, or a face, and small boys ask why, we will be able to say "Vietnam" and not mean a filthy obscene memory, but mean instead where America finally turned ... '

Now we are told that the men who fought there must watch quietly while American lives are lost so that we can exercise the incredible arrogance of "Vietnamising" the Vietnamese.

Each day, to facilitate the process by which the United States washes her hands of Vietnam, someone has to give up his life so that the United States doesn't have to admit something that the entire world already knows, so that we can't say that we have made a mistake. Someone has to die so that President Nixon won't be, and these are his words, "the first President to lose a war."

We are asking Americans to think about that, because how do you ask a man to be the last man to die in Vietnam? How do you ask a man to be the last man to die for a mistake? We are here in Washington to say that the problem of this war is not just a question of war and diplomacy. It is part and parcel of everything that we are trying, as human beings, to communicate to people in this country—the question of racism, which is rampant in the military, and so many other questions, such as the use of weapons: the hypocrisy in our taking umbrage at the Geneva Conventions and using that as justification for a continuation of this war, when we are more guilty than any other body of violations of those Geneva Conventions; in the use of free-fire zones; harassment-interdiction fire, search-and-destroy missions; the bombings; the torture of prisoners; all accepted policy by many units in South Vietnam. That is what we are trying to say. It is part and parcel of everything.

An American Indian friend of mine who lives in the Indian Nation of Alcatraz put it to me very succinctly. He told me how, as a boy on an Indian reservation, he had watched television, and he used to cheer the cowboys when they came in and shot the Indians, and then suddenly one day he stopped in Vietnam and he said, "my God, I am doing to these people the very same thing that was done to my people," and he stopped. And that is what we are trying to say, that we think this thing has to end.

We are here to ask, and we are here to ask vehemently, where are the leaders of our country? Where is the leadership? We're here to ask where are McNamara, Rostow, Bundy, Gilpatrick, and so many others? Where are they now that we, the men they sent off to war, have returned? These are the commanders who have deserted their troops. And there is no more serious crime in the laws of war. The Army says they never leave their wounded. The Marines say they never even leave their dead. These men have left all the casualties and retreated behind a pious shield of public rectitude. They've left the real stuff of their reputations bleaching behind them in the sun in this country....

We wish that a merciful God could wipe away our own memories of that service as easily as this administration has wiped away their memories of us. But all that they have done, and all that they can do by this denial, is to make more clear than ever our own determination to undertake one last mission: to search out and destroy the last vestige of this barbaric war; to pacify our own hearts; to conquer the hate and fear that have driven this country these last ten years and more. And more. And so, when, thirty years from now, our brothers go down the street without a leg, without an arm, or a face, and small boys ask why, we will be able to say "Vietnam" and not mean a desert, not a filthy obscene memory, but mean instead where América finally turned, and where soldiers like us helped it in the turning.

After delivering this speech, Kerry went to work as a high-profile prosecutor in Middlesex County, Massachusetts. He was elected Lieutenant Governor in 1982 and became a US Senator two years later. In 1988 Senator Kerry chaired the Senate Foreign Relations Subcommittee's investigation into the 'Iran/Contra Affair'. He was serving his fourth term when he announced his candidacy for the Democratic presidential nomination in 2003.

What happened to the earnest young man with the mop of black hair who dared to confront the US military leadership three decades before? Time knocked the edges off the young Vietnam Veteran and the American public ultimately rejected the smoothed-over politician that stood before them in 2004 in favour of four more years of George W Bush.

Richard M Nixon

'Farewell to the Whitehouse'

Washington DC, 9 August 1974.

Richard Milhous Nixon (1913-94) enjoyed a spectacular rise to prominence in US politics in the late 1940s and early 1950s. After his return from the political graveyard in 1968, six years later he became the first president in the history of the United States to resign from office.

Elected to the US Congress in 1946 after serving in the Navy during World War II, he had made a name for himself as a fervent 'anti-Communist' on the House Committee on Un-American Activities. In 1950 he was elected to the US Senate and as a high-profile opponent of President Truman's handling of the Korean War, he had enough clout to persuade the Californian delegation to throw their support behind Republican candidate Dwight D. Eisenhower in the 1952 presidential race. Eisenhower rewarded Nixon by choosing him as his running mate.

While the Republicans were holding their National Convention in September 1952 a sensational story appeared in the New York Post alleging that a 'secret rich men's trust fund' had kept Nixon in financial style far beyond his congressional salary. There was immediate pressure to remove Nixon from the Republican ticket but in a brilliant tactical move, Nixon appeared on national television in California to 'explain' to the American people his financial situation. Now known as the 'Checkers Speech' because of the reference to a pet dog given to his daughters by a Republican supporter, Richard Nixon turned the performance—part drama, part pathos—into a political triumph.

The Republican Party went on to win the election by a landslide but Nixon could not capitalise on his eight years as vice president and lost the 1960 presidential race to Senator John F. Kennedy. After a failed bid for the governorship of California in 1962 a bitter Nixon told the press, 'You won't have Nixon to kick around any more, gentlemen. This is my last Press Conference.' Almost seven years later to the day, Nixon was elected the 37th President of the United States.

In 1968 Richard Nixon returned from the political scrapheap and the anonymity of corporate life to win the Republican nomination and defeat a decimated Democratic Party to win the presidency. In January 1969 Nixon halted the bombing of North Vietnam but a year later only a token withdrawal of troops had taken place. Under Nixon the Vietnam War entered a new phase when he ordered troops into neighbouring Cambodia to clear out Vietcong training grounds, invaded Laos then resumed the bombing of North Vietnam. By 1972, Dr Henry Kissinger, Nixon's special representative at the Paris Peace talks, declared that peace was 'at hand'. This premature announcement, timed to make maximum impact on that year's presidential race, saw Nixon re-elected in a land-slide victory.

Nixon's second term as president was engulfed by 'Watergate'. The scandal grew from a bungled break-in by five burglars who entered the Democratic National Committee offices at the Watergate complex in Washington on the night of 17 June, 1972. Subsequent investigations, most famously by Washington Post reporters Carl Bernstein and Bob Woodward, linked the break-in to President Nixon's top aides, who were involved in an extensive cover-up of politically-sanctioned illegal activities. After a two year investigation by the news media, government agencies, the US Senate, the House of Representatives and the US Supreme Court, the extent of the White House cover-up consumed Nixon's Presidency. It gradually became apparent that Nixon would not survive a full impeachment vote in the Congress despite using the prestige and power of the presidency to stonewall the judicial process.

On August 8, 1974, President Richard M. Nixon appeared on television and became the first President in the history of the United States to resign from office. At 11:35 am the following day Nixon's assistant, Alexander Haig Jnr, tended the President's letter of resignation to Secretary of State Henry A. Kissinger in his White House office. Members of Nixon's staff then assembled to farewell the man they had served—in some cases stretching back to Nixon's time as Vice-President in the early 1950s. Nixon then delivered this revealing speech.

I think the record should show that this is one of those spontaneous things that we always arrange whenever the President comes in to speak, and it will be so reported in the press, and we don't mind, because they have to call it as they see it.

'Sure, we have done some things wrong in this Administration, and the top man always takes the responsibility, and I have never ducked it.'

But on our part, believe me, it is spontaneous.

You are here to say goodbye to us, and we don't have a good word for it in English—the best is au revoir. We'll see you again.

I just met with the members of the White House staff, you know, those who serve here in the White House day in and day out, and I asked them to do what I ask all of you to do to the extent that you can and, of course, are requested to do so: to serve our next President as you have served me and previous Presidents—because many of you have been here for many years—with devotion and dedication, because this office, great as it is, can only be as great as the men and women who work for and with the President.

This house, for example—I was thinking of it as we walked down this hall, and I was comparing it to some of the great houses of the world that I have been in. This isn't the biggest house. Many, and most, in even smaller countries, are much bigger. This isn't the finest house. Many in Europe, particularly, and in China, Asia, have paintings of great, great value, things that we just don't have here and, probably, will never have until we are 1,000 years old or older.

But this is the best house. It is the best house, because it has something far more important than numbers of people who serve, far more important than numbers of rooms or how big it is, far more important than numbers of magnificent pieces of art.

This house has a great heart, and that heart comes from those who serve. I was rather sorry they didn't come down. We said goodbye to them upstairs. But they are really great. And I recall after so many times I have made speeches, and some of them pretty tough, yet, I always come back, or after a hard day—and my days usually have run rather long—I would always get a lift from them, because I might be a little down but they always smiled.

RICHARD M NIXON   193

And so it is with you. I look around here, and I see so many on this staff that, you know, I should have been by your offices and shaken hands, and I would love to have talked to you and found out how to run the world—everybody wants to tell the President what to do, and boy, he needs to be told many times—but I just haven't had the time. But I want you to know that each and every one of you, I know, is indispensable to this Government.

I am proud of this Cabinet. I am proud of all the members who have served in our Cabinet. I am proud of our sub-Cabinet. I am proud of our White House Staff. As I pointed out last night, sure, we have done some things wrong in this Administration, and the top man always takes the responsibility, and I have never ducked it. But I want to say one thing: We can be proud of it—five and a half years. No man or no woman came into this Administration and left it with more of this world's goods than when he came in. No man or no woman ever profited at the public expense or the public till. That tells something about you.

Mistakes, yes. But for personal gain, never. You did what you believed in. Sometimes right, sometimes wrong. And I only wish that I were a wealthy man—at the present time, I have got to find a way to pay my taxes—and if I were, I would like to recompense you for the sacrifices that all of you have made to serve in government.

But you are getting something in government—and I want you to tell this to your children, and I hope the Nation's children will hear it, too—something in government service that is far more important than money. It is a cause bigger than yourself. It is the cause of making this the greatest nation in the world, the leader of the world, because without our leadership, the world will know nothing but war, possibly starvation or worse, in the years ahead. With our leadership it will know peace, it will know plenty.

We have been generous, and we will be more generous in the future as we are able to. But most important, we must be strong here, strong in our hearts, strong in our souls, strong in our belief, and strong in our willingness to sacrifice, as you have been willing to sacrifice, in a pecuniary way, to serve in government.

There is something else I would like for you to tell your young people. You know, people often come in and say, "What will I tell my kids?" They look at government and say, sort of a rugged life, and they see the mistakes that are made. They get the impression that everybody is here for the

'As we leave, we leave proud of the people who have stood by us and worked for us and served this country. We want you to be proud of what you have done.'

purpose of feathering his nest. That is why I made this earlier point— not in this Administration, not one single man or woman.

And I say to them, there are many fine careers. This country needs good farmers, good businessmen, good plumbers, good carpenters.

I remember my old man. I think that they would have called him sort of a little man, common man. He didn't consider himself that way. You know what he was? He was a streetcar motorman first, and then he was a farmer, and then he had a lemon ranch. It was the poorest lemon ranch in California, I can assure you. He sold it before they found oil on it. [Laughter] And then he was a grocer. But he was a great man, because he did his job, and every job counts up to the hilt, regardless of what happens.

Nobody will ever write a book, probably, about my mother. Well, I guess all of you would say this about your mother—my mother was a saint. And I think of her, two boys dying of tuberculosis, nursing four others in order that she could take care of my older brother for three years in Arizona, and seeing each of them die, and when they died, it was like one of her own.

Yes, she will have no books written about her. But she was a saint.

Now, however, we look to the future. I had a little quote in the speech last night from T.R. [Theodore Roosevelt]. As you know, I kind of like to read books. I am not educated, but I do read books—and the T.R. quote was a pretty good one. Here is another one I found as I was reading, my last night in the White House, and this quote is about a young man. He was a young lawyer in New York. He had married a beautiful girl, and they had a lovely daughter, and then suddenly she died, and this is what he wrote. This was in his diary.

He said, "She was beautiful in face and form and lovelier still in spirit. As a flower she grew and as a fair young flower she died. Her life had been always in the sunshine. There had never come to her a single great sorrow. None ever knew her who did not love and revere her for her bright and sunny temper and her saintly unselfishness. Fair, pure and joyous as a maiden, loving, tender and happy as a young wife. When she had just become a mother, when her life seemed to be just begun and when the years seemed so bright before her, then by a strange and terrible fate death came to her. And when my heart's dearest died, the light went from my life forever."

That was T.R. in his twenties. He thought the light had gone from his life forever—but he went on. And he not only became President but, as an ex-President, he served his country, always in the arena, tempestuous, strong, sometimes wrong, sometimes right, but he was a man.

And as I leave, let me say, that is an example I think all of us should remember. We think sometimes when things happen that don't go the right way; we think that when you don't pass the bar exam the first time—I happened to, but I was just lucky; I mean, my writing was so poor the bar examiner said, "We have just got to let the guy through." We think that when someone dear to us dies, we think that when we lose an election, we think that when we suffer a defeat that all is ended. We think, as T.R. said, that the light had left his life forever. Not true.

It is only a beginning, always. The young must know it; the old must know it. It must always sustain us, because the greatness comes not when things go always good for you, but the greatness comes and you are really tested, when you take some knocks, some disappointments, when sadness comes, because only if you have been in the deepest valley can you ever know how magnificent it is to be on the highest mountain.

And so I say to you on this occasion, as we leave, we leave proud of the people who have stood by us and worked for us and served this country. We want you to be proud of what you have done. We want you to continue to serve in government, if that is your wish.

Always give your best, never get discouraged, never be petty; always remember, others may hate you, but those who hate you don't win unless you hate them, and then you destroy yourself.

And so, we leave with high hopes, in good spirit, and with deep humility, and with very much gratefulness in our hearts. I can only say to each and every one of you, we come from many faiths, we pray perhaps to different gods—but really the same God in a sense—but I want to say for each and every one of you, not only will we always remember you, not only will we always be grateful to you but always you will be in our hearts and you will be in our prayers.

Thank you very much.

Richard Nixon's spontaneous speech exposed a flawed contradiction. Much was made of Nixon's references to his mother and his self-demeaning attitude towards his academic ability but his attempt to explain his behaviour as being 'not for personal gain' did not sit well with those who still remembered the 'Checkers' speech. (By choosing resignation over impeachment, Nixon also kept his presidential pension for the rest of his life.) Unlike Teddy Roosevelt, to whom he alluded in his speech, Nixon did not enjoy a vigorous public life in retirement. Although he re-entered the spotlight under the sponsorship of the Clinton administration—writing books, commenting on political issues and even attending official functions—he remained a national ghost, haunting the public from a time long gone.

Someone once wrote that the only thing history owes us is the truth. History will judge Nixon harshly.

Gough Whitlam

'Well May We Say, God Save the Queen'

Parliament House Steps, Canberra, Australia, 11 November 1975.

E dward Gough Whitlam, born in Melbourne on 11 July, 1916, is the only Australian Prime Minister to be dismissed from office. Moving to Sydney at the age of two, Whitlam studied law at Sydney University before joining the Royal Australian Air Force in World War II. In 1945, just before leaving the RAAF, he joined the Labor Party in Sydney. After unsuccessful forays into local and state politics, Whitlam won a seat in federal politics in 1952. He was Deputy Opposition leader to Arthur Calwell from 1960-66 but once he took control of the party, Whitlam swept through the old guard of 'laborites' and established a more democratic style of socialist leadership that appealed to Labor's left-wing and centre-right factions.

In December 1972—on the back of a memorable slogan 'It's Time'—the Labor Party was returned to government after 23 years in opposition. Whitlam's sharp wit and charismatic presence provided many Australians with the hope that the 1970s would be a progressive era after decades of conservative government.

Once in government, Whitlam's initial reforms took Australia by storm—removing race as a criterion for immigration (the 'White Australia' policy was still in unofficial operation), ending conscription, abolishing the British honours system, increasing government support for the arts (and reinvigorating the Australian film industry), reforming health services (and putting contraceptives on the medical benefits list), increasing social and educational opportunities for Aborigines and instituting equal pay for women. He was the first Prime Minister in 24 years to visit China, and he re-opened the Australian Embassey in Peking. Perhaps he moved too quickly.

Despite a booming economy and low inflation when he came to office Australia, like the rest of the world in the mid-1970s, was beset by international economic constraints—especially fuel prices and overseas loans. Whitlam's biggest

> 'Maintain your rage and enthusiasm through the campaign for the election now to be held.'

failing as Prime Minister was that he did not control his ministers, and with a mandate to conduct 'open' government, their economic mismanagement severely embarrassed him and eroded public confidence in his leadership.

Despite this perception, Whitlam was re-elected to a second three-year term in 1974 but with a greatly reduced majority.

The events leading up Whitlam's dismissal have become part of Australian political history. In 1974 Whitlam's Minister for Minerals and Energy, Rex Connor, negotiated a $4 billion loan (incredibly, to be repaid over 20 years) to finance the government's ambitious development projects. Although Whitlam knew of the negotiations, his cabinet did not. When the press reported the story the Federal Opposition, under Liberal leader Malcolm Fraser, went on the attack. Whitlam was then forced to sack his treasurer, Deputy Prime Minister Jim Cairns, who was involved in a messy affair with his Secretary (Juni Morosi) and Rex Connor resigned in October 1975 for misleading the parliament over his negotiations with Pakistani financier Tirath Khemlani.

When Malcolm Fraser used the Liberals' majority in the Senate to block the government's money bills—threatening to bring the country to halt in a bid to force an election in both houses of government—Whitlam had a constitutional crisis on his hands.

One of the quirks of Australia's parliamentary system, which is modelled on Britain's Westminster system, is that the head of state is actually the representative of the ruling monarch of England ... the Governor-General. In 1975, Queen Elizabeth II's representative was Sir John Kerr, the jurist and barrister who had been appointed to the post by his former law colleague, Gough Whitlam.

The Governor-General, in consultation with the Queen, asserted the power to dissolve both houses of parliament—effectively dismissing the elected government of the land—and appoint an interim government of his choosing. This Kerr did on 11 November 1975—a date that had long resonated with the Australian public. It was the date, in 1880, that bushranger Ned Kelly was hanged. It was the date, in 1918, that World War I ended. Now the country had another reason to remember it.

On advice of the Chief Justice of the High Court, Sir John Kerr called Gough Whitlam to Government House at 1:00 pm that afternoon. What Whitlam didn't know was that Liberal leader Malcolm Fraser was waiting in another room, although allegations of collusion between the Governor-General and the Opposition Leader proved unfounded.

Whitlam was dismissed at 1:15 pm, Fraser was commissioned as Prime Minister at 1:30 pm and barely half an hour later the Senate passed the Supply Bill that it had been blocking since October 16. Almost comically, when Fraser announced to the House of Representatives that he was the new Prime Minister and put forward the motion to adjourn the session, the move was defeated by the dismissed former government which still maintained a slender majority in the lower house.

Then, at 3:16 pm, Gough Whitlam sponsored a motion of no-confidence in the new Prime Minister which was passed. Parliament was patently unworkable and the Speaker of the House sought an urgent meeting with the Governor-General but was told that Kerr was not available until 4:45 pm. For the next hour, Australia effectively had no federal government.

At 4:50 pm that afternoon, the Governor-General's secretary, David Smith, went to the steps of Parliament House and read the proclamation dissolving Parliament.

A large, angry crowd mostly made up of Labor supporters had gathered at the base of the original Parliament House steps, with Gough Whitlam standing silently at Smith's shoulder. The proclamation concluded:

'Now therefore, I Sir John Robert Kerr, the Governor General of Australia, do by this my Proclamation dissolve the Senate and the House of Representatives.

Given under my Hand and the Great Seal of Australia on 11 November 1975.

By His Excellency's Command,

Malcolm Fraser

Prime Minister.

God Save the Queen!'

Gough Whitlam immediately addressed the crowd when David Smith finished. His spontaneous speech—a mixture of sarcastic word-play and controlled venom—has since passed into Australian folklore.

' Well may we say "God Save the Queen" because nothing will save the Governor-General. The proclamation which you have just heard read by the Governor-General's official secretary was countersigned "Malcolm Fraser" who will undoubtedly go down in Australian history from Remembrance Day, 1975 as "Kerr's cur". They won't silence the outskirts of Parliament House, even if the inside has been silenced for the next few weeks. The Governor-General's proclamation was signed after he already made an appointment to meet the Speaker at a quarter to five. The House of Representatives had requested the Speaker to give the Governor-General its decision that Mr Fraser did not have the confidence of the House and that the Governor-General should call me to form the Government ... Maintain your rage and enthusiasm through the campaign for the election now to be held and until polling day. '

But Whitlam misjudged the mood of the Australian people and the Labor Party lost the 13 December elections by the biggest majority in electoral history. Malcolm Fraser remained Prime Minister until defeated by Bob Hawke in 1983. Although Whitlam and many of Labor's hardcore supporters 'maintained the rage' in the three decades since, Whitlam's relationship towards Malcolm Fraser softened after he left politics in 1977. (Needless to say, Whitlam never again spoke to his former friend, Sir John Kerr, who died in London in 1993.)

The two former Prime Ministers formed something of an 'odd couple' during Australia's Republican debate in the late 1990s, but interestingly, given the opportunity to change the Head of State to an elected or nominated Australian representative, the nation opted to stay part of the British Commonwealth.

Anwar el-Sadat

'Peace With Justice'

Address to the Israeli Knesset, Tel Aviv, 20 November 1977.

Mohammed Anwar el-Sadat (1918-81) was born in the Tala District of Egypt. After the coup that ousted King Farouk in 1952, he succeeded Gamal Abdel Nasser as Egyptian president in 1970. As early as 1971 Sadat had raised the issue of signing a peace agreement with Israel providing that all occupied territories captured during the Six-Day War in 1967 were returned to neighbouring Arab states. During 1972-73 Sadat stated that war was inevitable unless the US forced Israel to accept the United Nations resolution to withdraw from occupied territories.

In 1973-74 Sadat also assumed the role of prime minister—a period in which he presided over Egyptian involvement in the 'Yom Kippur War' against Israel. On the feast of Yom Kippur, 6 October, 1973, the holiest day of the Jewish calendar, Egypt and Syria (backed by nine other Arab states) launched a surprise attack on Israel. The Israeli army recovered brilliantly and Egypt was on the brink of a disastrous defeat when, on 22 October, the United Nations directed all parties to immediately 'terminate all military activity'. With war a diplomatic and military failure, Sadat sought a peaceful end to the conflict by continuing to negotiate with the Israeli government and announced he would be willing to enter into a peace agreement with his country's former enemy.

In an historic move for both Egypt and Israel, Sadat was invited to address the Israeli parliament on 20 November 1977.

＇

In the name of God, Mr. Speaker of the Knesset, ladies and gentlemen, allow me first to thank deeply the Speaker of the Knesset for affording me this opportunity to address you.

As I begin my address I wish to say, peace and the mercy of God Almighty be upon you and may peace be with us all, God willing. Peace for us all, of the Arab lands and in Israel, as well as in every part of this big world, which is so beset by conflicts, perturbed by its deep contradictions, menaced now and then by destructive wars launched by man to annihilate his fellow men.

Finally, amidst the ruins of what man has built among the remains of the victims of mankind there emerges neither victor nor vanquished. The only vanquished remains always a man, God's most sublime creation. Man, whom God has created, as Gandhi, the apostle of peace puts it, to forge ahead, to mold the way of life and to worship God Almighty.

I come to you today on solid ground to shape a new life and to establish peace. We all love this land, the land of God, we all, Moslems, Christians and Jews, all worship God.

Under God, God's teachings and commandments are: love, sincerity, security and peace.

I do not blame all those who received my decision when I announced it to the entire world before the Egyptian People's Assembly. I do not blame all those who received my decision with surprise and even with amazement—some gripped even by violent surprise. Still others interpreted it as political, to camouflage my intentions of launching a new war.

I would go so far as to tell you that one of my aides at the presidential office contacted me at a late hour following my return home from the People's Assembly and sounded worried as he asked me: "Mr. President, what would be our reaction if Israel actually extended an invitation to you?"

I replied calmly: 'I would accept it immediately. I have declared that I would go to the ends of the earth. I would go to Israel, for I want to put before the people of Israel all the facts."

I can see the faces of all those who were astounded by my decision and had doubts as to the sincerity of the intentions behind the declaration of my decision. No one could have ever conceived that the President of the biggest Arab state, which bears the heaviest burden and the main responsibility pertaining to the cause of war and peace in the Middle East, should declare his readiness to go to the land of the adversary while we were still in a state of war.

We all still bear the consequences of four fierce wars waged within 30 years. All this at the time when the families of the 1973 October war are still mourning under the cruel pain of bereavement of father, son, husband and brother.

As I have already declared, I have not consulted as far as this decision is concerned with any of my colleagues or brothers, the Arab heads of state or the confrontation states.

Most of those who contacted me following the declaration of this decision expressed their objection because of the feeling of utter suspicion and absolute lack of confidence between the Arab states and the Palestine people on the one hand and Israel on the other that still surges in us all.

Many months in which peace could have been brought about have been wasted over differences and fruitless discussions on the procedure of convening the Geneva conference. All have shared suspicion and absolute lack of confidence.

But to be absolutely frank with you, I took this decision after long thought, knowing that it constitutes a great risk, for God Almighty has made it my fate to assume responsibility on behalf of the Egyptian people, to share in the responsibility of the Arab nation, the main duty of which, dictated by responsibility, is to exploit all and every means in a bid to save my Egyptian Arab people and the pan-Arab nation from the horrors of new suffering and destructive wars, the dimensions of which are foreseen only by God Himself.

After long thinking, I was convinced that the obligation of responsibility before God and before the people make it incumbent upon me that I should go to the far corners of the world—even to Jerusalem to address members of the Knesset and acquaint them with all the facts surging in me, then I would let you decide for yourselves.

Following this, may God Almighty determine our fate.

Ladies and gentlemen, there are moments in the lives of nations and peoples when it is incumbent upon those known for their wisdom and clarity of vision to survey the problem, with all its complexities and vain memories, in a bold drive toward new horizons.

Those who like us are shouldering the same responsibilities entrusted to us are the first who should have the courage to make determining decisions that are consonant with the magnitude of the circumstances. We must all rise above all forms of obsolete theories of superiority, and the most important thing is never to forget that infallibility is the prerogative of God alone.

'No one could have ever conceived that the President of the biggest Arab state, which bears the heaviest burden and the main responsibility pertaining to the cause of war and peace in the Middle East, should declare his readiness to go to the land of the adversary while we were still in a state of war.'

If I said that I wanted to avert from all the Arab people the horrors of shocking and destructive wars I must sincerely declare before you that I have the same feelings and bear the same responsibility toward all and every man on earth, and certainly toward the Israeli people.

Any life that is lost in war is a human life, be it that of an Arab or an Israeli. A wife who becomes a widow is a human being entitled to a happy family life, whether she be an Arab or an Israeli.

Innocent children who are deprived of the care and compassion of their parents are ours. They are ours, be they living on Arab or Israeli land.

They command our full responsibility to afford them a comfortable life today and tomorrow.

For the sake of them all, for the sake of the lives of all our sons and brothers, for the sake of affording our communities the opportunity to work for the progress and happiness of man, feeling secure and with the right to a dignified life, for the generations to come, for a smile on the face of every child born in our land—for all that I have taken my decision to come to you, despite all the hazards, to deliver my address.

I have shouldered the prerequisites of the historic responsibility and therefore I declared on February 4, 1971, that I was willing to sign a peace agreement with Israel. This was the first declaration made by a

> **'Any life that is lost in war is a human life, be it that of an Arab or an Israeli. A wife who becomes a widow is a human being entitled to a happy family life, whether she be an Arab or an Israeli.'**

responsible Arab official since the outbreak of the Arab-Israeli conflict. Motivated by all these factors dictated by the responsibilities of leadership on October 16, 1973, before the Egyptian People's Assembly, I called for an international conference to establish permanent peace based on justice. I was not heard.

I was in the position of man pleading for peace or asking for a cease-fire, motivated by the duties of history and leadership, I signed the first disengagement agreement, followed by the second disengagement agreement in Sinai.

Then we proceeded, trying both open and closed doors in a bid to find a certain road leading to a durable and just peace.

We opened our heart to the peoples of the entire world to make them understand our motivations and objectives and actually to convince them of the fact that we are advocates of justice and peacemakers. Motivated by all these factors, I also decided to come to you with an open mind and an open heart and with a conscious determination so that we might establish permanent peace based on justice.

It is so fated that my trip to you, which is a journey of peace, coincided with the Islamic feast the holy Feast of the Sacrifice when Abraham—peace be upon him—forefather of the Arabs and Jews, submitted to God, I say, when God Almighty ordered him not out of weakness, but through a giant spiritual force and by free will to sacrifice his very own son, personified a firm and unshakeable belief in ideals that had for mankind a profound significance.

Ladies and gentlemen, let us be frank with each other. Using straightforward words and a clear conception with no ambiguity, let us be frank with each other today while the entire world, both East and West, follows these unparalleled moments which could prove to be a radical turning point in the history of this part of the world if not in the history of the world as a whole.

Let us be frank with each other, let us be frank with each other as we answer this important question:

How can we achieve permanent peace based on justice? Well, I have come to you carrying my clear and frank answer to this big question, so that the people in Israel as well as the entire world may hear it. All those devoted prayers ring in my ears, pleading to God Almighty that this historic meeting may eventually lead to the result aspired to by millions.

Before I proclaim my answer, I wish to assure you that in my clear and frank answer I am availing myself of a number of facts which no one can deny.

The first fact is that no one can build his happiness at the expense of the misery of others.

The second fact: never have I spoken, nor will I ever speak, with two tongues; never have I adopted, nor will I ever adopt, two policies. I never deal with anyone except in one tongue, one policy and with one face.

The third fact: direct confrontation is the nearest and most successful method to reach a clear objective.

The fourth fact: the call for permanent and just peace based on respect for United Nations resolutions has now become the call of the entire world. It has become the expression of the will of the international community, whether in official capitals where policies are made and decisions taken, or at the level of world public opinion, which influences policymaking and decision-taking.

The fifth fact, and this is probably the clearest and most prominent, is that the Arab nation, in its drive for permanent peace based on justice, does not proceed from a position of weakness. On the contrary, it has the power and stability for a sincere will for peace.

The Arab declared intention stems from an awareness prompted by a heritage of civilization, that to avoid an inevitable disaster that will befall us, you and the whole world, there is no alternative to the establishment of permanent peace based on justice, peace that is not swayed by suspicion or jeopardised by ill intentions.

In the light of these facts which I meant to place before you the way I see them, I would also wish to warn you, in all sincerity I warn you, against some thoughts that could cross your minds.

Frankness makes it incumbent upon me to tell you the following:

First, I have not come here for a separate agreement between Egypt and Israel. This is not part of the policy of Egypt. The problem is not that of Egypt and Israel.

An interim peace between Egypt and Israel, or between any Arab confrontation state and Israel, will not bring permanent peace based on justice in the entire region.

Rather, even if peace between all the confrontation states and Israel were achieved in the absence of a just solution of the Palestinian problem, never will there be that durable and just peace upon which the entire world insists.

Second, I have not come to you to seek a partial peace, namely to terminate the state of belligerency at this stage and put off the entire problem to a subsequent stage. This is not the radical solution that would steer us to permanent peace.

Equally, I have not come to you for a third disengagement agreement in Sinai or in Golan or the West Bank. For this would mean that we are merely delaying the ignition of the fuse. It would also mean that we are lacking the courage to face peace, that we are too weak to shoulder the burdens and responsibilities of a durable peace based upon justice.

I have come to you so that together we should build a durable peace based on justice to avoid the shedding of one single drop of blood by both sides. It is for this reason that I have proclaimed my readiness to go to the farthest corner of the earth...

....I repeat with Zachariah: "Love, right and justice." From the holy Koran I quote the following verses: "We believe in God and in what has been revealed to us and what was revealed to Abraham, Ishmael, Isaac, Jacob and the 13 Jewish tribes. And in the books given to Moses and Jesus and the Prophets from their Lord, who made no distinction between them." So we agree, Salam Aleikum—peace be upon you. '

The peace agreement between Egypt and Israel was sponsored by newly-elected US President Jimmy Carter in 1978. Carter invited the Egyptian

President and Israeli Prime Minister Menachem Begin to his presidential retreat at Camp David, resulting in the 1978 Camp David Accord. Sadat and Begin were jointly awarded the Nobel Peace Prize for their efforts, but Sadat was severely criticised for his initiative by other Arab leaders and hard-line Muslims from within his own country. On 6 October, 1981 Sadat was attending a military parade when he was fired upon by five gunmen dressed in black ceremonial uniforms who were part of the official parade. The Egyptian president and five other people were killed in the attack. Sadat's successor, former vice-president Hosni Mubarak, pledged to honour all treaties with the Israelis.

Jimmy Carter

'A Crisis of Confidence'

TV broadcast, Washington DC, 15 July 1979.

Jimmy Carter seemed to be the perfect solution to America's ailing self-belief after Nixon's Watergate scandal and Gerald Ford's inept presidency. Born in Plains, Georgia in 1924, the quietly-spoken, perennially smiling and deeply religious peanut farmer was swept into power during America's Bicentennial Year on a promise that he would never tell the American public a lie. The amazing thing for many commentators was not that the former Georgia governor won the election—that in itself was a miracle (Carter was unheard of before the primaries)—but that he wanted to run in the first place.

Carter faced an uphill struggle to win public confidence but his presidency was ham-strung from the beginning. Although down-to-earth and unassuming, Carter lacked political astuteness to ask for help when he needed it. Rising inflation, stagnant economic growth, unemployment and rising interest rates—compounded by soaring international fuel prices—saw America gripped by an energy crisis in the late 1970s.

The crisis engulfed the Carter administration, which seemed unable to offer any viable solutions to the economic mess in which America found itself. In July 1979 Carter retired to Camp David for eight days to consider recommendations before delivering the following speech to the American people on the night of Sunday, 15 July.

'Exactly three years ago, on July 15, 1976, I accepted the nomination of my party to run for President of the United States.

I promised you a President who is not isolated from the people, who feels your pain, and who shares your dreams and who draws his strength and his wisdom from you.

During the past three years I've spoken to you on many occasions about national concerns, the energy crisis, reorganising the Government, our Nation's economy, and issues of war and especially peace. But over those years the subjects of the speeches, the talks, and the press conferences have become increasingly narrow focused more and more on what the isolated world of Washington thinks is important. Gradually, you've heard more and more about what the Government thinks or what the Government should be doing and less and less about our Nation's hopes, our dreams, and our vision of the future.

> 'The threat is nearly invisible in ordinary ways. It is a crisis of confidence. It is a crisis that strikes at the very heart and soul and spirit of our national will. We can see this crisis in the growing doubt about the meaning of our own lives and in the loss of ... purpose for our Nation.'

Ten days ago I had planned to speak to you again about a very important subject—energy. For the fifth time I would have described the urgency of the problem and laid out a series of legislative recommendations to the Congress. But as I was preparing to speak, I began to ask myself the same question that I now know has been troubling many of you. Why have we not been able to get together as a nation to resolve our serious energy problem?

It's clear that the true problems of our Nation are much deeper— deeper than gasoline lines or energy shortages, deeper even than inflation or recession. And I realise more than ever that as President I need your help. So, I decided to reach out and listen to the voices of America.

I invited to Camp David people from almost every segment of our society—business and labor, teachers and preachers, Governors, mayors, and private citizens. And then I left Camp David to listen to other Americans, men and women like you ... [Carter then outlined a series of comments garnered from the meetings.]

... The threat is nearly invisible in ordinary ways. It is a crisis of confidence. It is a crisis that strikes at the very heart and soul and spirit of our national will. We can see this crisis in the growing doubt about the meaning of our own lives and in the loss of a unity of purpose for our Nation.

The erosion of our confidence in the future is threatening to destroy the social and the political fabric of America.

The confidence that we have always had as a people is not simply some romantic dream or a proverb in a dusty book that we read just on the Fourth of July.

It is the idea which founded our Nation and has guided our development as a people. Confidence in the future has supported everything else—public institutions and private enterprise, our own families, and the very Constitution of the United States. Confidence has defined our course and has served as a link between generations. We've always believed in something called progress. We've always had a faith that the days of our children would be better than our own.

Our people are losing that faith, not only in government itself but in the ability as citizens to serve as the ultimate rulers and shapers of our democracy. As a people we know our past and we are proud of it. Our progress has been part of the living history of America, even the world. We always believed that we were part of a great movement of humanity itself called democracy, involved in the search for freedom, and that belief has always strengthened us in our purpose. But just as we are losing our confidence in the future, we are also beginning to close the door on our past.

In a nation that was proud of hard work, strong families, close-knit communities, and our faith in God, too many of us now tend to worship self- indulgence and consumption. Human identity is no longer defined by what one does, but by what one owns. But we've discovered that owning things and consuming things does not satisfy our longing for meaning. We've learned that piling up material goods cannot fill the emptiness of lives which have no confidence or purpose.

The symptoms of this crisis of the American spirit are all around us. For the first time in the history of our country a majority of our people believe that the next five years will be worse than the past five years. Two-thirds of our people do not even vote. The productivity of American workers is actually dropping, and the willingness of Americans to save for the future has fallen below that of all other people in the Western world.

As you know, there is a growing disrespect for government and for churches and for schools, the news media, and other institutions. This is not a message of happiness or reassurance, but it is the truth and it is a warning.

> 'For the first time in the history of our country a majority of our people believe that the next five years will be worse than the past five years.'

These changes did not happen overnight. They've come upon us gradually over the last generation, years that were filled with shocks and tragedy.

We were sure that ours was a nation of the ballot, not the bullet, until the murders of John Kennedy and Robert Kennedy and Martin Luther King, Jr. We were taught that our armies were always invincible and our causes were always just, only to suffer the agony of Vietnam. We respected the Presidency as a place of honor until the shock of Watergate.

We remember when the phrase "sound as a dollar" was an expression of absolute dependability, until 10 years of inflation began to shrink our dollar and our savings. We believed that our Nation's resources were limitless until 1973, when we had to face a growing dependence on foreign oil.

These wounds are still very deep. They have never been healed. Looking for a way out of this crisis, our people have turned to the Federal Government and found it isolated from the mainstream of our Nation's life. Washington, D.C., has become an island. The gap between our citizens and our Government has never been so wide. The people are looking for honest answers, not easy answers; clear leadership, not false claims and evasiveness and politics as usual.

What you see too often in Washington and elsewhere around the country is a system of government that seems incapable of action. You see a Congress twisted and pulled in every direction by hundreds of well-financed and powerful special interests. You see every extreme position defended to the last vote, almost to the last breath by one unyielding group or another. You often see a balanced and a fair approach that demands sacrifice, a little sacrifice from everyone,

> **'The solution of our energy crisis can also help us to conquer the crisis of the spirit in our country. It can rekindle our sense of unity, our confidence in the future, and give our nation and all of us individually a new sense of purpose.'**

abandoned like an orphan without support and without friends.

Often you see paralysis and stagnation and drift. You don't like it, and neither do I. What can we do? [Carter then proposed six points of government intervention to correct the energy problems facing America in the late 1970s.]

... Our Nation must be fair to the poorest among us, so we will increase aid to needy Americans to cope with rising energy prices. We often think of conservation only in terms of sacrifice. In fact, it is the most painless and immediate way of rebuilding our Nation's strength. Every gallon of oil each one of us saves is a new form of production. It gives us more freedom, more confidence, that much more control over our own lives.

So, the solution of our energy crisis can also help us to conquer the crisis of the spirit in our country. It can rekindle our sense of unity, our confidence in the future, and give our Nation and all of us individually a new sense of purpose.

You know we can do it. We have the natural resources. We have more oil in our shale alone than several Saudi Arabias. We have more coal than any nation on Earth. We have the world's highest level of technology. We have the most skilled work force, with innovative genius, and I firmly believe that we have the national will to win this war.

I do not promise you that this struggle for freedom will be easy. I do not promise a quick way out of our Nation's problems, when the truth is that the only way out is an all-out effort. What I do promise you is that I will lead our fight, and I will enforce fairness in our struggle, and I will ensure honesty.

And above all, I will act. We can manage the short-term shortages more effectively and we will, but there are no short-term solutions to our long-range problems. There is simply no way to avoid sacrifice.

Twelve hours from now I will speak again in Kansas City, to expand and to explain further our energy program. Just as the search for solutions to our energy shortages has now led us to a new awareness of our Nation's deeper problems, so our willingness to work for those solutions in energy can strengthen us to attack those deeper problems.

I will continue to travel this country, to hear the people of America. You can help me to develop a national agenda for the 1980s. I will listen and I will act. We will act together. These were the promises I made three years ago, and I intend to keep them.

Little by little we can and we must rebuild our confidence. We can spend until we empty our treasuries, and we may summon all the wonders of science. But we can succeed only if we tap our greatest resources-America's people, America's values, and America's confidence.

I have seen the strength of America in the inexhaustible resources of our people. In the days to come, let us renew that strength in the struggle for an energy secure nation.

In closing, let me say this: I will do my best, but I will not do it alone. Let your voice be heard. Whenever you have a chance, say something good about our country. With God's help and for the sake of our Nation, it is time for us to join hands in America. Let us commit ourselves together to a rebirth of the American spirit ... working together with our common faith we cannot fail.

Thank you and good night.'

It was Jimmy Carter's handling of foreign policy that finally brought about his political downfall. He had several important international victories—handing back control of the Panama Canal, normalising relations with China and sponsoring talks between Egypt and Israel.

But when 52 Americans were taken hostage by Iranian extremists in Teheran on 4 November 1979, his presidency was shaken to its core. Carter's inability to resolve the issue through diplomatic means, and a failed military rescue that resulted in the loss of lives in April 1980, saw him soundly defeated by

Republican candidate Ronald Reagan at the end of the year.

Despite his openness and earnestness, Carter had failed to inspire the nation's imagination and restore the confidence it so badly wanted.

However, since his defeat over 25 years ago, Jimmy Carter has continued to grow in statesmanship. Dedicating his public life to humanitarian causes he has been involved an international observer and mediator in many of the world's conflicts—Nicaragua, Panama, Sudan, Ethiopia and North Korea—and remains an important advocate for the rights of the poor and oppressed.

The Big Chill
1980-1989

Indira Gandhi

'True Liberation of Women'

New Delhi, India, 26 March 1980.

The Nehru-Gandhi 'dynasty' in modern Indian politics is as important—and equally tragic—as the Kennedy family in the United States of America. Indira Gandhi (1917-84) was the daughter of Jawaharla Nehru, the first Prime Minister of India. After studying at Oxford she married Feroze Khan in 1942, a Moslem, and converted from her family's Hindu religion against the wishes of her parents. In order to facilitate the inter-caste marriage, Mahatma Gandhi 'adopted' Khan (whose mother's maiden name was the Persian derivative 'Ghandy') but although the marriage produced two sons (Rajiv and Sanjay) it was not a success. Indira Gandhi later became president of the Indian Congress Party (1959-60) and following the death of Lal Shastri, Prime Minister of India in 1966. During the 1970s she struggled to contain national sectarian violence. After her conviction for electoral malpractice in 1975, she declared a state of emergency that was kept in place for two years. Defeated in 1977 she returned for a second term as Prime Minister in 1980.

In March 1980 she outlined the true liberation of women at the inauguration of the All-India Women's Conference Building Complex in New Delhi.

'For several decades the All-India Women's Conference has been the organised voice of the women of India. I have never been a member of any women's organisation but have been interested enough to keep track of their activities and to lend the helping hand whenever I could.

I am glad that at long last the All-India Women's Conference has a home of its own and it is named after one of the best known and most remarkable women of our times, Sarojini Naidu, feminine to the core but well able to hold her own in the world of men, whether in letters or in politics.

> 'There is no time to lose and it involves a tremendous task of educating. We want to walk together and in step with all others, but if men hesitate, should not women show the way?'

To add to the importance of the occasion and to give it a touch of elegance, we have in our midst His Highness the Aga Khan and Her Highness the Begum Aga Khan. They are friends of India and have founded or encouraged many projects for education, health and other aspects of welfare. But for their timely and generous help, this complex would not have been ready today. Nor would we have before us the attractive Aga Khan Hall. We welcome them and wish them well in their work.

I see before me a number of eminent women who have distinguished themselves in various professions—in social work, in education, in science, in administration, in law and, of course, in politics. They must all feel gratified to see the completion of this building. I have often said that I am not a feminist. Yet, in my concern for the underprivileged, how can I ignore women who, since the beginning of history, have been dominated over and discriminated against in social customs and in laws. How insidious and all-pervasive is this attitude of male' superiority is revealed in the vocabulary of the languages the world over. And this is unquestioningly accepted and acquiesced in by all but a minuscule minority of men and also women. Currently I am reading a book titled World and Women. I learned from it what Mr. Ling White, the President of Mills College in the USA, wrote of the use of masculine generic pronouns. I quote: "The penetration of the habit of language into the minds of little girls as they grow up to be women is more profound than most people, including most women, have realised. For, it implies that personality is really a male attribute and that women are a sub or a human sub-species." The author goes on to say that it is time we looked more carefully where the thoughtless use of stereotypes is taking us. "Man as leader, woman as

> **'By excluding women, men are depriving themselves of a fuller emancipation or growth for themselves.'**

follower; man as producer, woman as consumer; man as strength, woman as weakness; this is the cosmography that has brought us to man as aggressor and humanity the victim."

Hence, by excluding women, men are depriving themselves of a fuller emancipation or growth for themselves.

In the West, women's so-called freedom is often equated with imitation of man. Frankly, I feel that is merely an exchange of one kind of bondage for another. To be liberated, woman must feel free to be herself, not in rivalry to man but in the context of her own capacity and her personality. We need women to be more interested, more alive and more active not because they are women but because they do comprise half the human race. Whether they like it or not, they cannot escape their responsibility nor should they be denied its benefits. Indian women are traditionally conservative but they also have the genius of synthesis, to adapt and to absorb. That is what gives them resilience to face suffering and to meet upheavals with a degree of calm, to change constantly and yet remain changeless, which is the quality of India herself.

Today's major concerns are: first, economic and social inequality and injustice between the affluent and developing countries and within countries. Secondly, the anxiety whether human wisdom will prevail over what can only be called a death wish in which the desire to dominate expresses itself in countless ways, the most dangerous being the armament race. And, thirdly, the need to protect this, our only Earth, from human rapacity and exploitation. Only recently have we awakened to the awareness of ancient truths regarding our own utter dependence on the balance of Nature and its resources.

These enormous challenges cannot be met only by some sections, however advanced they may be, while others pull in different directions or watch apathetically. The effort has to be a universal one, conscious and concerted, considering no one too small to contribute. The effort must embrace all nationalities and all classes regardless of religion, caste or sex.

There is no time to lose and it involves a tremendous task of educating. We want to walk together and in step with all others, but if men hesitate, should not women show the way? So, while complimenting the All-India Women's Conference, especially its President, Smt. Lakshmi Raghuramaiah, on their achievements, I dedicate to the nation this building complex of the All-India Women's Conference. '

One of the great ironies of Indira Gandhi's political career was that a predominantly non-Christian country (Hindu/Muslim) would democratically elect a woman as its leader (twice) when some western governments (USA and Australia) have yet to cross that gender barrier. On 31 October 1984 Indira Gandhi was gunned down by her Sikh body guards as she walked through the garden of her New Delhi home to meet with actor Peter Ustinov who was making a documentary about her.

In June that year, Indian troops had stormed the Golden Temple in Amritsar in order to end a four-day siege by Sikh militants. (Most commentators saw this as the reason for her murder.) She was succeeded as Prime Minister by her eldest son, Rajiv Gandhi. The elder Gandhi heir was a pilot of India Airlines but his mother sponsored his political career following the death of his younger brother Sanjiv, in 1980.

When general elections were held later that year, Gandhi's Congress Party won with a record majority. In November 1989, Rajiv Gandhi resigned as Premier but suffered a similar fate to his mother when he was assassinated by Tamil separatists in May 1991 while campaigning in Madras.

Margaret Thatcher

'The Falklands War'

Cheltenham, England, 3 July 1982.

The 'Iron Lady' of world politics during the 1980s and Britain's first female Prime Minister was born Margaret Hilda Roberts above a shop in Grantham, Lincolnshire in 1925. An Oxford graduate and research chemist, she married Dennis Thatcher in 1951 before becoming a lawyer. The Conservative Party member for Finchley in 1959, she replaced Edward Heath as Opposition Leader in 1975. In 1979, the Conservative Party was swept to power and Margaret Thatcher duly became Britain's first female Prime Minister.

Under Thatcher's leadership, the Conservative Party privatised national industries and institutions such as education, health care and local government services. Despite presiding over the worst unemployment figures since the Depression, Thatcher's government was re-elected with an increased majority in 1983. The reasons for this were two-fold: the lack of an organised Opposition Party and public support for her after the Falklands War in 1982.

On 2 April, 1982 Argentinean troops invaded the Falkland Islands in the southern Atlantic Ocean. The Falklands, 770 kilometres north-east of Cape Horn, had been a British Crown Colony since 1833 but for many years Argentina had laid claim to the islands (which they called Islas Malvinas). As Prime Minister, Margaret Thatcher immediately sent a task force of 30 warships, and some 10 000 troops, to liberate the two larger islands, East and West Falkland.

By 12 April Britain had established a 200-mile exclusion zone around the islands and had recaptured South Georgia, a Falklands dependency to the south-west, by the end of the month. On 1 May the RAF conducted a Vulcan bomber raid on Stanley, the islands' capital, on East Falkland. Many lives were lost on both sides; most notably for Britain on the HMS Antelope and HMS Coventry, while the HMS Sheffield was hit by Exocet missile and the Atlantic

Conveyor was also sunk. Then, on 28 May, the second battalion of the Parachute Regiment recaptured Goose Green, on the south-west part of East Falkland, and infantry brigades landed at San Carlos, in the north-west corner, three days later.

Although the war had turned in Britain's favour it suffered massive losses on 8 June when the RFA Sir Galahad and RFA Sir Tristram were attacked during the transfer of troops to Fitzroy, south-west of Stanley, and the HMS Fearless was sunk in Choiseul Sound. Within a week, General Mario Menendez, the leader of the Argentinean troops in the Falklands surrendered. The Falklands were recaptured, at a price—255 Britons killed and 777 wounded, 635 Argentineans killed and 1068 wounded.

This speech exemplifies the way Margaret Thatcher used Britain's military success to reverse her polls rating as the 'least popular' Prime Minister of modern times to win the 1983 general election. Thatcher remarked at the time: 'It's exciting to have a real crisis on your hands, when you have spent half your political life dealing with humdrum issues like the environment.'

'Today we meet in the aftermath of the Falklands Battle. Our country has won a great victory and we are entitled to be proud. This nation had the resolution to do what it knew had to be done—to do what it knew was right.

We fought to show that aggression does not pay, and that the robber cannot be allowed to get away with his swag. We fought with the support of so many throughout the world: the Security Council, the Commonwealth, the European Community, and the United States. Yet we also fought alone—for we fought for our own people and for our own sovereign territory.

Now that it is all over, things cannot be the same again, for we have learnt something about ourselves -a lesson which we desperately needed to learn. When we started out, there were the waverers and the faint-hearts: the people who thought that Britain could no longer seize

'For we have learnt something about ourselves—a lesson which we desperately needed to learn. When we started out, there were the waverers and the faint-hearts: the people who thought that Britain could no longer seize the initiative for herself.'

the initiative for herself; the people who thought we could no longer do the great things which we once did; and those who believed that our decline was irreversible—that we could never again be what we were. There were those who would not admit it—even perhaps some here today—people who would have strenuously denied the suggestion but—in their heart of hearts—they too had their secret fears that it was true: that Britain was no longer the nation that had built an Empire and ruled a quarter of the world.

Well, they were wrong. The lesson of the Falklands is that Britain has not changed and that this nation still has those sterling qualities which shine through our history. This generation can match their fathers and grandfathers in ability, in courage, and in resolution. We have not changed. When the demands of war and the dangers to our own people call us to arms—then we British are as we have always been—competent, courageous and resolute.

When called to arms—ah, that's the problem. It took the battle in the South Atlantic for the shipyards to adapt ships way ahead of time; for dockyards to refit merchantmen and cruise liners, to fix helicopter platforms, to convert hospital ships—all faster than was thought possible; it took the demands of war for every stop to be pulled out and every man and woman to do their best.

British people had to be threatened by foreign soldiers and British territory invaded and then—why then—the response was incompar¬able. Yet why does it need a war to bring out our qualities and reassert our pride? Why do we have to be invaded before we throw aside our selfish aims and begin to work together as only we can work, and achieve as only we can achieve?

That really is the challenge we as a nation face today. We have to see that the spirit of the South Atlantic—the real spirit of Britain—is kindled not only by war but can now be fired by peace.

We have the first prerequisite. We know we can do it-we haven't lost the ability. That is the Falklands Factor. We have proved ourselves to ourselves. It is a lesson we must not now forget. Indeed, it is a lesson which we must apply to peace just as we have learnt it in war. The faltering and the self-doubt has given way to achievement and pride.

We have the confidence and we must use it.

Just look at the Task Force as an object lesson. Every man had his own task to do and did it superbly. Officers and men, senior NCO and newest recruit—every one realised that his contribution was essential for the success of the whole. All were equally valu¬able—each was differently qualified. By working together, each was able to do more than his best. As a team they raised the average to the level of the best and by each doing his utmost together they achieved the impossible. That's an accurate picture of Britain at war— not yet of Britain at peace. But the spirit has stirred and the nation has begun to assert itself. Things are not going to be the same again.'

'But the spirit has stirred and the nation has begun to assert itself. Things are not going to be the same again.'

In 1987 Margaret Thatcher became the first Prime Minister since the nineteenth century to win three consecutive elections. But Thatcher's autocratic prime ministerial style and her attitude towards the European Community ultimately split her own cabinet and led to her downfall. When Sir Geoffrey Howe, the Leader of the Commons and the last remaining member of her original cabinet in 1979, was publicly critical of her when announcing his resignation in November 1990, Thatcher's days as Prime Minister were numbered. Michael Heseltine was the first to challenge for the leadership of the Conservative Party and when Thatcher could not gather the necessary support to survive the first round of voting, she withdrew from the leadership race. John Major was elected her eventual successor.

Margaret Thatcher was made a life peer of the realm, becoming Lady Thatcher, in 1992.

Jesse Jackson

'Keep Hope Alive'

Atlanta, Georgia, 19 July, 1988

The first African American presidential candidate in US history to be a major political force, Jesse Louis Jackson was born in 1941 in Greenville, South Carolina, the son of a 17-year-old, unmarried high school student. When his mother married Charles Jackson, Jesse took his stepfather's surname and later won a football scholarship to the University of Illinois. Jackson returned to the South during his first year of University and transferred to North Carolina Agricultural and Technical College and received a BA in Sociology. He then accepted a Rockefeller grant to attend the Chicago Theological Seminary where he planned to train as a Baptist minister. There Jackson became involved in the Civil Rights movement and although he was later ordained a minister, he left CTS in 1966 without finishing his course work.

Jackson joined Martin Luther King Jnr and the Southern Christian Leadership Conference in 1965 and was directly involved in the 'Chicago Freedom' movement the following year. In April 1968 Jackson was with King in Alabama when the Civil Rights leader was assassinated. He later resigned from the SCLC to found his own organisation, People United to Save Humanity (PUSH) in 1971.

Jackson's bold ambition, and his alleged misrepresentation of his role in the Civil Rights movement, put him offside with many black leaders but he continually proved himself to be an articulate and charismatic speaker on such as issues as education, welfare support and political representation.

In 1984 Jackson launched his first campaign for the Democratic presidential nomination and performed well in several southern states including Alabama, Georgia, Louisiana and Florida, but not enough to secure the nomination. Four years later his political campaign was better co-ordinated and his 'Rainbow Coalition' attracted widespread support from urban blacks, feminists and other minorities.

Although Michael Dukakis was the party's eventual choice as presidential nominee, Jackson's 19 July speech saw him accept the nomination for Vice-President:

'And then, for our children, young America, hold your head high now. We can win. We must not lose you to drugs and violence, premature pregnancy, suicide, cynicism, pessimism and despair. We can win.'

'I'm often asked, "Jesse, why do you take on these tough issues? They're not very ... political. We can't win that way."

If an issue is morally right, it will eventually be political. It may be political and never be right. Fannie Lou Hamer didn't have the most votes in Atlantic City, but her principles have outlasted every delegate who voted to lock her out. Rosa Parks did not have the most votes, but she was morally right. Dr King didn't have the most votes about the Vietnam War, but he was morally right. If we're principled first, our politics will fall in place.

"Jesse, why did you take these big bold initiatives?" A poem by an unknown author went something like this: We mastered the air, we've conquered the sea, and annihilated distance and prolonged life, we were not wise enough to live on this earth without war and without hate.

As for Jesse Jackson, I'm tired of sailing my little boat, far inside the harbor bar. I want to go out where the big ships float, out on the deep where the great ones are. And should my frail craft prove too slight, the waves that sweep those billows o'er, I'd rather go down in a stirring fight than drown to death in the sheltered shore. We've got to go out, my friends, where the big boats are.

And then, for our children, young America, hold your head high now. We can win. We must not lose you to drugs and violence, premature pregnancy, suicide, cynicism, pessimism and despair. We can win.

Wherever you are tonight, I challenge you to hope and to dream. Don't submerge your dreams. Exercise above all else, even on drugs, dream of the day you're drug-free. Even in the gutter, dream of the day that you'll be upon your feet again. You must never stop dreaming. Face reality, yes. But don't stop with the way things are; dream of things as they ought to be. Dream. Face pain, but love, hope, faith, and dreams will help you rise above the pain.

Use hope and imagination as weapons of survival and progress, but you keep on dreaming, young America. Dream of peace. Peace is rational and reasonable. War is irrational in this age and unwinnable.

Dream of teachers who teach for life and not for living. Dream of doctors who are concerned more about public health than private wealth. Dream of lawyers more concerned about justice than a judgeship. Dream of preachers who are concerned more about prophecy than profiteering. Dream on the high road of sound values. And in America, as we go forth to September, October and November and then beyond, America must never surrender to a high moral challenge.

Do not surrender to drugs. The best drug policy is a no first use. Don't surrender with needles and cynicism. Let's have no first use on the one hand, or clinics on the other. Never surrender, young America.

Go forward. America must never surrender to malnutrition. We can feed the hungry and clothe the naked. We must never surrender. We must go forward. We must never surrender to illiteracy. Invest in our children. Never surrender; and go forward.

We must never surrender to inequality. Women cannot compromise ERA [the Equal Rights Amendment] or comparable worth. Women are making 60 cents on the dollar to what a man makes. Women cannot buy milk cheaper. Women deserve to get paid for the work that you do. It's right and it's fair. Don't surrender, my friends. Those who have AIDS tonight, you deserve our compassion. Even with AIDS you must not surrender in your wheelchairs. I see you sitting here tonight in those wheelchairs. I've starved with you. I've reached out to you across our nation. Don't you give up. I know it's tough sometimes. People look down on you. It took you a little more effort to get here tonight.

And no one should look down on you, but sometimes mean people do. The only justification we have for looking down on someone is that we're going to stop and pick them up. But even in your wheelchairs, don't you give up. We cannot forget fifty years ago when our backs were against the wall, [Franklin D.] Roosevelt was in a wheelchair. I would rather have Roosevelt in a wheelchair than Reagan and [George] Bush on a horse. Don't you surrender and don't give up.

Don't surrender and don't give up. Why can I challenge you this way? "Jesse Jackson, you don't understand my situation. You be on television. You don't understand. I see you with the big people. You don't understand my situation." I understand.

> '**I wasn't born in the hospital [but] in a three-room house, bathroom in the backyard, slop jar by the bed, no hot and cold running water. I understand.**'

You're seeing me on TV but you don't know the me that makes me, me. They wonder why does Jesse run, because they see me running for the White House. They don't see the house I'm running from.

I have a story. I wasn't always on television. Writers were not always outside my door. When I was born late one afternoon, October 8th, in Greenville, SC, no writers asked my mother her name. Nobody chose to write down her address. My mama was not supposed to make it. And I was not supposed to make it. You see, I was born to a teenage mother who was born to a teenage mother.

I understand. I know abandonment and people being mean to you, and saying you're nothing and nobody, and can never be anything. I understand. Jesse Jackson is my third name. I'm adopted. When I had no name, my grandmother gave me her name. My name was Jesse Burns until I was twelve. So I wouldn't have a blank space, she gave me a name to hold me over. I understand when nobody knows your name. I understand when you have no name. I understand.

I wasn't born in the hospital—Mama didn't have insurance. I was born in the bed at the house. I really do understand. Born in a three-room house, bathroom in the backyard, slop jar by the bed, no hot and cold running water. I understand. Wallpaper used for decoration—No. For a windbreaker. I understand. I'm a working person's person, that's why I understand you whether you're black or white.

I understand work. I was not born with a silver spoon in my mouth. I had a shovel programmed for my hand. My mother, a working woman. So many days she went to work with runs in her stockings. She knew better, but she wore runs in her stockings so that my brother and I could have matching socks and not be laughed at at school.

I understand. At three o'clock on Thanksgiving Day we couldn't eat turkey because mama was preparing someone else's turkey at three o'clock. We had to play football to entertain ourselves and then around six o'clock she would get off the Alta Vista bus when we would bring up the leftovers and eat our turkey—leftovers, the carcass, the cranberries around eight o'clock at night. I really do understand.

Every one of these funny labels they put on you, those of you who are watching this broadcast tonight in the projects, on the corners, I understand. Call you outcast, low down, you can't make it, you're nothing, you're from nobody, subclass, underclass—when you see Jesse Jackson, when my name goes in nomination, your name goes in nomination.

I was born in the slum, but the slum was not born in me. And it wasn't born in you, and you can make it. Wherever you are tonight you can make it. Hold your head high, stick your chest out. You can make it. It gets dark sometimes, but the morning comes. Don't you surrender. Suffering breeds character. Character breeds faith. In the end faith will not disappoint.

You must not surrender. You may or may not get there, but just know that you're qualified and you hold on and hold out. We must never surrender. America will get better and better. Keep hope alive. Keep hope alive. Keep hope alive. On tomorrow night and beyond, keep hope alive.

I love you very much. I love you very much.'

The 1988 Presidential race was won by Republican candidate George Bush and Jackson moved from Chicago to Washington DC where he was elected the District of Columbia's 'statehood senator'–a position created to press for the district's statehood. During the 1980s and 1990s Jackson often acted as international peace negotiator and although there were some important successes, he drew criticism for embracing the PLO, Fidel Castro and the Marxist Sandinista government of Nicaragua (his description of New York as 'Hymie Town' was another error of judgment). In 2000 he finally graduated from the Chicago Theological Seminary.

Ryan White

'I Have AIDS'

Testimony before the President's Commission on AIDS, Washington DC, 1988.

In the early 1980s, cases of a retrovirus that infected the cells of the human immune system were first diagnosed in the United States and Europe (although it was later thought the disease had its origins in Africa). Human Immunodeficiency Virus, which was researched by scientists on both sides of the Atlantic, was not officially named until 1986. Although it was known that HIV was the underlying cause of AIDS (Acquired Immune Deficiency Syndrome) the causes, methods of trans-mission and suitable treatment was originally the source of much controversy.

Originally viewed as a disease that only affected the homosexual community, it soon became clear that HIV/AIDS was indiscriminate in choosing its victims and was transferable through penetrative sexual contact, blood transfusion, the sharing of contaminated needles and between mother and infant during pregnancy, childbirth and breast-feeding.

Kokomo, Indiana schoolboy Ryan White contacted HIV/AIDS in 1984 when he was given a blood transfusion during an operation to remove part of his lung. A haemophiliac since birth, the 13-year-old was unknowingly susceptible to contracting the disease and was given only six months to live. Despite the fact that he was determined to live his life as normally as possible, Ryan White and his family came up against systematic discrimination and small-town prejudice.

His school tried to keep him from attending and, after several legal battles, the White family settled with the school and agreed to use separate bathrooms and disposable servery materials in the cafeteria. Even then, the discrimination did not stop; ignorance and misunderstanding about Ryan's condition led the White family to pack up home and move from Kokomo, Indiana to Cicero, Indiana.

> 'I was labelled a troublemaker, my mom an unfit mother, and I was not welcome anywhere. People would get up and leave so they would not have to sit anywhere near me. Even at church, people would not shake my hand.'

In 1988, as the world gradually began to understand the causes and effects—especially the social effects—of contracting HIV/AIDS, Ryan White addressed the President's Commission on AIDS, Washington DC. White's story did more to combat AIDS-related discrimination and shamed the Reagan government to become more proactive in its research funding and education programs than any other person.

'Thank You, Commissioners:

My name is Ryan White. I am sixteen years old. I have haemophilia, and I have AIDS.

When I was three days old, the doctors told my parents I was a severe haemophiliac, meaning my blood does not clot. Lucky for me, there was a product just approved by the Food and Drug Administration. It was called Factor VIII, which contains the clotting agent found in blood.

While I was growing up, I had many bleeds or haemorrhages in my joints which make it very painful. Twice a week I would receive injections or IVs of Factor VIII which clotted the blood and then broke it down. A bleed occurs from a broken blood vessel or vein. The blood then had nowhere to go so it would swell up in a joint. You could compare it to trying to pour a quart of milk into a pint-sized container of milk.

The first five to six years of my life were spent in and out of the hospital. All in all I led a pretty normal life. Most recently my battle has been against AIDS and the discrimination surrounding it. On December 17, 1984, I had surgery to remove two inches of my left lung due to pneumonia. After two hours of surgery the doctors told my mother I had AIDS. I contracted AIDS through my Factor VIII which is made from blood. When I came out of surgery, I was on a respirator and had a tube in my left lung. I spent Christmas and the next thirty days in the hospital. A lot of my time was spent searching, thinking and planning my life.

I came face to face with death at thirteen years old. I was diagnosed with AIDS: a killer. Doctors told me I'm not contagious. Given six months to live, and being the fighter that I am, I set high goals for myself. It was my decision to live a normal life, go to school, be with my friends, and enjoying day to day activities. It was not going to be easy.

'AIDS can destroy a family if you let it, but luckily for my sister and me, Mom taught us to keep going. Don't give up, be proud of who you are, and never feel sorry for yourself.'

The school I was going to said they had no guidelines for a person with AIDS. The school board, my teachers, and my principal voted to keep me out of the classroom even after the guidelines were set by the I.S.B.H., for fear of someone getting AIDS from me by casual contact. Rumors of sneezing, kissing, tears, sweat, and saliva spreading AIDS caused people to panic.

We began a series of court battles for nine months, while I was attending classes by telephone. Eventually, I won the right to attend school, but the prejudice was still there. Listening to medical facts was not enough. People wanted one hundred percent guarantees. There are no one hundred percent guarantees in life, but concessions were made by Mom and me to help ease the fear. We decided to meet them halfway:

- Separate restrooms
- No gym
- Separate drinking fountains
- Disposable eating utensils and trays

Even though we knew AIDS was not spread through casual contact. Nevertheless, parents of twenty students started their own school. They were still not convinced. Because of the lack of education on AIDS, discrimination, fear, panic, and lies surrounded me:

- I became the target of Ryan White jokes
- Lies about me biting people
- Spitting on vegetables and cookies

- Urinating on bathroom walls
- Some restaurants threw away my dishes
- My school locker was vandalised inside and folders were marked FAG and other obscenities.

I was labelled a troublemaker, my mom an unfit mother, and I was not welcome anywhere. People would get up and leave so they would not have to sit anywhere near me. Even at church, people would not shake my hand.

This brought on the news media, TV crews, interviews, and numerous public appearances. I became known as the AIDS boy. I received thousands of letters of support from all around the world, all because I wanted to go to school. Mayor Koch, of New York, was the first public figure to give me support. Entertainers, athletes, and stars started giving me support. I met some of the greatest like Elton John, Greg Louganis, Max Headroom, Alyssa Milano (my teen idol), Lyndon King (Los Angeles Raiders), and Charlie Sheen. All of these plus many more became my friends, but I had very few friends at school. How could these people in the public eye not be afraid of me, but my whole town was?

'**Hamilton Heights High School is proof that AIDS education in schools works.**'

It was difficult, at times, to handle; but I tried to ignore the injustice, because I knew the people were wrong. My family and I held no hatred for those people because we realised they were victims of their own ignorance. We had great faith that with patience, understanding, and education, that my family and I could be helpful in changing their minds and attitudes around. Financial hardships were rough on us, even though Mom had a good job at G.M. The more I was sick, the more work she had to miss. Bills became impossible to pay. My sister, Andrea, was a championship roller skater who had to sacrifice too. There was no money for her lessons and travel. AIDS can destroy a family if you let it, but luckily for my sister and me, Mom taught us to keep going. Don't give up, be proud of who you are, and never feel sorry for yourself.

After two and a half years of declining health, two attacks of pneumocystis, shingles, a rare form of whooping cough, and liver problems, I faced fighting chills, fevers, coughing, tiredness, and vomiting. I was very ill and being tutored at home. The desire to move into a bigger house, to avoid living AIDS daily, and a dream to be accepted by a community and school, became possible and a reality with a movie about my life, The Ryan White Story.

My life is better now. At the end of the school year (1986-87), my family and I decided to move to Cicero, Indiana. We did a lot of hoping and praying that the community would welcome us, and they did. For the first time in three years, we feel we have a home, a supportive school, and lots of friends. The communities of Cicero, Atlanta, Arcadia, and Noblesville, Indiana, are now what we call "home." I'm feeling great. I am a normal happy teenager again. I have a learner's permit. I attend sports functions and dances. My studies are important to me. I made the honor role just recently, with 2 As and 2 Bs. I'm just one of the kids, and all because the students at Hamilton Heights High School listened to the facts, educated their parents and themselves, and believed in me.

I believe in myself as I look forward to graduating from Hamilton Heights High School in 1991.

Hamilton Heights High School is proof that AIDS education in schools works.'

Ryan White's story focused national and international attention on HIV/AIDS. Congress later passed the $1.8 billion Ryan White Comprehensive AIDS Resources Emergency (CARE) Act that sought to address the unmet health needs of people living with HIV by funding primary health care and support services. Ryan White passed away from the effects of his disease on April 8 1990, aged 18, but his short life made an extraordinary impact.

The Dawn of Enlightment 1990-1999

Mikhail Gorbachev

'Dissolving the Soviet Union'

Televised address, 25 December 1991.

Mikhail Sergeyevich Gorbachev was born in Privolyne, Russia in 1931. A member of the Communist Party since 1952, he rose through the ranks of the Party Central Committee and upon the death of Konstantin Chernenko in 1985, became party general secretary of the Central Committee. In the 1980s Gorbachev undertook two wide-reaching programs—openness (glasnost) and reconstruction (perestroika)—to modernise the Soviet Union and its failing economy. In 1988 he became chairman of the Presidium of the Supreme Soviet and two years later was named the first—and last—executive president of the USSR.

Paradoxically, Gorbachev's reforms brought about the end of the Communist regime that he sought to maintain. Gorbachev's reforms created greater domestic freedoms, reduced military spending and promoted a healthier relationship with the West.

In 1989 Soviet troops withdrew from Afghanistan, the Communist Party voted to end 'one party rule' and Soviet republics threatened to leave the Union to govern themselves.

One of the most powerful undertakings Gorbachev was involved in was to publicly 'reinstate' the reputations of thousands of citizens jailed and executed under the Stalin regime in the 1930s and 1940s. This had a strong effect on the nation's consciousness and how the country viewed itself nationally.

In August 1991 Gorbachev survived an attempted coup in Moscow—rescued by newly elected Russian Federative President Boris Yelstsin who organised the seizure of government buildings in Moscow and then banned the Communist Party. This shift in the political and social mood of the country led to the establishment of the Commonwealth of Independent States.

On (Western Christendom's) Christmas Day, 1991, Mikhail Gorbachev resigned as president of the Union of Soviet Socialist Republics. This was the final act in an ironically peaceful dissolution of a communist (socialist) nation that had been borne in so much bloodshed and maintained by fear and oppression since the October Revolution in 1917.

'Dear compatriots, fellow citizens, as a result of the newly formed situation, creation of the Commonwealth of Independent States, I cease my activities in the post of the USSR president. I am taking this decision out of considerations based on principle. I have firmly stood for independence, self-rule of nations, for the sovereignty of the republics, but at the same time for preservation of the union state, the unity of the country.

Events went a different way. The policy prevailed of dismembering this country and disuniting the state, with which I cannot agree. And after the Alma-Ata meeting and the decisions taken there, my position on this matter has not changed. Besides, I am convinced that decisions of such scale should have been taken on the basis of a popular expression of will.

Yet, I will continue to do everything in my power so that agreements signed there should lead to real accord in the society, (and) facilitate the escape from the crisis and the reform process. Addressing you for the last time in the capacity of president of the USSR, I consider it necessary to express my evaluation of the road we have travelled since 1985, especially as there are a lot of contradictory, superficial and subjective judgments on that matter.

'The society was suffocating … doomed to serve ideology and bear the terrible burden of the arms race. We could not go on living like that. Everything had to be changed radically.'

Fate had it that when I found myself at the head of the state it was already clear that all was not well in the country. There is plenty of everything: land, oil and gas, other natural riches, and God gave us lots of intelligence and talent, yet we lived much worse than developed countries and keep falling behind them more and more.

The reason could already be seen: The society was suffocating in the vice of the command-bureaucratic system, doomed to serve ideology and bear the terrible burden of the arms race. It had reached the limit of its possibilities. All attempts at partial reform, and there had been many, had suffered defeat, one after another. The country was losing perspective. We could not go on living like that. Everything had to be changed radically.

The process of renovating the country and radical changes in the world turned out to be far more complicated than could be expected. However, what has been done ought to be given its due. This society acquired freedom, liberated itself politically and spiritually, and this is the foremost achievement which we have not yet understood completely, because we have not learned to use freedom.

However, work of historic significance has been accomplished. The totalitarian system which deprived the country of an opportunity to become successful and prosperous long ago has been eliminated. A breakthrough has been achieved on the way to democratic changes. Free elections, freedom of the press, religious freedoms, representative organs of power, a multiparty (system) became a reality; human rights are recognised as the supreme principle.

The movement to a diverse economy has started, equality of all forms of property is becoming established, people who work on the land are coming to life again in the framework of land reform, farmers have appeared, millions of acres of land are being given over to people who live in the countryside and in towns.

Economic freedom of the producer has been legalised, and entrepreneurship, shareholding, privatisation are gaining momentum. In turning the economy toward a market, it is important to remember that all this is done for the sake of the individual. At this difficult time, all should be done for his social protection, especially for senior citizens and children.

We live in a new world. The Cold War has ended, the arms race has stopped, as has the insane militarisation which mutilated our economy, public psyche and morals. The threat of a world war has been removed. Once again I want to stress that on my part everything was done during the transition period to preserve reliable control of the nuclear weapons.

We opened ourselves to the world, gave up interference into other people's affairs, the use of troops beyond the borders of the country, and trust, solidarity and respect came in response.

'**Economic freedom of the producer has been legalised, and entrepreneurship, shareholding, privatisation are gaining momentum.**'

The nations and peoples of this country gained real freedom to choose the way of their self-determination. The search for a democratic reformation of the multinational state brought us to the threshold of concluding a new Union Treaty. All these changes demanded immense strain. They were carried out with sharp struggle, with growing resistance from the old, the obsolete forces.

The old system collapsed before the new one had time to begin working, and the crisis in the society became even more acute.

The August coup brought the general crisis to its ultimate limit. The most damaging thing about this crisis is the break-up of the statehood. And today I am worried by our people's loss of the citizenship of a great country. The consequences may turn out to be very hard for everyone.

I am leaving my post with apprehension, but also with hope, with faith in you, your wisdom and force of spirit. We are the heirs of a great civilization, and its rebirth into a new, modern and dignified life now depends on one and all.

Some mistakes could surely have been avoided, many things could have been done better, but I am convinced that sooner or later our common efforts will bear fruit, our nations will live in a prosperous and democratic society.

I wish all the best to all of you.'

The following day the Russian government took over the offices of the former USSR. Gorbachev was now politically dead—the former leader of a system of government that no longer existed. Slow to call for democratic elections, he had failed to see the threat from hardline communists within his own party and underestimated the power of the truth to erode the credibility—from both outside and within the Soviet Union—of a discredited regime.

Nelson Mandela

'Release from Prison'

Address to a rally upon release from prison at Cape Town, 11 February 1990.

Nelson Mandela fought against the brutal apartheid regime of South Africa and became the national and international symbol of the struggle for black South Africa's self-determination.

He was born Rolihlahla Dalibhunga Mandela, the son of a Thembu tribal chieftain on 18 July 1918 in a small village in the Transkei province in South Africa. Given the English name 'Nelson' by a schoolteacher, Mandela was raised by the acting regent of the Thembu people after the death of his father in 1927. Mandela later attended Fort Hare University, became a lawyer in Johannesburg and joined the African National Congress (ANC) in 1944. With friends Oliver Tambo and Walter Sisulu, Mandela formed the Youth League of the ANC when he felt the ANC leadership was too conservative. The same year he married his first wife, Evelyn Mase, the mother of his first three children.

For the next 20 years Mandela was involved in a campaign of non-violent defiance against the South African government's apartheid policies. In 1952 he was arrested for violating the Suppression of Communism Act (which was intended to crush any mass movement against apartheid) and banned from attending meetings for the next two years. In 1955 the 'Freedom Charter' adopted at the Congress of the People called for equal rights for blacks and equal share of the country's wealth with whites.

The following year, Nelson Mandela, along with 155 other political activists, was accused of attempting to overthrow the South African government by violent means. Charged with high treason, the charges were dropped against Mandela after a four-year trial. During this time, Mandela divorced his first wife and married Winnie Madikizela in 1958.

On 21 March, 1960 South African police opened fire on unarmed anti-apartheid protestors in Sharpeville, killing 69 civilians—most of whom were shot in the back as they ran away from the police. The government declared a State of Emergency and banned the ANC and other opposition minority groups. Nelson Mandela responded to the banning of the ANC by forming the underground Umkhonto we Sizwe ('Spear of the Nation' or 'MK') movement whose policy was to target and destroy government utilities and symbols of apartheid—but not people. In 1961 Mandela 'illegally' escaped the country and studied guerrilla warfare in Africa and Europe. Returning from overseas after a year on the run, Mandela was arrested by South African security police and sentenced to five years jail on Robben Island. In 1964 the government brought further charges including sabotage, high treason and conspiracy to overthrow the government against him.

Although Nelson Mandela and the other accused escaped execution they were sentenced to life imprisonment. At Robben Island Prison, Mandela was confined to a small cell without a bed or plumbing and was forced to do hard labour in a quarry. He could write and receive a letter every six months and was allowed to meet with a visitor for thirty minutes once every year. In the late 1960s his mother and eldest son were killed in separate car accidents but Mandela was not allowed to attend either funeral. But even when confined to prison, Mandela led a protest of civil disobedience at Robben Island that effectively forced the South African government to improve prison conditions.

During the 1970s and 1980s Mandela became the symbolic leader of an international movement (led by exiled colleague Oliver Tambo) to end apartheid in South Africa. In the last nine years of his sentence, after contracting tuberculosis, Mandela was moved to Pollsmoor Prison where he effectively lived under house arrest whilst the Botha government negotiated with him. In 1989 F W de Klerk became South African president and bowing to political, social and economic pressures, immediately instigated a program to end apartheid. International sanctions had cost the country $4 billion between 1988 and 1990 and de Klerk knew that the apartheid goal of congregating blacks into separate homelands was impossible to maintain. The South African president lifted the ban on the ANC, suspended executions and released most of the prisoners from the Rivonia Trial in 1964.

Finally, in February 1990, de Klerk ordered Mandela's release. Nelson delivered this speech to acknowledge the litany of people who had been involved in the struggle to end apartheid.

'Friends, comrades and fellow South Africans.

I greet you all in the name of peace, democracy and freedom for all.

I stand here before you not as a prophet but as a humble servant of you, the people. Your tireless and heroic sacrifices have made it possible for me to be here today. I therefore place the remaining years of my life in your hands.

'Today the majority of South Africans, black and white, recognise that apartheid has no future. It has to be ended by our own decisive mass action in order to build peace and security.'

On this day of my release, I extend my sincere and warmest gratitude to the millions of my compatriots and those in every corner of the globe who have campaigned tirelessly for my release.

I send special greetings to the people of Cape Town, this city which has been my home for three decades. Your mass marches and other forms of struggle have served as a constant source of strength to all political prisoners.

I salute the African National Congress. It has fulfilled our every expectation in its role as leader of the great march to freedom. I salute our President, Comrade Oliver Tambo, for leading the ANC even under the most difficult circumstances.

I salute the rank and file members of the ANC. You have sacrificed life and limb in the pursuit of the noble cause of our struggle.

I salute combatants of Umkhonto we Sizwe, like Solomon Mahlangu and Ashley Kriel who have paid the ultimate price for the freedom of all South Africans.

I salute the South African Communist Party for its sterling contribution to the struggle for democracy. You have survived 40 years of unrelenting persecution. The memory of great communists like Moses Kotane, Yusuf Dadoo, Bram Fischer and Moses Mabhida will be cherished for generations to come.

I salute General Secretary Joe Slovo, one of our finest patriots. We are heartened by the fact that the alliance between ourselves and the Party remains as strong as it always was.

I salute the United Democratic Front, the National Education Crisis Committee, the South African Youth Congress, the Transvaal and

Natal Indian Congresses and COSATU and the many other formations of the Mass Democratic Movement.

I also salute the Black Sash and the National Union of South African Students. We note with pride that you have acted as the conscience of white South Africa. Even during the darkest days in the history of our struggle you held the flag of liberty high. The large-scale mass mobilisation of the past few years is one of the key factors which led to the opening of the final chapter of our struggle.

I extend my greetings to the working class of our country. Your organised strength is the pride of our movement. You remain the most dependable force in the struggle to end exploitation and oppression.

I pay tribute to the many religious communities who carried the campaign for justice forward when the organisations for our people were silenced.

I greet the traditional leaders of our country—many of you continue to walk in the footsteps of great heroes like Hintsa and Sekhukune.

I pay tribute to the endless heroism of youth, you, the young lions. You, the young lions, have energised our entire struggle. I pay tribute to the mothers and wives and sisters of our nation. You are the rock-hard foundation of our struggle. Apartheid has inflicted more pain on you than on anyone else.

On this occasion, we thank the world community for their great contribution to the anti-apartheid struggle. Without your support our struggle would not have reached this advanced stage. The sacrifice of the frontline states will be remembered by South Africans forever.

My salutations would be incomplete without expressing my deep appreciation for the strength given to me during my long and lonely years in prison by my beloved wife and family. I am convinced that your pain and suffering was far greater than my own.

Before I go any further I wish to make the point that I intend making only a few preliminary comments at this stage. I will make a more complete statement only after I have had the opportunity to consult with my comrades.

Today the majority of South Africans, black and white, recognise that apartheid has no future. It has to be ended by our own decisive mass action in order to build peace and security. The mass campaign of defiance and other actions of our organisation and people can only culminate in the establishment of democracy. The destruction caused by apartheid on our sub-continent is incalculable. The fabric of family life of millions of my people has been shattered. Millions are homeless and unemployed. Our economy lies in ruins and our people are embroiled in political strife. Our resort to the armed struggle in 1960 with the formation of the military wing of the ANC, Umkhonto we Sizwe, was a purely defensive action against the violence of apartheid. The factors which necessitated the armed struggle still exist today. We have no option but to continue. We express the hope that a climate conducive to a negotiated settlement will be created soon so that there may no longer be the need for the armed struggle. I am a loyal and disciplined member of the African National Congress. I am therefore in full agreement with all of its objectives, strategies and tactics. The need to unite the people of our country is as important a task now as it always has been. No individual leader is able to take on this enormous task on his own. It is our task as leaders to place our views before our organisation and to allow the democratic structures to decide. On the question of democratic practice, I feel duty bound to make the point that a leader of the movement is a person who has been democratically elected at a national conference. This is a principle which must be upheld without any exceptions.

Today, I wish to report to you that my talks with the government have been aimed at normalising the political situation in the country. We have not as yet begun discussing the basic demands of the struggle. I wish to stress that I myself have at no time entered into negotiations about the future of our country except to insist on a meeting between the ANC and the government. Mr. De Klerk has gone further than any other Nationalist president in taking real steps to normalise the situation. However, there are further steps as outlined in the Harare

> 'I have fought against white domination and I have fought against black domination. I have cherished the ideal of a democratic and free society in which all persons live together.'

Declaration that have to be met before negotiations on the basic demands of our people can begin. I reiterate our call for—inter alia—the immediate ending of the State of Emergency and the freeing of all, and not only some, political prisoners. Only such a normalised situation, which allows for free political activity, can allow us to consult our people in order to obtain a mandate. The people need to be consulted on who will negotiate and on the content of such negotiations. Negotiations cannot take place above the heads or behind the backs of our people. It is our belief that the future of our country can only be determined by a body which is democratically elected on a non-racial basis. Negotiations on the dismantling of apartheid will have to address the overwhelming demand of our people for a democratic, non-racial and unitary South Africa. There must be an end to white monopoly on political power and a fundamental restructuring of our political and economic systems to ensure that the inequalities of apartheid are addressed and our society thoroughly democratised.

It must be added that Mr. De Klerk himself is a man of integrity who is acutely aware of the dangers of a public figure not honouring his undertakings. But as an organisation we base our policy and strategy on the harsh reality we are faced with. And this reality is that we are still suffering under the policy of the Nationalist government.

Our struggle has reached a decisive moment. We call on our people to seize this moment so that the process towards democracy is rapid and uninterrupted. We have waited too long for our freedom. We can no longer wait. Now is the time to intensify the struggle on all fronts. To relax our efforts now would be a mistake which generations to come will not be able to forgive. The sight of freedom looming on the horizon should encourage us to redouble our efforts.

It is only through disciplined mass action that our victory can be assured. We call on our white compatriots to join us in the shaping of a new South Africa. The freedom movement is a political home for you too. We call on the international community to continue the campaign to isolate the apartheid regime. To lift sanctions now would be to run the risk of aborting the process towards the complete eradication of apartheid.

Our march to freedom is irreversible. We must not allow fear to stand in our way. Universal suffrage on a common voters' role in a united democratic and non-racial South Africa is the only way to peace and racial harmony.

In conclusion I wish to quote my own words during my trial in 1964. They are true today as they were then:

"I have fought against white domination and I have fought against black domination. I have cherished the ideal of a democratic and free society in which all persons live together in harmony and with equal opportunities. It is an ideal which I hope to live for and to achieve. But if needs be, it is an ideal for which I am prepared to die." '

After his release from prison in 1990, Nelson Mandela led the ANC in its negotiations with the minority National Party government to bring an end to apartheid, the armed struggle in the Natal province and to establish a multiracial government. But the battle was not won without bloodshed. The ANC adopted a policy of a 'rolling mass action' of protests and strikes to show the government that people supported an end to violence. In September 1992 Mandela and de Klerk signed the 'Record of Understanding' which promised to investigate the role of the police in propagating violence and established an elected constitutional assembly to develop a new South African constitution. The following year Mandela and the South African President were jointly awarded the Nobel Peace Prize for their efforts.

Nelson Mandela's achievement in leading his country to freedom did not come without personal sacrifice—even after his release. In 1992 he separated from his wife Winnie after she was convicted of kidnapping and being an accessory to assault by men acting as her bodyguards in the murder of 13-year-old Stompie Seipei. Mandela married Graca Machel, the widow of the former president of Mozambique, in 1998, a year before he retired to private life.

In 1994 the ANC won 252 of the 400 seats in the country's first free elections with Nelson Mandela elected South African President on 10 May 1994. At age 76, the 'walk to freedom' had taken an entire lifetime.

Earl Spencer

'Eulogy for Diana, Princess of Wales'

Westminster Abbey, London, 9 September 1997.

The tragic death of Princess Diana in a car accident in Paris in 1997 created an unprecedented outpouring of emotion in England and around the world.

Lady Diana Frances Spencer was born in Norfolk, England on 1 July, 1961, the third child of Earl Spencer and his first wife. On 29 July, 1981, shortly after her 20th birthday and in a frenzied atmosphere of world-wide media scrutiny, Diana married Charles, the Prince of Wales and heir to the British throne. Diana bore two sons, Princes William (b.1982) and Henry 'Harry' (b.1984) and threw her considerable position and newfound celebrity behind several charitable causes—notably children, the homeless, AIDS sufferers and a Red Cross campaign to ban land mines world-wide.

But her marriage to Prince Charles was doomed—a mismatch from the start—and the pair grew increasingly alienated before announcing their separation in 1992 and eventual divorce four years later. Diana kept her title, the Princess of Wales, and continued her charitable works. But her public comments on the failings of her marriage and her relationship with the Royal Family only increased media interest in her personal life. Hounded by Europe's voracious 'paparazzi' she was killed in a car accident on the night of 31 August, 1997, along with boyfriend Dodi Fayed, as their driver sped away from a media pack in Paris.

Diana's tragic death shocked the Royal Family into making a formal announcement of regret, which the Queen delivered at 6:00pm from Buckingham Palace on Friday, 5 September. Four days later, Diana's coffin was borne in procession from Kensington Palace to Westminster Abbey with her brother, Earl Spencer, Prince William, Prince Harry, The Prince of Wales and The Duke of Edinburgh walking behind.

At the funeral at Westminster Abbey, her brother—the ninth Earl Spencer— delivered a moving eulogy.

'I stand before you today, the representative of a family in grief, in a country in mourning, before a world in shock.

We are all united, not only in our desire to pay our respects to Diana, but rather in our need to do so, because such was her extraordinary appeal that the tens of millions of people taking part in this service all over the world via television and radio who never actually met her feel that they too lost someone close to them in the early hours of Sunday morning.

It is a more remarkable tribute to Diana then I can ever hope to offer to her today.

Diana was the very essence of compassion, of duty, of style, of beauty. All over the world she was the symbol of selfless humanity. A standard bearer for the rights of the truly downtrodden. A very British girl who transcended nationality. Someone with a natural nobility who was classless and who proved in the last year that she needed no royal title to continue to generate her particular brand of magic.

> 'Diana was the very essence of compassion, of duty, of style, of beauty.'

Today is our chance to say 'thank you' for the way you brightened our lives, even though God granted you but half a life. We will all feel cheated always that you were taken from us so young and yet we must learn to be grateful that you came at all.

Only now you are gone do we truly appreciate what we are without, and we want you to know that life without you is very, very difficult.

We have all despaired for our loss over the past week and only the strength of the message you gave us through your years of giving has afforded us the strength to move forward.

There is a temptation to rush, to canonise your memory. There is no need to do so. You stand tall enough as a human being of unique qualities, and do not need to be seen as a saint.

Indeed, to sanctify your memory would be to miss out on the very core of your being—your wonderfully mischievous sense of humour with a laugh that bent you double, your joy for life transmitted wherever you took your smile and the sparkle in those unforgettable eyes, your boundless energy which you could barely contain.

But your greatest gift was your intuition and it was a gift you used wisely. This is what underpinned all your other wonderful attributes.

And if we look to analyse what it was about you that had such a wide appeal we find it in your instinctive feel for what was really important in all our lives.

Without your God-given sensitivity, we would be immersed in greater ignorance at the anguish of Aids and HIV sufferers, the plight of the homeless, the isolation of lepers, the random destruction of land mines.

Diana explained to me once that it was her innermost feelings of suffering that made it possible for her to connect with her constituency of the rejected.

And here we come to another truth about her.

For all the status, the glamour, the applause, Diana remained throughout a very insecure person at heart, almost childlike in her desire to do good for others so she could release herself from deep feelings of unworthiness of which her eating disorders were merely a symptom.

The world sensed this part of her character and cherished her vulnerability.

The last time I saw Diana was on July 1st, her birthday, in London when typically she was not taking time to celebrate her special day with friends but was guest of honour at a fund-raising charity evening. She sparkled, of course.

But I would rather cherish the days I spent with her in March when she came to visit me and my children at our home in South Africa. I am proud of the fact that, apart from when she was on public display meeting President Mandela, we managed to contrive to stop the ever-present paparazzi from getting a single picture of her. That meant a lot to her.

These are days I will always treasure. It was as if we were transported back to our childhood when we spent such an enormous amount of time together as the two youngest in the family.

Fundamentally she hadn't changed at all from the big sister who mothered me as a baby, fought with me at school, who endured those long journeys between our parents' home with me at weekends.

It is a tribute to her level-headedness and strength that despite the most bizarre life after her childhood, she remained intact, true to herself.

There is no doubt she was looking for a new direction in her life at this time.

She talked endlessly of getting away from England, mainly because of the treatment that she received at the hands of the newspapers.

I don't think she ever understood why her genuinely good intentions were sneered at by the media, why there appeared to be a permanent quest on their behalf to bring her down. It is baffling.

My own and only explanation is that genuine goodness is threatening to those at the opposite end of the moral spectrum.

It is a point to remember that of all the ironies about Diana, perhaps the greatest was this: a girl given the name of the ancient goddess of hunting was, in the end, the most hunted person of the modern age.

She would want us today to pledge ourselves to protecting her beloved boys, William and Harry, from a similar fate, and I do this here, Diana, on your behalf.

We will not allow them to suffer the anguish that used regularly to drive you to tearful despair. And beyond that, on behalf of your mother and sisters, I pledge that we, your blood family, will do all we can to continue the imaginative and loving way in which you were steering these two exceptional young men so that their souls are not simply immersed by duty and tradition but can sing openly as you planned.

> 'Of all the ironies about Diana, perhaps the greatest was this: a girl given the name of the ancient goddess of hunting was, in the end, the most hunted person of the modern age.'

We fully respect the heritage into which they have both been born and will always respect and encourage them in their royal role. But we, like you, recognise the need for them to experience as many different aspects of life as possible to arm them spiritually and emotionally for the years ahead. I know you would have expected nothing less from us.

William and Harry, we all care desperately for you today. We are all chewed up with sadness at the loss of a woman who wasn't even our mother. How great your suffering is we cannot even imagine.

I would like to end by thanking God for the small mercies he has shown us at this dreadful time, for taking Diana at her most beautiful and radiant and when she had joy in her private life.

Above all, we give thanks for the life of a woman I'm so proud to be able to call my sister the unique, the complex, the extraordinary and irreplaceable Diana whose beauty, both internal and external, will never be extinguished from our minds.'

As Earl Spencer spoke, a spontaneous wave of applause from the thousands of mourners outside the Abbey swept over the congregation inside. While many applauded his condemnation of the role the media played in his sister's death and agreed with his stinging criticism of the conditions that had allowed Diana's life to be so publicly exposed, just as many thought the eulogy ungracious to the Royal Family.

That afternoon Diana's body was interred on the Spencer family home, Althorp, in Northamptonshire on a landscaped island known as 'The Oval'. Diana, the 'Princess of Hearts', was finally at rest away from the prying eyes of the public.

Tony Blair

'Address to the Irish Parliament'

Irish Parliament, Dublin, 26 November 1998.

Tony Blair is the longest serving Labour Prime Minister in British history. On Thursday, 26 November 1998 Tony Blair also made history when he became the first British Prime Minister to address the Irish Parliament.

Tony Charles Lynton Blair was born in Edinburgh on 6 May 1953, the son of a barrister and lecturer. After spending most of his childhood in Durham, Blair returned to Edinburgh with his family at the age of 14 before studying law at Oxford and becoming a barrister. He stood unsuccessfully as a Labour Party candidate in a bi-election before winning the seat of Sedgefield in the 1983 General Election at age 30. Blair served in the Shadow Ministry for the next decade until the sudden death of Labour Party leader John Smith in 1994 saw him gain widespread support to take on the role. The new leader set about modernising the Labour Party, coining the term 'New Labour', and led the Party to a landslide victory in 1997 after 18 years in opposition.

Blair's government immediately implemented a program of constitutional change—reducing the number of hereditary peers in the House of Lords to just 92, offering referendums on home rule to Scotland and Wales before taking on the most divisive and violent issue in Britain during the twentieth century—relations with Ireland. Southern Ireland had won its independence from England in the early 1920s, but with the province of Northern Ireland annexed to Britain, decades of violence and animosity between the two nations had followed.

In this speech Blair recalled his own Irish heritage and extended hope for heartfelt reconciliation by declaring an end to more than 800 years of enmity between England and Ireland.

'Members of the Dail and Seanad, after all the long and torn history of our two peoples, standing here as the first British prime minister ever to address the joint Houses of the Oireachtas, I feel profoundly both the history in this event, and I feel profoundly the enormity of the honour that you are bestowing upon me. From the bottom of my heart, *go raibh mile maith agaibh*.

Ireland, as you may know, is in my blood. My mother was born in the flat above her grandmother's hardware shop on the main street of Ballyshannon in Donegal. She lived there as a child, started school there and only moved when her father died; her mother remarried and they crossed the water to Glasgow.

We spent virtually every childhood summer holiday up to when the troubles really took hold in Ireland, usually at Rossnowlagh, the Sands House Hotel, I think it was. And we would travel in the beautiful countryside of Donegal. It was there in the seas off the Irish coast that I learned to swim, there that my father took me to my first pub, a remote little house in the country, for a Guinness, a taste I've never forgotten and which it is always a pleasure to repeat.

Even now, in my constituency of Sedgefield, which at one time had 30 pits or more, all now gone, virtually every community remembers that its roots lie in Irish migration to the mines of Britain.

So, like it or not, we—the British and the Irish—are irredeemably linked.

We experienced and absorbed the same waves of invasions: Celts, Vikings, Normans—all left their distinctive mark on our countries. Over a thousand years ago, the monastic traditions formed the basis for both our cultures. Sadly, the power games of medieval monarchs and feudal chiefs sowed the seeds of later trouble.

Yet, it has always been simplistic to portray our differences as simply Irish versus English—or British. There were, after all, many in Britain too who suffered greatly at the hands of powerful absentee landlords, who were persecuted for their religion, or who were for centuries disenfranchised.

And each generation in Britain has benefited, as ours does, from the contribution of Irishmen and women.

Today the links between our parliaments are continued by the British-Irish Parliamentary Body, and last month 60 of our MPs set up a new all-party "Irish in Britain Parliamentary Group."

Irish parliamentarians have made a major contribution to our shared parliamentary history. Let me single out just two:

- Daniel O'Connell, who fought against injustice to extend a franchise restricted by religious prejudice;
- Charles Stewart Parnell, whose statue stands today in the House of Commons and whose political skills and commitment to social justice made such an impact in that House.

So much shared history, so much shared pain.

And now the shared hope of a new beginning.

The peace process is at a difficult juncture. Progress is being made, but slowly. There is an impasse over the establishment of the executive; there is an impasse over decommissioning. But I have been optimistic the whole way through. And I am optimistic now. Let us not underestimate how far we have come; and let us agree that we have come too far to go back now.

Politics is replacing violence as the way people do business. The Good Friday Agreement, overwhelmingly endorsed by the people on both sides of the Border, holds out the prospect of a peaceful long-term future for Northern Ireland, and the whole island of Ireland.

The Northern Ireland Bill provides for the new Assembly and Executive, the North-South Ministerial Council, and the British-Irish Council. It incorporates the principle of consent into British constitutional law and repeals the Government of Ireland Act of 1920. It establishes a Human Rights Commission with the power to support individual cases. We will have an Equality Commission to police a new duty on all public bodies in Northern Ireland to promote equality of opportunity. We have set up the Patten Commission to review policing. We are scaling down the military presence. Prisoners are being released.

> **'Let us not underestimate how far we have come; and let us agree that we have come too far to go back now.'**

None of this is easy. I get many letters from the victims of violence asking why we are freeing terrorist prisoners. It is a tough question but my answer is clear: the agreement would never have come about if we had not tackled the issue of prisoners. That agreement heralds the prospect of an end to violence and a peaceful future for Northern Ireland. Our duty is to carry it out. That is a duty I feel more strongly than ever, having seen for myself the horror of Omagh. This was not the first such atrocity. But with all of my being, I will it to be the last. I will never forget the meeting I had, with Bill Clinton, with survivors, and with relatives of those who died. Their suffering and their courage was an inspiration. They will never forget their loved ones. Nor must we. We owe it to them above all to build a lasting peace, when we have the best opportunity in a generation to do so.

The Taoiseach's personal contribution has been immense. I pay tribute to his tireless dedication. I value his friendship. I also salute the courage of our predecessors, Deputy Albert Reynolds, Deputy John Bruton and John Major; and I also salute Deputy Dick Spring, whose role in this process goes back a long way.

Like us, you are living up to your side of the bargain too. You have voted to end the territorial claim over Northern Ireland, essential to the agreement.

It is time now for all the parties to live up to all their commitments. Time for North/South bodies to be established to start a new era of co-operation between you and Northern Ireland—I hope agreement on these is now close. Time to set up the institutions of the new government. Time for the gun and the threat of the gun to be taken out of politics once and for all; for decommissioning to start.

I am not asking anyone to surrender. I am asking everyone to declare the victory of peace.

In Belfast or Dublin, people say the same thing: make the agreement work.

It is never far from my mind. My sense of urgency and mission comes from the children in Northern Ireland. I reflect on those who have been victims of violence, whose lives are scarred and twisted through the random wickedness of a terrorist act, on those who grow up in fear, those whose parents and loved ones have died.

And I reflect on those, who though untouched directly by violence, are nonetheless victims -- victims of mistrust and misunderstanding who through lack of a political settlement miss the chance of new friendships, new horizons, because of the isolation from others that the sectarian way of life brings.

I reflect on the sheer waste of children taught to hate when I believe passionately children should be taught to think.

Don't believe anyone who says the British people don't care about the peace process. People in my country care deeply about it, are willing it to work. And in our two countries, it is not just the politicians who have a role to play.

No one should ignore the injustices of the past, or the lessons of history. But too often between us, one person's history has been another person's myth.

We need not be prisoners of our history. My generation in Britain sees Ireland differently today and probably the same generation here feels differently about Britain.

We can understand the emotions generated by Northern Ireland's troubles, but we cannot really believe, as we approach the 21st century, there is not a better way forward to the future than murder, terrorism and sectarian hatred.

We see a changed Republic of Ireland today:

- a modern, open economy;
- after the long years of emigration, people beginning to come back for the quality of life you now offer;
- a country part of Europe's mainstream, having made the most of European structural funds but no longer reliant on them;
- some of the best business brains in the business world;
- leaders in popular culture, U2, the Corrs, Boyzone, B-Witched;

- a country that had the courage to elect its first woman president and liked it so much, you did it again; and the politics of Northern Ireland would be better for a few more women in prominent positions too.

And you see, I hope, a Britain emerging from its post-Empire malaise, modernising, becoming as confident of its future as it once was of its past.

The programme of the new Labour government: driving up standards in education; welfare reform; monetary and fiscal stability as the foundation of a modern economy; massive investment in our public services tied to the challenge of modernisation; a huge programme of constitutional change; a new positive attitude to Europe—it is a program of national renewal as ambitious as any undertaken in any western democracy in recent times.

It is precisely the dramatic changes in both countries that allow us to see the possibilities of change in our relationship with each other.

It will require vision, but no more than the vision that has transformed Ireland. It will require imagination, but no more than that shown by the British people in the last two years. The old ways are changing between London and Dublin. And this can spur the change and healing in Northern Ireland too. The old notions of unionist supremacy and of narrow nationalism are gradually having their fingers prised from their grip on the future.

Different traditions have to understand each other. Just as we must understand your yearning for a united Ireland, so too must you understand what the best of unionism is about. They are good and decent people, just like you. They want to remain part of the UK—and I have made it clear that I value that wish. They feel threatened. Threatened by the terrorism with which they have had to live for so long. Threatened, until the Good Friday Agreement, that they would be forced into a united Ireland against the will of the people of Northern Ireland.

Yet they realise now that a framework in which consent is guaranteed is also one in which basic rights of equality and justice are guaranteed, and that those who wish a united Ireland are free to make that claim, provided it is democratically expressed, just as those who believe in the Union can make their claim.

It is all about belonging. The wish of unionists to belong to the UK. The wish of nationalists to belong to Ireland. Both traditions are reasonable. There are no absolutes. The beginning of understanding is to realise that.

My point is very simple. Those urges to belong, divergent as they are, can live together more easily if we, Britain and the Irish Republic, can live closer together too.

Down through the centuries, Ireland and Britain have inflicted too much pain, each on the other. But now, the UK and Ireland as two modern countries, we can try to put our histories behind us, try to forgive and forget those age-old enmities.

We have both grown up now. A new generation is in power in each country.

We now have a real opportunity to put our relations on a completely new footing, not least through working together in Europe. I know that is what our peoples want and I believe we can deliver it.

Our ties are already rich and diverse:

- the UK is the largest market for Irish goods. And you are our fifth most important market in the world;
- in trade unions, professional bodies and the voluntary sector, our people work together to help their communities; in culture, sport and academic life there is an enormous crossover. Our theatres are full of Irish plays. Our television is full of Irish actors and presenters. Your national football team has a few English accents too;
- above all, at the personal level, millions of Irish people live and work in Britain, and hundreds of thousands of us visit you every year.

As ties strengthen, so the past can be put behind us. Nowhere was this better illustrated than at the remarkable ceremony at Messines earlier this month. Representatives of nationalists and unionists travelled together to Flanders to remember shared suffering. Our army bands played together. Our heads of state stood together. With our other European neighbours, such a ceremony would be commonplace. For us it was a first. It shows how far we have come. But it also shows we still have far to go.

The relationships across these islands are also changing in a significant way.

The Taoiseach has spoken of the exciting new relationships that will unfold as the people of Scotland and Wales, as well as Northern Ireland, express their wishes through their own parliaments and assemblies. The new British Irish Council must reflect and explore these opportunities. We have much to gain by co-operating better across these islands in areas like transport, education, the fight against illegal drugs.

But I want our co-operation to be wider and more fundamental still—above all in Europe.

It is 25 years since we both joined what was then the EEC. We have had different approaches to agriculture, to monetary union, to defence. But increasingly we share a common agenda and common objectives:

- completion of the Single Market and structural economic reform;
- better conditions for growth and jobs in Europe;
- successful enlargement;
- a united and coherent foreign policy voice for Europe;
- a more effective fight against crime, drugs, illegal immigration and environmental damage;
- flexible, open and accountable European institutions.

We must work to make the single currency a success. Unlike Ireland, we are not joining in the first wave. But we have made clear that we are prepared to join later if the economic benefits are clear and unambiguous. For my government, there is no political or constitutional barrier to joining. There is no resistance to full-hearted European co-operation wherever this brings added value to us all.

Enlargement will increasingly test our political and economic imaginations, as we struggle with policy reform and future financing. The international financial system must be reformed. We must learn to apply real political will and harness our skills and resources far more effectively to solve regional problems—notably in the Balkans and the Middle East. Above all, Europe must restate its vision for today's world, so that our people understand why it is so important. This means defining the priorities where common European action makes obvious sense and can make a real difference, like economic co-ordination, foreign and security policy, the environment, crime and drugs. It also means distinguishing them from areas where countries or regions can best continue to make policy themselves, to suit local circumstances, while still learning from each other—for example, tax, education, health, welfare.

> 'I do not believe Northern Ireland can or should any longer define the relationship between us. Our common interests, what we can achieve together, go much, much wider than that.'

That is why I want to forge new bonds with Dublin. Together we can have a stronger voice in Europe and work to shape its future in a way which suits all our people. It is said there was a time when Irish diplomats in Europe spoke French in meetings to ensure they were clearly distinguished from us. I hope those days are long behind us. We can accomplish much more when our voices speak in harmony.

Our ministers and officials are increasingly consulting and coordinating systematically. We can do more. I believe we can transform our links if both sides are indeed ready to make the effort. For our part, we are.

This must also involve a dramatic new effort in bilateral relations, above all to bring our young generations together. We need new youth and school exchanges, contact through the new University for Industry, better cultural programs in both directions. We need to work much more closely to fight organised crime and drugs. We can do much more to enrich each other's experience in areas like health care and welfare.

None of this threatens our separate identities. Co-operation does not mean losing distinctiveness.

What the Taoiseach and I seek is a new dimension to our relationships—a real partnership between governments and peoples, which will engage our societies at every level.

We have therefore agreed to launch a new intensive process. The Taoiseach and I will meet again next spring in London, with key ministerial colleagues, to give this the necessary impetus and agenda, and will thereafter meet at least once a year to review progress. This will be part of the work of the new Intergovernmental Conference. The objective is threefold:

- first, revitalised and modernised bilateral relations where we can finally put the burden of history behind us;
- second, a habit of close consultation on European issues, marked by a step-change in contacts at every level, particularly in key areas such as agriculture, justice and home affairs, employment and foreign and security policy;
- third, working together on international issues more widely, for example UN peacekeeping, to which both our countries have been important contributors, arms proliferation and the Middle East.

What I welcome above all is that, after keeping us apart for so long, Northern Ireland is now helping to bring us closer together. But I do not believe Northern Ireland can or should any longer define the relationship between us. Our common interests, what we can achieve together, go much, much wider than that.

Our two countries can look to the future with confidence in our separate ways. But we will be stronger and more prosperous working together.

That is my ambition. I know it is shared by the Taoiseach. I believe it is an ambition shared by both our nations. The 21st century awaits us. Let us confront its challenge with confidence, and together give our children the future they deserve.'

Elie Wiesel

'The Perils of Indifference'

East Room, White House, Washington DC, 12 April 1999.

An impassioned insight into the causes and nature of the Holocaust during World War II came from a scholar born in Sighet, Transylvania (now part of Romania). Eliezer Wiesel was born on 30 September 1928 in a small village, his life revolving around 'family, religious study, community and God'.

In the summer of 1944, 15-year-old Elie Wiesel, along with his father, mother and sisters, was deported by the Nazis to the Auschwitz death camp in occupied Poland. Wiesel and his father were selected for slave labour and were set to work at the nearby Buna rubber factory. Daily life was a constant struggle against overwhelming despair—starvation rations, brutal discipline and, as Wiesel later wrote, the memory of children whose bodies were 'turned into wreaths of smoke beneath a silent blue sky'.

Wiesel and his father were hurriedly evacuated from Auschwitz by a forced march to Gleiwitz in January 1945 as the Russian Army drew near, and then to Buchenwald via an open train car. There, his father, mother, and a younger sister eventually died but Elie Wiesel was liberated by American troops in April 1945. After the war, he moved to Paris and became a journalist. Originally vowing to remain silent on his Holocaust experiences, he was encouraged to write about them by French Nobel laureate Francois Mauriac. Since then, Wiesel has written over 40 books including Night, which was first published in 1960. Settling in New York and becoming an American citizen, he has been Andrew Mellon Professor in the Humanities at Boston University since 1976 and has received numerous awards and honours including the 1986 Nobel Peace Prize and the Presidential Medal of Freedom.

The Founding Chair of the United States Holocaust Memorial, Elie Wiesel was invited to participate in a series of Millennium Lectures hosted by President Bill Clinton and First Lady Hillary Rodham Clinton at the White House leading up to the year 2000. Here, in his speech in the East Room of the White House, Wiesel reiterated his belief that 'to remain silent and indifferent is the greatest sin of all'

'Mr President, Mrs Clinton, members of Congress, Ambassador Holbrooke, Excellencies, friends.

Fifty-four years ago to the day, a young Jewish boy from a small town in the Carpathian Mountains woke up, not far from Goethe's beloved Weimar, in a place of eternal infamy called Buchenwald. He was finally free, but there was no joy in his heart. He thought there never would be again.

Liberated a day earlier by American soldiers, he remembers their rage at what they saw. And even if he lives to be a very old man, he will always be grateful to them for that rage, and also for their compassion. Though he did not understand their language, their eyes told him what he needed to know—that they, too, would remember, and bear witness.

And now, I stand before you, Mr. President—Commander-in-Chief of the army that freed me, and tens of thousands of others—and I am filled with a profound and abiding gratitude to the American people.

'Of course, indifference can be tempting—more than that, seductive. It is so much easier to look away from victims.'

Gratitude is a word that I cherish. Gratitude is what defines the humanity of the human being. And I am grateful to you, Hillary—or Mrs. Clinton—for what you said, and for what you are doing for children in the world, for the homeless, for the victims of injustice, the victims of destiny and society. And I thank all of you for being here.

We are on the threshold of a new century, a new millennium. What will the legacy of this vanishing century be? How will it be remembered in the new millennium? Surely it will be judged, and judged severely, in both moral and metaphysical terms. These failures have cast a dark shadow over humanity: two World Wars, countless civil wars, the senseless chain of assassinations—

> 'Indifference is always the friend of the enemy, for it benefits the aggressor.'

Gandhi, the Kennedys, Martin Luther King, Sadat, Rabin—bloodbaths in Cambodia and Nigeria, India and Pakistan, Ireland and Rwanda, Eritrea and Ethiopia, Sarajevo and Kosovo; the inhumanity in the gulag and the tragedy of Hiroshima. And, on a different level, of course, Auschwitz and Treblinka. So much violence, so much indifference.

What is indifference? Etymologically, the word means "no difference." A strange and unnatural state in which the lines blur between light and darkness, dusk and dawn, crime and punishment, cruelty and compassion, good and evil.

What are its courses and inescapable consequences? Is it a philosophy? Is there a philosophy of indifference conceivable? Can one possibly view indifference as a virtue? Is it necessary at times to practice it simply to keep one's sanity, live normally, enjoy a fine meal and a glass of wine, as the world around us experiences harrowing upheavals?

Of course, indifference can be tempting—more than that, seductive. It is so much easier to look away from victims. It is so much easier to avoid such rude interruptions to our work, our dreams, our hopes. It is, after all, awkward, troublesome, to be involved in another person's pain and despair. Yet, for the person who is indifferent, his or her neighbor are of no consequence. And, therefore, their lives are meaningless. Their hidden or even visible anguish is of no interest. Indifference reduces the other to an abstraction.

Over there, behind the black gates of Auschwitz, the most tragic of all prisoners were the "Muselmanner," as they were called. Wrapped in their torn blankets, they would sit or lie on the ground, staring vacantly into space, unaware of who or where they were, strangers to their surroundings. They no longer felt pain, hunger, thirst. They feared nothing. They felt nothing. They were dead and did not know it.

Rooted in our tradition, some of us felt that to be abandoned by humanity then was not the ultimate. We felt that to be abandoned by

God was worse than to be punished by Him. Better an unjust God than an indifferent one. For us to be ignored by God was a harsher punishment than to be a victim of His anger. Man can live far from God—not outside God. God is wherever we are. Even in suffering? Even in suffering.

In a way, to be indifferent to that suffering is what makes the human being inhuman. Indifference, after all, is more dangerous than anger and hatred. Anger can at times be creative. One writes a great poem, a great symphony, one does something special for the sake of humanity because one is angry at the injustice that one witnesses. But indifference is never creative. Even hatred at times may elicit a response. You fight it. You denounce it. You disarm it. Indifference elicits no response. Indifference is not a response.

Indifference is not a beginning, it is an end. And, therefore, indifference is always the friend of the enemy, for it benefits the aggressor—never his victim, whose pain is magnified when he or she feels forgotten. The political prisoner in his cell, the hungry children, the homeless refugees—not to respond to their plight, not to relieve their solitude by offering them a spark of hope is to exile them from human memory. And in denying their humanity we betray our own.

Indifference, then, is not only a sin, it is a punishment. And this is one of the most important lessons of this outgoing century's wide-ranging experiments in good and evil.

In the place that I come from, society was composed of three simple categories: the killers, the victims, and the bystanders. During the darkest of times, inside the ghettoes and death camps—and I'm glad that Mrs. Clinton mentioned that we are now commemorating that event, that period, that we are now in the Days of Remembrance—but then, we felt abandoned, forgotten. All of us did.

And our only miserable consolation was that we believed that Auschwitz and Treblinka were closely guarded secrets; that the leaders of the free world did not know what was going on behind those black gates and barbed wire; that they had no knowledge of the war against the Jews that Hitler's armies and their accomplices waged as part of the war against the Allies.

If they knew, we thought, surely those leaders would have moved heaven and earth to intervene. They would have spoken out with great outrage and conviction. They would have bombed the railways leading to Birkenau, just the railways, just once.

And now we knew, we learned, we discovered that the Pentagon knew, the State Department knew. And the illustrious occupant of the White House then, who was a great leader—and I say it with some anguish and pain, because, today is exactly 54 years marking his death—Franklin Delano Roosevelt died on April the 12th, 1945, so he is very much present to me and to us.

No doubt, he was a great leader. He mobilised the American people and the world, going into battle, bringing hundreds and thousands of valiant and brave soldiers in America to fight fascism, to fight dictatorship, to fight Hitler. And so many of the young people fell in battle. And, nevertheless, his image in Jewish history—I must say it—his image in Jewish history is flawed.

The depressing tale of the St. Louis is a case in point. Sixty years ago, its human cargo—maybe 1,000 Jews—was turned back to Nazi Germany. And that happened after the Kristallnacht, after the first state sponsored pogrom, with hundreds of Jewish shops destroyed, synagogues burned, thousands of people put in concentration camps. And that ship, which was already on the shores of the United States, was sent back.

I don't understand. Roosevelt was a good man, with a heart. He understood those who needed help. Why didn't he allow these refugees to disembark? A thousand people—in America, a great country, the greatest democracy, the most generous of all new nations in modern history. What happened? I don't understand. Why the indifference, on the highest level, to the suffering of the victims?

But then, there were human beings who were sensitive to our tragedy. Those non-Jews, those Christians, that we called the "Righteous Gentiles," whose selfless acts of heroism saved the honor of their faith. Why were they so few? Why was there a greater effort to save SS murderers after the war than to save their victims during the war?

> 'Have we really learned from our experiences? Are we less insensitive to the plight of victims of ethnic cleansing and other forms of injustices in places near and far?'

Why did some of America's largest corporations continue to do business with Hitler's Germany until 1942? It has been suggested, and it was documented, that the Wehrmacht could not have conducted its invasion of France without oil obtained from American sources. How is one to explain their indifference?

And yet, my friends, good things have also happened in this traumatic century: the defeat of Nazism, the collapse of communism, the rebirth of Israel on its ancestral soil, the demise of apartheid, Israel's peace treaty with Egypt, the peace accord in Ireland. And let us remember the meeting, filled with drama and emotion, between Rabin and Arafat that you, Mr. President, convened in this very place. I was here and I will never forget it.

And then, of course, the joint decision of the United States and NATO to intervene in Kosovo and save those victims, those refugees, those who were uprooted by a man whom I believe that because of his crimes, should be charged with crimes against humanity. But this time, the world was not silent. This time, we do respond. This time, we intervene.

Does it mean that we have learned from the past? Does it mean that society has changed? Has the human being become less indifferent and more human? Have we really learned from our experiences? Are we less insensitive to the plight of victims of ethnic cleansing and other forms of injustices in places near and far? Is today's justified intervention in Kosovo, led by you, Mr. President, a lasting warning that never again will the deportation, the terrorisation of children and their parents be allowed anywhere in the world? Will it discourage other dictators in other lands to do the same?

What about the children? Oh, we see them on television, we read about them in the papers, and we do so with a broken heart. Their fate is always the most tragic, inevitably. When adults wage war, children perish. We see their faces, their eyes. Do we hear their pleas? Do we feel their pain, their agony? Every minute one of them dies of disease, violence, famine. Some of them—so many of them—could be saved.

And so, once again, I think of the young Jewish boy from the Carpathian Mountains. He has accompanied the old man I have become throughout these years of quest and struggle. And together we walk towards the new millennium, carried by profound fear and extraordinary hope.'

When introduced by Hillary Clinton, the First Lady stated, 'It was more than a year ago that I asked Elie if he would be willing to participate in these Millennium Lectures ... I never could have imagined that when the time finally came for him to stand in this spot and to reflect on the past century and the future to come, that we would be seeing children in Kosovo crowded into trains, separated from families, separated from their homes, robbed of their childhoods, their memories, their humanity.'

She could just as easily have commented that those who refuse to heed the lessons of history are condemned to repeat it.

The New Millennium 2000-

George W Bush

'A Great People Has Been Moved'

Washington, DC, 11 September 2001.

The ramifications of the passenger jet attacks in New York and Washington on 11 September 2001 changed global politics and the position of the United States within it. This speech, given on the night of the attack by US President George W Bush, marked the beginning of America and its allies' 'war on terror' at the start of the new millennium.

George Walker Bush was born in New Haven, Connecticut on 6 July, 1946, the oldest son of George and Barbara Bush. The Bush family grew up in Midland and Houston, Texas, with George W. attending Yale University (his father George H Bush's alma mater) and earned an MBA from Harvard Business School. When Bush ran for the presidency in 2000 much was made of his wild youth, his national guard service during the Vietnam War and his shift to sobriety after his marriage in 1976. The millions he made from the oil industry and his stake in the Texas Rangers baseball franchise—all while his father was President of the United States—also raised concerns, but didn't stop him from being electable in his own right.

In 1978 Bush tried to follow his father into the House of Representatives, but was defeated by his Democratic rival, Kent Hance. In 1994, after his father had been voted out of the White House, George W was elected governor of Texas and went onto become the first Texas governor to be elected to a second four-year term.

In 2001 George W (nicknamed 'Dubya' by a sceptical press) became the 42nd President of the United States after one of the closest and most controversial elections in American history. Bush defeated former Democratic Vice-President Al Gore by a mere five electoral votes (despite Gore securing 500 000 more primary votes). The outcome was ultimately decided in Florida, where

Bush's younger brother Jeb was the governor, but it was a result contested by the Gore camp until mid-December 2000.

In his first year as president, Bush faced the biggest test of any world leader in a generation. On Tuesday, 11 September, 2001, two fully-fuelled passenger jets were deliberately crashed into the twin towers of the World Trade Centre in New York. The impact and subsequent fire caused both 110-story towers to collapse, killing 2792 people, including hundreds of New York rescue workers—police, fire and ambulance personnel.

Another aeroplane, with 64 people on board, was diverted to Washington, D.C., and crashed into the Pentagon killing 125 military personnel inside the building as well as the passengers and crew on board. A fourth jet, with 44 people on board crashed in Pennsylvania when the passengers apperently overpowered the terrorists .

President Bush was visiting a primary school in Sarasota, Florida when he was informed of the attacks. He made a brief statement that morning then flew to Barksdale Air Force Base in Louisiana. That evening he returned to the White House and addressed the American people:

> 'A great people has been moved to defend a great nation. Terrorist attacks can shake the foundations of our biggest buildings, but they cannot touch the foundation of America.'

‘ Good evening.

Today, our fellow citizens, our way of life, our very freedom came under attack in a series of deliberate and deadly terrorist acts. The victims were in airplanes or in their offices: secretaries, business men and women, military and federal workers, moms and dads, friends and neighbors. Thousands of lives were suddenly ended by evil, despicable acts of terror. The pictures of airplanes flying into buildings, fires burning, huge structures collapsing have filled us with disbelief, terrible sadness, and a quiet, unyielding anger. These acts of mass murder were intended to frighten our nation into chaos and retreat. But they have failed. Our country is strong.

A great people has been moved to defend a great nation. Terrorist attacks can shake the foundations of our biggest buildings, but they cannot touch the foundation of America. These acts shatter steel, but they cannot dent the steel of American resolve. America was targeted for attack because we're the brightest beacon for freedom and opportunity in the world. And no one will keep that light from shining. Today, our nation saw evil—the very worst of human nature—and we responded with the best of America. With the daring of our rescue workers, with the caring for strangers and neighbors who came to give blood and help in any way they could.

Immediately following the first attack, I implemented our government's emergency response plans. Our military is powerful, and it's prepared. Our emergency teams are working in New York city and Washington D.C. to help with local rescue efforts. Our first priority is to get help to those who have been injured, and to take every precaution to protect our citizens at home and around the world from further attacks. The functions of our government continue without interruption. Federal agencies in Washington which had to be evacuated today are reopening for essential personnel tonight and will be open for business tomorrow. Our financial institutions remain strong, and the American economy will be open for business as well.

The search is underway for those who were behind these evil acts. I have directed the full resources of our intelligence and law enforcement communities to find those responsible and to bring them to justice. We will make no distinction between the terrorists who committed these acts and those who harbor them.

I appreciate so very much the members of Congress who have joined me in strongly condemning these attacks. And on behalf of the American people, I thank the many world leaders who have called to offer their condolences and assistance. America and our friends and allies join with all those who want peace and security in the world, and we stand together to win the war against terrorism.

Tonight, I ask for your prayers for all those who grieve, for the children whose worlds have been shattered, for all whose sense of safety and security has been threatened. And I pray they will be comforted by a Power greater than any of us, spoken through the ages in Psalm 23:

"Even though I walk through the valley of the shadow of death, I fear no evil for you are with me."

This is a day when all Americans from every walk of life unite in our resolve for justice and peace. America has stood down enemies before, and we will do so this time. None of us will ever forget this day, yet we go forward to defend freedom and all that is good and just in our world.

Thank you. Good night. And God bless America.'

History now shows that the United States of America responded to the attack with all its military might. Afghanistan was 'liberated' from Taliban rule in 2002 and Iraq was invaded on a false premise (in search of 'weapons of mass destruction') against the wishes of the United Nations in 2003. The world would never be the same again.

Arundhati Roy

'Peace and the New Corporate Liberation Theology'

Sydney Peace Prize, Australia, 3 November 2004.

Indian novelist and peace activist Arundhati Roy wa. born in 1961 to a Hindu father and Christian mother. At the age of 16 she moved to Delhi where she lived a subsistence lifestyle selling empty bottles out of a tin hut. Roy later studied architecture at university and married her first husband, also an architect, before turning to writing. She married her second husband, filmmaker Pradeep Kishen, in 1984 and wrote several screenplays. In 1997 she won the prestigious Booker Prize for her semi-autobiographical novel The God of Small Things. A noted peace activist, Roy criticise. India's nuclear weapons program, America's invasion of Afghanistan and was convicted (she was sentenced to a single day's 'symbolic' imprisonment and fined) for contempt of court because of her demonstrations against the Narmada Dam Project.

In May 2004, Arundhati Roy was awarded the Sydney Peace Prize. Her acceptance speech delivered the following November—a stinging critique of the Bush administration's decision to invade Iraq without United Nations authority—provides a thoughtful antidote to post-9/11 war rhetoric.

'Today, it is not merely justice itself, but the idea of justice that is under attack. The assault on vulnerable, fragile sections of society is at once so complete, so cruel and so clever—all encompassing and yet specifically targeted, blatantly brutal and yet unbelievably insidious— that its sheer audacity has eroded our definition of justice. It has forced us to lower our sights, and curtail our expectations. Even among the well-intentioned, the expansive, magnificent concept of justice is gradually being substituted with the reduced, far more fragile discourse of 'human rights'.

If you think about it, this is an alarming shift of paradigm. The difference is that notions of equality, of parity have been pried loose and eased out of the equation. It's a process of attrition. Almost unconsciously, we begin to think of justice for the rich and human rights for the poor. Justice for the corporate world, human rights for its victims. Justice for Americans, human rights for Afghans and Iraqis. Justice for the Indian upper castes, human rights for Dalits and Adivasis (if that.) Justice for white Australians, human rights for Aboriginals and immigrants (most times, not even that.)

It is becoming more than clear that violating human rights is an inherent and necessary part of the process of implementing a coercive and unjust political and economic structure on the world. Without the violation of human rights on an enormous scale, the neo-liberal project would remain in the dreamy realm of policy. But increasingly Human Rights violations are being portrayed as the unfortunate, almost accidental fallout of an otherwise acceptable political and economic system. As though they're a small problem that can be mopped up with a little extra attention from some NGOs. This is why in areas of heightened conflict—in Kashmir and in Iraq for example—Human Rights Professionals are regarded with a degree of suspicion. Many resistance movements in poor countries who are fighting huge injustice and questioning the underlying principles of what constitutes "liberation" and "development", view Human Rights NGOs as modern day missionaries who've come to take the ugly edge off Imperialism. To defuse political anger and to maintain the status quo.

It has been only a few weeks since a majority of Australians voted to re-elect Prime Minister John Howard who, among other things, led Australia to participate in the illegal invasion and occupation of Iraq. The invasion of Iraq will surely go down in history as one of the most cowardly wars ever fought. It was a war in which a band of rich nations, armed with enough nuclear weapons to destroy the world several times

> 'It is becoming more than clear that violating human rights is an inherent and necessary part of the process of implementing a coercive and unjust political and economic structure on the world.'

over, rounded on a poor nation, falsely accused it of having nuclear weapons, used the United Nations to force it to disarm, then invaded it, occupied it and are now in the process of selling it.

I speak of Iraq, not because everybody is talking about it, (sadly at the cost of leaving other horrors in other places to unfurl in the dark), but because it is a sign of things to come. Iraq marks the beginning of a new cycle. It offers us an opportunity to watch the Corporate-Military cabal that has come to be known as 'Empire' at work. In the new Iraq the gloves are off.

As the battle to control the world's resources intensifies, economic colonialism through formal military aggression is staging a comeback. Iraq is the logical culmination of the process of corporate globalisation in which neo-colonialism and neo-liberalism have fused. If we can find it in ourselves to peep behind the curtain of blood, we would glimpse the pitiless transactions taking place backstage. But first, briefly, the stage itself.

In 1991 US President George Bush senior mounted Operation Desert Storm. Tens of thousands of Iraqis were killed in the war. Iraq's fields were bombed with more than 300 tonnes of depleted uranium, causing a fourfold increase in cancer among children. For more than 13 years, twenty four million Iraqi people have lived in a war zone and been denied food and medicine and clean water. In the frenzy around the US elections, let's remember that the levels of cruelty did not fluctuate whether the Democrats or the Republicans were in the White House. Half a million Iraqi children died because of the regime of economic sanctions in the run up to Operation Shock and Awe. Until recently, while there was a careful record of how many US soldiers had lost their lives, we had no idea of how many Iraqis had been killed. US General Tommy Franks said "We don't do body counts" (meaning Iraqi body counts). He could have added "We don't do the Geneva Convention either." A new, detailed study, fast-tracked by The Lancet medical journal and extensively peer reviewed, estimates that 100 000

Iraqis have lost their lives since the 2003 invasion. That's one hundred halls full of people—like this one. That's one hundred halls full of friends, parents, siblings, colleagues, lovers ... like you. The difference is that there aren't many children here today ... let's not forget Iraq's children. Technically that bloodbath is called precision bombing. In ordinary language, it's called butchering.

Most of this is common knowledge now. Those who support the invasion and vote for the invaders cannot take refuge in ignorance. They must truly believe that this epic brutality is right and just or, at the very least, acceptable because it's in their interest.

> 'So the 'civilised' 'modern' world—built painstakingly on a legacy of genocide, slavery and colonialism—now controls most of the world's oil. And most of the world's weapons, most of the world's money, and most of the world's media.'

So the 'civilised' 'modern' world—built painstakingly on a legacy of genocide, slavery and colonialism—now controls most of the world's oil. And most of the world's weapons, most of the world's money, and most of the world's media. The embedded, corporate media in which the doctrine of Free Speech has been substituted by the doctrine of Free If You Agree Speech.

The UN's Chief Weapons Inspector Hans Blix said he found no evidence of nuclear weapons in Iraq. Every scrap of evidence produced by the US and British governments was found to be false—whether it was reports of Saddam Hussein buying uranium from Niger, or the report produced by British Intelligence which was discovered to have been plagiarised from an old student dissertation. And yet, in the prelude to the war, day after day the most 'respectable' newspapers and TV channels in the U.S., headlined the 'evidence' of Iraq's arsenal of weapons of nuclear weapons. It now turns out that the source of the manufactured 'evidence' of Iraq's arsenal of nuclear weapons was Ahmed Chalabi who, (like General Suharto of Indonesia, General Pinochet of Chile, the Shah of Iran, the Taliban and of course, Saddam Hussein himself)—was bankrolled with millions of dollars from the good old CIA.

And so, a country was bombed into oblivion. It's true there have been some murmurs of apology. Sorry 'bout that folks, but we have really have to move on. Fresh rumours are coming in about nuclear weapons in Iran and Syria. And guess who is reporting on these fresh rumours? The same reporters who ran the bogus 'scoops' on Iraq. The seriously embedded 'A Team'.

The head of Britain's BBC had to step down and one man committed suicide because a BBC reporter accused the Blair administration of 'sexing up' intelligence reports about Iraq's WMD programme. But the head of Britain retains his job even though his government did much more than 'sex up' intelligence reports. It is responsible for the illegal invasion of a country and the mass murder of its people.

Visitors to Australia like myself, are expected to answer the following question when they fill in the visa form: Have you ever committed or been involved in the commission of war crimes or crimes against humanity or human rights? Would George Bush and Tony Blair get visas to Australia? Under the tenets of International Law they must surely qualify as war criminals.

However, to imagine that the world would change if they were removed from office is naive. The tragedy is that their political rivals have no real dispute with their policies. The fire and brimstone of the US election campaign was about who would make a better 'Commander-in-Chief' and a more effective manager of the American Empire. Democracy no longer offers voters real choice. Only specious choice.

Even though no weapons of mass destruction have been found in Iraq—stunning new evidence has revealed that Saddam Hussein was planning a weapons programme. (Like I was planning to win an Olympic Gold in synchronised swimming.) Thank goodness for the doctrine of pre-emptive strike. God knows what other evil thoughts he harbored—sending Tampax in the mail to American senators, or releasing female rabbits in burqas into the London underground. No doubt all will be revealed in the free and fair trial of Saddam Hussein … that's coming up soon in the New Iraq.

All except the chapter in which we would learn of how the U.S. and Britain plied him with money and material assistance at the time he was carrying out murderous attacks on Iraqi Kurds and Shias. All except the chapter in which we would learn that a 12,000 page report submitted by the Saddam Hussein government to the UN, was censored by the United States because it lists twenty-four US corporations who participated in Iraq's pre-Gulf War nuclear and conventional weapons programme. (They include Bechtel, DuPont, Eastman Kodak, Hewlett Packard, International Computer Systems and Unisys.)

So Iraq has been 'liberated.' Its people have been subjugated and its markets have been 'freed'. That's the anthem of neo-liberalism. Free the markets. Screw the people.

The US government has privatised and sold entire sectors of Iraq's economy. Economic policies and tax laws have been re-written. Foreign companies can now buy 100% of Iraqi firms and expatriate the profits. This is an outright violation of international laws that govern an occupying force, and is among the main reasons for the stealthy, hurried charade in which power was 'handed over' to an 'interim Iraqi government'. Once handing over of Iraq to the Multi-nationals is complete, a mild dose of genuine democracy won't do any harm. In fact it might be good PR for the Corporate version of Liberation Theology, otherwise known as New Democracy...

In New Iraq, privatisation has broken new ground. The US Army is increasingly recruiting private mercenaries to help in the occupation. The advantage with mercenaries is that when they're killed they're not included in the US soldiers' body count. It helps to manage public opinion, which is particularly important in an election year. Prisons have been privatised. Torture has been privatised. We have seen what that leads to. Other attractions in New Iraq include newspapers being shut down. Television stations bombed. Reporters killed. US soldiers have opened fire on crowds of unarmed protestors killing scores of people. The only kind of resistance that has managed to survive is as crazed and brutal as the occupation itself. Is there space for a secular, democratic, feminist, non-violent resistance in Iraq? There isn't really.

That is why it falls to those of us living outside Iraq to create that mass-based, secular and non-violent resistance to the US occupation.

If we fail to do that, then we run the risk of allowing the idea of resistance to be hijacked and conflated with terrorism and that will be a pity because they are not the same thing.

So what does peace mean in this savage, corporatised, militarised world? What does it mean in a world where an entrenched system of appropriation has created a situation in which poor countries, which have been plundered by colonising regimes for centuries, are steeped in debt to the very same countries that plundered them and have to repay that debt at the rate of 382 billion dollars a year? What does peace mean in a world in which the combined wealth of the world's 587 billionaires exceeds the combined gross domestic product of the world's 135 poorest countries? Or when rich countries—that pay farm subsidies of a billion dollars a day—try and force poor countries to drop their subsidies? What does peace mean to people in occupied Iraq, Palestine, Kashmir, Tibet and Chechnya? Or to the Aboriginal people of Australia? Or the Ogoni of Nigeria? Or the Kurds in Turkey? Or the Dalits and Adivasis of India? What does peace mean to non-Muslims in Islamic countries or to women in Iran, Saudi Arabia and Afghanistan? What does it mean to the millions who are being uprooted from their lands by dams and development projects? What does peace mean to the poor who are being actively robbed of their resources and for whom everyday life is a grim battle for water, shelter, survival and, above all, some semblance of dignity? For them, peace is war.

We know very well who benefits from war in the age of Empire. But we must also ask ourselves honestly who benefits from peace in the Age of Empire? War mongering is criminal, but talking of peace without talking of justice could easily become advocacy for a kind of capitulation. And talking of justice without unmasking the institutions and the systems that perpetrate injustice, is beyond hypocritical.

It's easy to blame the poor for being poor. It's easy to believe that the world is being caught up in an escalating spiral of terrorism and war. That's what allows the American President to say: "You're either with us or with the terrorists." But we know that that's a spurious choice. We know that terrorism is only the privatisation of war. That terrorists are the free marketers of war. They believe that the legitimate use of violence is not the sole prerogative of the state.

It is mendacious to make moral distinction between the unspeakable brutality of terrorism and the indiscriminate carnage of war and occupation. Both kinds of violence are unacceptable. We cannot support one and condemn the other.

The real tragedy is that most people in the world are trapped between the horror of a punative peace and the terror of war. Those are the two sheer cliffs we're hemmed in by. The question is: How do we climb out of this crevasse?

For those who are materially well-off, but morally uncomfortable, the first question you must ask yourself is do you really want to climb out of it? How far are you prepared to go? Has the crevasse become too comfortable?

If you really want to climb out, there's good news and bad news.

The good news is that the advance party began the climb some time ago. They're already halfway up. Thousands of activists across the world have been hard at work preparing footholds and securing the ropes to make it easier for the rest of us. There isn't only one path up. There are hundreds of ways of doing it. There are hundreds of battles being fought around the world that need your skills, your minds, your resources. No battle is irrelevant. No victory is too small.

The bad news is that colourful demonstrations, weekend marches and annual trips to the World Social Forum are not enough. There have to be targetted acts of real civil disobedience with real consequences. Maybe we can't flip a switch and conjure up a revolution, but there are several things we could do. For example, you could make a list of those corporations who have profited from the invasion of Iraq and have offices here in Australia. You could name them, boycott them, occupy

'The bad news is that colourful demonstrations, weekend marches and annual trips to the World Social Forum are not enough. There have to be targeted acts of real civil disobedience with real consequences.'

their offices and force them out of business. If it can happen in Bolivia, it can happen in India. It can happen in Australia. Why not?

That's only a small suggestion, but remember that if the struggle were to resort to violence, it will lose vision, beauty and imagination. Most dangerous of all, it will marginalise and eventually victimise women. And a political struggle that does not have women at the heart of it, above it, below it and within it is no struggle at all.

The point is that the battle must be joined. As the wonderful American historian Howard Zinn put it: "You can't be neutral on a moving train".'

Sources

Print

Andrews, James and David Zarefsky, (1989), *American Voices*, Longman, White Plains, NY.

Berkman, Alexander, *Anarchism on Trial: Speeches of Alexander Berkman and Emma Goldman Before the United States District Court in the City of New York*, July, 1917,' New York, Mother Earth Publishing Association.

Ferrell, Robert H. 1980, *Off the Record: The Private Papers of Harry S. Truman*, New York, Harper and Row.

Graham, John, 1970, *Great American Speeches*, 1898-1963, Text Studies, New York: Meredith Corporation.

Lenin, VI, *Collected Works*, Volume 28.

'Live Aid' CD (2004) Warner Vision Australia.

MacArthur, Brian, *The Penguin Book of Twentieth Century Speeches* (1999), Penguin, London.

McPherson, James M. ed. (2000), *To the Best of My Ability: The American Presidents*, Dorling Kindersley, New York.

'Public Papers of the Presidents of the United States', Washington, D. C. Government Printing Office, various.

Stalin, J, 'From the Pamphlet Collection', J. Stalin, *Speeches Delivered at Meetings of Voters of the Stalin Electoral District*, Foreign Languages Publishing House, Moscow, 1950.

Tojo, *Washington Post*, 30 November, 1941.

Electronic

www.amercianrhetoric.com.

www.anc.org.za

Fidel Castro, by Robert E. Quirk (1993) www.fiu.edu

Castro Speech Data Base (www.lanic.utexas)

Chase Smith, US Senate Website, www.senate.gov.

Chamberlain, www.lib.byu.edu, www.mtholyoke.edu, www.historyplace.com.

Churchill, W, www.raf.mod.uk, www.espeeches.com.

Darrow, Clarence, www.federalobserver.com

Edward VIII, www.thamesweb.co.uk.

Einstein and Russell, www.ppu.org.uk, www.velapanthi.com, www.ppu.org.uk

www.ex.ac.uk

www.elf.net/bjordan

www.ford.utexas.edu

Ghandi, www.mkgandhi.org.

Gehrig, Lou, www.nationalpastime.com and www.baseballhalloffame.org.

www.theremnant.com

www.historyplace.com

Adolf Hitler: An Apolitical Historical Website (www.adolfhitler.ws/lib/speeches)

www.ibiblio.org

www.international.activism.uts.edu.au

Krushchev, www.sovietrevolution.net

www.librarylink.org.ph

Lindbergh, Charles, www.charleslindbergh.com

An Early Spring: Mao Tse-tung, the Chinese Intellectuals and the Hundreds Flowers Campaign by John M. Jackson (2004) www.filebox.vt.edu

McArthur, www.hundredpercenter.com

McCarthy, Joe, www.mnstate.edu

McMillan, www.africanhistory.about.com, www.africanhistory.about.com

Golda Meir, www.localvoter.com/speech.

Nixon, www.nixonfoundation.org

Pearse, Padraic, www.easter1916.net/oration.htm.

Patton, www.famousquotes.me.uk, worldatwar.net, www.pattonhq.com.
www.pbs.org
www.rainbowpush.org
www.reaganfoundation.org
Australian Federal Parliament, opening, www.chr.org.au, www.peo.gov.au/resources/federation.htm.
Roosevelt, www.historyplace.com.
Ryan White, www.ryanwhite.com
www.spacerace.com
www.spaceguy.com
Terrell, Mary Church, www.gos.sbc.edu.
www.thinkingpeace.com
www.tungate.com
www.usconstitution.com
Von Galen, www.geocities.com, www.oldion.com.
Whitlam, www.pandora.nla.gov.au, transcript of ATN Channel 7 news report, 11 November 1975.
Wilson, Woodrow, www.historyplace.com/speeches.
www.worldhistory.com
Women's Library: Women's Internet Information Network (www.undelete.org/library).

About the Author

Alan J Whiticker was born in Sydney, Australia, in 1958 and attended St Dominic's College in Penrith. Alan has been a teacher for 25 years and is currently the Assistant Principal of a Western Sydney Catholic School. He lives in Penrith with his wife, Karen and children, Timothy and Melanie.

His previous books include *The Encyclopedia of Rugby League Players* (1993, 1995, 1999, 2002 and 2005, with Glen Hudson), *Jimmy Barnes: Say it Loud* (2002), *Wanda: The Untold Story of the Wanda Beach Murders* (2003), *A History of Rugby League Clubs* (with Ian Collis), and his first children's book, *The Battle for Troy: An Adaptation of Homer's Iliad* (2004). His latest book, *12 Crimes That Shocked a Nation*, was released by New Holland Publishers in 2007.